Information Systems and School Improvement

INVENTING THE FUTURE

Edited by
ADRIANNE BANK and **RICHARD C. WILLIAMS**

Teachers College, Columbia University
New York and London

LB
1028.46
.I53
1987

The conference at which these chapters were first presented as papers was supported by a grant from the National Institute of Education to UCLA's Center for the Study of Evaluation, as was the subsequent work editing the volume. The work reported by Bank and Williams and by Sirotnik and Burstein (Chapter 18) was similarly funded. However, the opinions expressed herein do not necessarily reflect the position or policy of the National Institute of Education, and no official endorsement by the National Institute of Education should be inferred.

Chapter 7, "The School Profile: An Information System for Managing School Improvement," was previously published, in a slightly different form, under the title, "Managing Improvement by Profiling" (*Educational Leadership*, March 1985, pp. 54–58), and is reprinted with permission of the publisher and the authors. Copyright © 1985 by the Association for Supervision and Curriculum Development. All rights reserved.

Chapter 8, "Developing an Elementary School Information System: The Computer-Assisted Professional," is adapted from chapter 6 and case history 8 in W. W. Cooley and W. E. Bickel, *Decision-Oriented Educational Research* (Boston: Kluwer-Nijhoff, 1986), and is reprinted by permission of the publisher.

Chapter 11, "Information Systems for School Improvement: What's Coming in the New Technologies?" copyright © 1985 by Steven M. Frankel. Reprinted by permission.

Published by Teachers College Press, 1234 Amsterdam Avenue, New York, N.Y. 10027

Copyright © 1987 by Teachers College, Columbia University

All rights reserved. No part of this publication may be reproduced or transmitted in any form or by any means, electronic or mechanical, including photocopy, or any information storage and retrieval system, without permission from the publisher.

Library of Congress Cataloging-in-Publication Data

Information systems and school improvement.

(Computers and education series)
Papers from the proceedings of a two-day conference held at UCLA in Feb. 1985.
Bibliography: p.
Includes index.
1. Computer managed instruction—United States—Congresses. 2. Computer-assisted instruction—United States—Congresses. I. Bank, Adrianne. II. Williams, Richard C., 1933–
LB1028.46.I53 1987   371.3'9445   86-30148

ISBN 0-8077-2842-X

Manufactured in the United States of America

92 91 90 89 88 87   1 2 3 4 5 6 7

COMPUTERS AND EDUCATION SERIES
Keith A. Hall, Editor

The Educational Software Selector (TESS)
 EPIE Institute

Computer Keyboarding for Children
 Edward B. Fry

Microcomputer Applications in
Educational Planning and Decision Making
 C. Kenneth Tanner and C. Thomas Holmes

Teaching Children to Use Computers:
A Friendly Guide
 Stephen D. Savas and E. S. Savas

The Teacher's Computer Book: 40 Student Projects
to Use with Your Classroom Software
 Patricia Moser Shillingburg,
 with Kenneth Craig Bareford,
 Joyce A. Paciga, and Janis Lubawsky Townsend

Information Systems and School Improvement:
Inventing the Future
 Adrianne Bank and Richard C. Williams, *Editors*

Contents

Preface ix

Acknowledgments xiii

Part I
Instructional Information Systems in Education: How Should We View Them?

1. The Coming of Instructional Information Systems — *Adrianne Bank & Richard C. Williams* — 3
2. Instructional Information Systems: Dream or Nightmare? — *Michael Quinn Patton* — 11
3. What About Information Systems and Educational Improvement? — *J. Richard Harsh* — 16
4. Some Lessons for Educators from Management Information Systems Literature — *Adrianne Bank & Elaine Craig* — 22

Part II
Alternative Types of Instructional Information Systems

5. The Computer as an Administrative Tool: A Survey of 30 High Schools — *Terence R. Cannings & Linda Polin* — 39
6. We'll Create the Future But Keep It Secret — *Peter Idstein* — 57
7. The School Profile: An Information System for Managing School Improvement — *Robert E. Blum & Jocelyn A. Butler* — 76
8. Developing an Elementary School Information System: The Computer-Assisted Professional — *William Cooley* — 86
9. Reactions to an Elementary School's Computerized Office Management System — *William M. Carey* — 97

Part III
The Technical Aspects of Instructional Information Systems

10. Technological Issues Relating to
    Information Systems — *Elaine Craig* — 105
11. Information Systems for School
    Improvement: What's Coming in the
    New Technologies? — *Steven M. Frankel* — 112
12. A Practical Assessment of
    Computerization in Schools — *John Leslie King* — 119
13. Technology and Assumptions: Let's
    Take Another Look — *Saul Rockman* — 136

Part IV
Instructional Information Systems and Educational Realities

14. Realities and Scenarios: Instructional
    Information Systems in Classrooms of
    the Future — *Richard C. Williams & Adrianne Bank* — 145
15. Hopes and Possibilities for
    Educational Information Systems — *Walter E. Hathaway* — 152
16. Superintendents Don't Type—Advice
    for Those Setting Up IIS Training
    Programs for Administrators — *Brian Stecher* — 159
17. Integrating Instructional Information
    Systems with Instructional Processes — *Nicholas F. Dussault* — 167
18. Making Sense Out of Comprehensive
    School-Based Information Systems:
    An Exploratory Investigation — *Kenneth A. Sirotnik & Leigh Burstein* — 185
19. Making Instructional Information
    Systems Teacher-Friendly — *Jean A. King* — 210

Part V
Inventing the Future: The Development of Instructional Information Systems

20. An Agenda for Developing
    Instructional Information Systems — *Adrianne Bank & Richard C. Williams* — 225

21. An Agenda for Research and Inquiry   *Richard C. Williams &*
    on Instructional Information Systems   *Adrianne Bank*   234

About the Contributors   241
Index   247

Preface

This book is about a new and timely topic—the melding of the computer's capacity to store and analyze masses of data with the need of educators to more effectively manage instruction for a diverse and mobile student population.

Computers are changing the world of work. And as computers change the world of work, so they will change the world of education. We now experience in our daily life computerized banking services, computer analyses of our voting patterns, and computerized inventory control at the checkout lines in the supermarket. We are becoming familiar with terms used by the media such as "office automation" and "computer commuters" who, while working at home, have worldwide communication access. But as educators, we are just starting to understand how the computer revolution will affect our students' work lives over the next 40 years—and indeed, how it will affect our own professional lives over the next 10 years.

For a long time, we at the UCLA Center for the Study of Evaluation (CSE) have been tracking selected aspects of the computer revolution in education. Our Instructional Information Systems (IIS) project has called attention to three different arenas in which the educational application of computers can operate. In the classroom—the first arena—more than a million computers have been purchased for use by students (Marcom & Bellew, 1985). In the business office—the second arena—automation has come to payroll, inventory, budgeting, and record-keeping in many of the larger school districts.

The third arena in which the computer revolution may come to operate doesn't have a geographic location within a school or district. This is currently the least well-defined of the three. It is the arena of instructional management. And instructional management takes place wherever and whenever people make decisions that affect the substance or organization of instruction. The third arena is what this book is about.

We believe that computer-based information systems to support instructional management decisions have, potentially, a wide range of uses. We believe that such Instructional Information Systems contain the possibility for improving the way teachers teach and students learn.

Instructional management means deciding how all the resources—organizational, curricular, and personnel—for delivering instruction to students will be arranged and configured. Instructional management decisions are made by teachers in the classroom when students are placed in reading groups or when remedial or enrichment materials are assigned. Instructional management decisions are made in the school when the principal and faculty decide on textbooks, the assignment of teacher aides, or the scheduling of special programs. Instructional management decisions are made in the central office when curriculum supervisors put together instructional objectives for a subject area or when staff development coordinators plan in-service courses for teachers. And instructional management decisions are made at the board level when budgets are considered, when policies to deal with particular problems are articulated, or when monitoring and evaluation of programs are mandated. We see that computerized Instructional Information Systems to support these decisions might contain data about such things as student characteristics, achievements, attendance, and instructional history. Such data could then be analyzed by individual, group, class, or school to give instructional managers snapshots of complex relationships that can now only be guessed at.

Our intent in this book is to begin a discussion about whether and how computerized information systems can be of assistance to instructional managers in the classroom, the principal's office, and the central district office. The chapters that follow take an important first step in conceptualizing this newest arena for the computer revolution in education. They represent the proceedings of a two-day conference called "Information Systems and School Improvement: Inventing the Future" that was held at UCLA in February 1985 and was sponsored by CSE's Instructional Information Systems Project under the leadership of Adrianne Bank and Richard C. Williams.

The participants at the conference were individuals who are authorities in their own fields. They include district and state policymakers, school superintendents, directors of research offices, and professors from business, computer science, and education departments. All have only recently become interested in the instructional management implications arising out of the ready availability of computers. They believe that the potential of Instructional Information Systems for improving education in our schools needs much exploration.

The contributions present conceptual, technical, administrative, and organizational perspectives on Instructional Information Systems. Some of the chapters take an advocacy position—either pro or con information systems. A few authors are very optimistic and see information systems as a potent force for bringing to education such various goods as increased efficiency, increased productivity, increased individualization, and increased student achievement. A few are very cautious, noting that American education has seen many fads come and go. They wonder whether computerized information systems to assist instructional management will be just another expensive fad, or, if they become a permanent fixture, whether they will change education for the worse. Some of the authors present analyses of work in progress; others describe their struggles and achievements as they attempt to break new ground in computerized instructional management.

But whether the authors are optimistic, cautious, pessimistic, or analytic, most of them address a number of common issues that are either explicitly raised or form an undercurrent in their remarks.

One cluster of issues relates to the sociotechnical complexities of Instructional Information Systems. Will technology become the tail wagging the educational dog? Will what we *can* do with information in education become the unthinking motor driving our view of what we *should* do with it? If we dedicate resources to setting up an Instructional Information System that includes state-of-the-art hardware and software, will we be creating a system that nobody will use? A system that can be easily misused? A system that can abuse its users?

A second cluster of issues relates to the effect of information systems on people within education. How will we anticipate and resolve the "people problems" that may occur on many levels and at many points in the creation, management, and use of information systems? These people problems might include the need for retraining and reallocation of personnel who run the system, the possible shifting of power over educational decision making between schools and the district office, the concerns of teachers about the use of information to evaluate their performance, and the loss of privacy for students when many kinds of information about their background and history can be aggregated in a single place.

A third set of issues relates to the compatibility or incompatibility of assumptions and values underlying education on the one hand and management information systems on the other. Those who see education as an art rather than as a science, or who look at teaching as craft rather than as technology, warn of dangers in moving too quickly to create information systems that might subvert the personal and clinical aspects of classroom interactions. Those who want educational institutions and the administrators and teachers in them to become more open and more responsive to the human needs of students and of society, and those who have visions of harnessing technology to increase the standardization and efficiency of instruction, may approach the idea of Instructional Information Systems from opposing viewpoints.

Yet another group of issues relates to the change process itself, with information systems seen as innovations that must go through a cycle of initiation, development, implementation, and incorporation. Who will participate in conceptualizing information systems, controlling them, using them, and paying for them? How will change be managed, supported, or resisted? Who will gain from the change? Who will lose?

The 21 chapters in this volume are organized into five parts, each of which begins with a summary of its contents. In several of the parts a background essay introduces the topic. Part V suggests an agenda for developing an Instructional Information System and an agenda for research and inquiry.

Readers with particular interests may approach this book in a number of different ways. For example, school and district-level administrators may be interested in details about the planning and design of an IIS. Although all sections of the book relate in some way to IIS planning and design, Parts II and IV focus most directly on reports from schools and districts. Part V contains some "how-to-do-its." Administrators who will be involved in decisions regarding technology will also benefit from Part III.

Teachers also will want to focus on Parts II and IV for discussions of IIS uses most directly related to classroom needs.

School board members and parent or community representatives will probably want to become familiar with most of the key issues raised in this book, so that they can respond to requests from school officials for funding for an IIS, or so they can explore with school officials the possible benefits for a particular school or district of installing an IIS.

Professors in schools or departments of education might use this volume as a supplementary text in administration, instruction, or evaluation courses. Students who could benefit from the background provided by this book include those training to be administrators, those specializing in uses of computers in education, and those doing research on technology or innovation in education. Students might be particularly interested in the conceptual chapters in Part I and in the research and policy agenda in Part V.

Technical consultants who work with computerized information systems could use this book to gain insight into the needs and problems associated with information systems in educational settings. Evaluators who work with schools in connecting testing programs with instructional improvement might use the book to find out what several districts are doing with their IIS.

In short, this book is a diverse collection with appeal to many types of readers. It documents the challenges raised by the possibility of creating Instructional Information Systems.

REFERENCE

Marcom, J., Jr., & Bellew, P. A. (1985, April 17). Slow response. *The Wall Street Journal*, pp. 1, 23.

Acknowledgments

It is customary practice for authors or editors to thank those closely involved with the production of a book and to indicate that there are others too numerous to name who have also contributed. We would like to do it differently.

There are, indeed, numerous individuals whose efforts have contributed to this volume, even before there was the idea that this volume would come to be. And we would like to name them, apologizing in advance to those whom we may inadvertently have left out.

This volume has its roots in work begun at the UCLA Center for the Study of Evaluation in 1975 and continuing to the present. There were those who were involved with conceptualizing and conducting the first-ever nationwide survey and analysis of school district research and development offices. They include Eva Baker, Larry Barber, James Burry, Linda Cullian, Lynn Doscher, Oscar Grusky, Egon Guba, Michael Kean, Catherine Lyon, Pam McGranahan, Charles O'Reilly, David O'Shea, Janet Sutton, and Lynn Zucker.

And then there were those practitioners and academics who worked with us or provided our case studies of heroic districts. These include Marvin Alkin, Brad Barrett, Grant Behnke, Emily Brizendine, Leigh Burstein, James Catterall, Jim Cox, Larry Crabbe, Liza Daniels, Don Dorr-Bremme, Joe Felix, Joe Gastright, David Hatton, Joan Herman, Mary Kennedy, Dorothy Maloney, Michele Marcus, Joan McDonald, Donna Mitroff, Ken Moffett, George Plumleigh, Magdala Raupp, Jerry Richardson, Ken Sirotnik, Bill Spady, Theron Swainston, Carol Thomas, and Dale Woolley.

And all those who have shared in the development of the CSE Instructional Information Systems Network and the related conferences and meetings. They include Eleanor Anderson, Paul Beck, Bonnie Bowman, Clint Boutwell, Beverly Cabello, Phyllis Catz, Don Cody, Hal Connolly, Betty Coogan, John Davey, Thomas Davis, Virginia DeBoer, Phil Ender, Phil Esbrandt, Jane Favero, Frederica Frost, Jill Hartley Fulton, Bruce Givner, John Goodlad, C. Wayne Gordon, Terence Gray, Judy Guilkey, Mike Hartmann, Arlene Hartry, Molly Helms, Wayne Hervi, Evangeline Hill, James Holton, Gail Houghton, Allan Jacobs, Phyllis Jacobson, Charles Kondrit, Bruce Kowalski, Terry Larsen, Merle Lauderdale, Phil Linscomb, Vince Madden, Dorothy Maloney, Stuart Mandell, John Marshall,

Tom Martin, Steve McMahon, Dave Meaney, Ed Meyers, Patricia Milazzo, Richard Miller, Shirley Mills, Ian Mitroff, Linda Murai, Milly Murray, Bruce Newlin, William Norin, Robert Peterson, Ann Picker, Lewis Prilliman, Claire Quinlan, Curt Rethmeyer, Robert Ryan, Neil Schmidt, Georgette Silva, Glenn Smartschan, Harris Sokoloff, Jane St. John, Les Stahler, Floraline Stevens, Lories Tolbert, Gene Tucker, A. J. Viscovich, Chuck Weis, Robert Wenkert, Joseph C. White, Lynn Winters, Linda Wisher, Milton Woolsey, and Frederique Wynberg.

These individuals have all been part of our lives for the past 10 years, as have those conference presenters whose thoughts have formed the basis for this book.

We especially want to thank our project monitors at the National Institute of Education—first, Mary Ann Millsap, then Norman Gold, and most recently, Susan M. Klein—for their advice and guidance, and for their never-failing encouragement and support.

We want to acknowledge the essential contribution to the organization of the 1985 IIS and School Improvement conference and to this book made by Elaine Craig, who also capably provided research assistance for several chapters. And, finally and most importantly, we want to thank our friend, Katharine Fry, who with skill and great care attended to the manuscript production of every single word in this book.

INFORMATION SYSTEMS AND SCHOOL IMPROVEMENT
Inventing the Future

PART I

Instructional Information Systems in Education: How Should We View Them?

The four chapters of Part I are quite diverse. Bank and Williams, in their introductory essay "The Coming of Instructional Information Systems," note that there is no standard or generally accepted definition of Instructional Information System. In order to place wide rather than narrow bounds on this newly emergent phenomenon, they describe information systems as sociotechnical arrangements whereby data can be stored on computers and retrieved by a variety of users in order to understand and manage the connection between children's learning and elements of the instructional environment. The authors point out four major factors stimulating the emergence of Instructional Information Systems: (1) rapid social transformations, which increase the need for standardized information; (2) increasing availability of inexpensive computer technology; (3) the efficiency-oriented legacy of previous and current school reforms; and (4) increasing interest by the testing and evaluation communities in providing management-oriented information about instruction.

In "Instructional Information Systems: Dream or Nightmare?" Patton asks us to start any discussion of information systems by examining two major issues: What is worth knowing and how we can focus people's attention on important information. His chapter suggests that information has meaning only within context, that the questions we ask of data influence the kind of answers we get back. Above all, he stresses that "information is for people."

In "What About Information Systems and Educational Improvement?" Harsh expresses skepticism about the assumption that information systems will automatically lead to educational improvement. He cites the lack of public and professional agreement about what constitutes improvement, emphasizing that previous technological innovations such as educational TV and computer-assisted instruction have not led to sustained changes in schools. He does see some promise for Instructional Information Systems if we keep our expectations modest and learn from previous experience.

"Some Lessons for Educators from Management Information Systems Literature," by Bank and Craig, compares the evaluation literature with the management information literature and observes that both fields began with expectations that technical systems would work miracles in organizations, and moved very quickly to disappointment that implementation was more complex than anticipated, and that impact on organizations was diffuse rather than immediately apparent. Bank and Craig delineate eight steps in what has come to be known as the management information system life cycle, and note the implications for educators of each step. Finally, they contrast educational organizations with business organizations and suggest some lessons that can be transferred from one sector to the other.

The authors of Part I share some assumptions and sound several common warnings. They all believe that information systems are an emerging phenomenon that educators will have to deal with in one way or another during the next decade. School or district information systems are not now commonplace. However, the technology that makes them possible is becoming more available and less expensive. There are social forces and marked pressures on schools to buy new technology so as to more efficiently keep records and reduce costs. There is great but unexplored potential for using information systems to answer important questions about learning and instruction. Whether most schools will accept or reject these pressures or proceed to explore the potential is not yet clear, but at a minimum, all schools and districts will soon have to consider these issues and arrive at their own decisions. The authors believe that Instructional Information Systems can increase our ability to understand, predict, and control education, but at the same time they see the possibilities of misuse, abuse, or nonuse of expensively installed systems.

1
The Coming of Instructional Information Systems

ADRIANNE BANK and RICHARD C. WILLIAMS

We both have childhood memories—although one of us grew up in Minnesota and the other in the heart of Manhattan—of adults saying to us, "Spring is coming, you can feel it in the air." Nothing much seemed to have changed from the day before. The snow was still on the ground, the wind still nippy, and there were no bird sounds. Yet, they sensed—and we came to be able to sense it too—that the seasons were ready to change. The signs were small, some even invisible, but you could feel it. Every once in a while the adults were wrong. Spring was delayed, and weeks or even months passed before the buds appeared and the sun brought warmth instead of just light. But whatever its timing, spring did come.

We know that the emergence of a man-made phenomenon such as computerized Instructional Information Systems should not be compared with the natural inevitability of spring. But it does feel to us that there are numerous small, almost invisible signs that we are ready for something we call information systems. We are aware that components of Instructional Information Systems are beginning to be developed in some schools and districts. This book and the conference on which it is based attest to the awakening interest of some academics and educational researchers. We can't be sure yet whether Instructional Information Systems will never come, will come and then go again like the spring, or will come and remain as a permanent part of the educational landscape.

WHAT ARE INSTRUCTIONAL INFORMATION SYSTEMS?

Before pointing to signs that may indicate our readiness for such systems, we should define what we mean by the term. We cannot supply precise definitions but can talk around the subject a bit.

We will start by placing Instructional Information Systems within the general field of information management. "Information management can be viewed as the keystone of information science and technology. Every activity in this eclectic profession—from user requirements, system design and evaluation, to document knowledge representation, database organization, storage and retrieval techniques, hard and soft technology applications . . . relates to the complex process of managing information" (Levitan, 1982, p. 227).

Within this comprehensive and theoretical notion of total information management are nested smaller systems for managing specific classes of information for specific users. In the business world, the term Management Information System (MIS) refers to one such specific class of information targeted to middle managers. That is, a Management Information System is intended to bring accurate, timely, relevant, precise information in easy-to-understand report formats to middle managers dealing with functions such as accounting and finance, marketing, production and operations, and administrative support.

A Decision Support System (DSS) acquires, stores, and makes available for access another specific class of information—that needed by top managers in business to support strategic planning. Decision Support Systems differ from Management Information Systems; they are not intended to provide large numbers of routine reports. Rather, a DSS is organized so that users may query the system to get answers to unique questions, pursue a line of inquiry, explore "what if" situations, and spot trouble areas or generate solutions to ill-defined problems (Mitroff, Killman, & Barabba, 1979).

There are some in the world of business who believe that in the future both of these systems, along with an automated office system, could be formed into one grand institutional information management system.

By contrast, in the world of education we are not yet thinking either conceptually or technically about the big picture called information management. Rather, in a few schools and districts, individuals are thinking about smaller, more discrete computerized systems that might be created to serve specific groups of users. Some of these can be thought of as Instructional Information Systems; others should not be.

The first group of computer users that educators think about are the students in their classrooms. "The computer invasion of education is nothing short of phenomenal. Recent national surveys reveal that most high schools and over half of all elementary schools now have more than one microcomputer used for instruction, with the majority having acquired their computers in only the last few years" (Rumberger, 1984, p. 1).

However, classroom use of computers by students does not fall within our definition of Instructional Information Systems. Neither do the computerized systems set up to perform administrative and business tasks (e.g., to record attendance, do scheduling, maintain student records, send letters to parents, process suspensions, make class lists, and compile ethnic surveys). We want to distinguish these administrative information systems designed primarily to make the running of the school more efficient from another group of systems that we are labeling Instructional Information Systems.

An Instructional Information System (IIS) is designed primarily to make the management of instruction more effective. It may provide a variety of users—such as school board members, administrators, and teachers—with information that will help them make better instructional management decisions. An IIS can link data on pupil characteristics (for example, ethnicity, primary language, and socioeconomic status) with pupil performance on tests; with their instructional history; and with student, parent, and teacher attitudes and opinions. These data may then be combined in any number of ways to provide information to decision makers about how to better manage instruction (Williams & Bank, 1984).

Instructional Information Systems can contain much of the data that is now normally stored in different locations in the school or central office and used only by those concerned about a specific aspect of instruction. Examples include data about student test scores, health records, and career plans. Instructional Information Systems, by making it possible to analyze multiple data sources, can greatly increase our understanding of individual students, groups of students, classes, and entire schools.

> The basic premise . . . is that while a variety of types of information (e.g., test, demographic, survey, interview and observational) can be and sometimes is collected from sources (e.g., pupils, teachers, administrators, parents) at multiple levels (individuals, instructional groups, classes, schools, districts) of the local educational system, these data are not commonly used in a manner consistent with existing knowledge about the possibilities and limits of data from multilevel social structures. (Burstein, 1983, p. 1)

Instructional Information Systems offer the potential of providing many types of users with data to serve their decision-making needs. We noted above that Management Information Systems and Decision Support Systems in business serve different users, the former providing information primarily for middle managers and the latter information for top-level managers and strategic planners. It may be that Instructional Information Systems, as they become operational in school districts and schools, will also split into two such discrete systems, one for teachers, perhaps, and one for administrators. Or one system might be for the school site and another for the district office. Alternatively, it may be more desirable to devise a way in which a single system can aggregate and report out the same data differently for teachers and school superintendents, or for parents and school boards.

An Instructional Information System might be able to help a teacher analyze the learning problems of a single student, locate the resources to provide remedial or supplementary instruction, place the child in an appropriate instructional group, or keep track of his or her progress through a continuum of skills. An IIS might help a principal check out the homogeneity or heterogeneity of class assignments; compare the progress of this year's students with last year's; examine the school's profile of achievement in reading as compared with math; or within the reading area, find out how students are doing in decoding skills as compared with comprehension skills. A superintendent or a school board member might query an IIS about the changing achievement pattern of the school as it relates to the changing demographic makeup of the area; or he or she might want to understand how additional funds for bilingual or special education affect the youngsters in those programs.

The creation and installation of Instructional Information Systems is a complex and costly sociotechnical process with many problems that must be solved before such systems become commonplace. However, we believe that Instructional Information Systems are on their way in some schools and in some school districts. What are these signs—some prominent, some almost invisible—that tell us that within perhaps five years Instructional Information Systems will be an important agenda item for schools and districts?

SIGNS INDICATING EDUCATIONAL READINESS FOR INSTRUCTIONAL INFORMATION SYSTEMS

In a recent article (Bank & Williams, 1985), we said that there are four factors that might predispose schools or districts to want an Instructional Information System. The first factor is the increasing diversity of the student population and the increasing complexity of the educational mission. The mobility of the American population is extraordinary. Children move with their families from state to state, from district to district, and frequently from school to school within districts. It becomes more and more important, therefore, that accurate and detailed records of instructional progress accompany students so that their needs can be accommodated in the receiving school.

The heterogeneity in our schools is also remarkable. We are only beginning to understand how differences in primary language, family relationships, and income level affect children's learning and how teaching and the organization of instruction should be modified accordingly. It becomes more and more important, therefore, that we begin analysis of learning patterns so as to assist schools in tailoring instruction to meet individual needs.

The task of education itself is becoming more complex. The future of our society is likely to require a large number of technically skilled individuals as well as people who can cope economically with shifting job requirements. We must begin to address not only basic skills but advanced skills. We must help meet the psychological and social needs of children in order to prepare them for the adult world of rapid change and uncertainty. We have to find ways to maintain better records on children so as to monitor and evaluate instructional effectiveness and student mastery of knowledge and skills.

The second factor contributing to educators' readiness for an IIS is the availability of technology. More and more areas of our society are making use of computers—in business, in entertainment, in daily life. We are becoming comfortable, as a culture, with the microchip. And as we do so in our daily lives, computer phobia and resistance to computerized information systems in the educational enterprise are diminishing. Concurrently, as education comes to be seen as a lucrative market for both hardware and software, vendors are paying more attention to the needs of administrators and teachers. Better and cheaper components of Instructional Information Systems are becoming available commercially. And there is a growing pool of people both technically qualified and experienced as educators, who can assist in the process of producing customized systems for schools and districts.

A third factor preparing the way for the introduction of information systems is the public's attitudes towards school reform. For example, accountability strategies adopted from business and government operations are popular with legislators. Such accountability strategies promote the use of specified, comparable, quantifiable data to determine whether an educational program has achieved its objectives. For many years now, legislators, program managers, and educational evaluators have struggled with developing such quantifiable and standardized measures of student achievement in the basic skills. Although the testing movement has not resolved all the difficulties in generalizing about students' knowledge from their performance on limited samples of multiple choice test items, progress has been made in designing tests that measure what they are intended to measure and whose results can be interpreted in relation to the individual, environmental, and instructional factors that might have influenced performance.

The federal government's 20-year involvement in education, starting in 1965, consistently supported the value of evaluation as a tool of local program reform. This support expressed itself in legislation mandating evaluation of federal programs as well as in substantial funding. Federal money encouraged the development of a research and evaluation community. Federal impact on school districts varied considerably. In some of the larger districts, research and development offices were created and large, trained staffs were assembled. Smaller districts handled evaluation requirements by routinely applying one of three federally developed evaluation models (Millsap, 1985).

The last factor that points to the likely emergence of Instructional Information Systems is almost invisible. Within a number of districts and schools are "idea champions" (Daft & Becker, 1978) who, usually without knowledge of one another or of the term "Instructional Information Systems," are developing components of such systems. Some of these individuals are extending their earlier evaluation efforts into a new field. Others are fascinated by the possibilities opened up by computers. For 10 years, our research at the UCLA Center for the Study of Evaluation (CSE) has sought out and identified a number of these districts (Bank & Williams, 1982; Williams & Bank, 1984). Currently, the CSE mailing list for the Instructional Information Systems Network includes over 150 interested districts and schools, primarily in the California area.

INFORMATION SYSTEMS NOW COME IN MANY SHAPES AND SIZES

We know that these district and school-level Instructional Information Systems are rarely named as such by the people who are working with them. Rather, they are seen as part of school improvement efforts, or of criterion-referenced testing programs, or of program evaluation activities. However, using a framework derived from the Management Information Systems literature, we can put an overlay on what the districts are doing. We will briefly compare four districts on core components of an IIS, such as specified users, specified uses, specified types of information inputs and outputs, specified information delivery procedures, and specified monitoring procedures for system functioning (Williams & Bank, 1985).

One small suburban district we know well has a centralized, highly coordinated system that includes a districtwide curriculum scope and sequence, districtwide criterion-referenced testing, districtwide staff development activities, clear expectations for principal supervision, and classroom supports in the form of learning and media specialists. Its purpose is to provide ongoing information and resources to classroom teachers, who then differentiate their instruction to meet individual needs. Its users are principals and teachers who examine the criterion-referenced test scores in order to plan instruction, monitor student progress, and communicate with parents. The information comes to them in the form of quarterly printouts. Teacher "debugging committees" keep the test items valid and the procedures free of frustration.

Another, a medium-sized urban district, has a school-oriented information system. The district sends out a variety of testing and survey data to help school planning teams do their own resource allocation. The district's purpose is to provide information and support to site teams who then help them solve school-level problems. School site council members and principals are the system's users, and they use annual school survey data combined with standardized test scores to identify school problems and generate solution strategies. The information comes to users in the form of annual school profiles.

A third district covers a large, sparsely settled geographic area and has an Instructional Information System consisting of three components. The first component outlines "what should be" in the form of goals, objectives, and a set of 10 elements of quality. The second component contains data about "what is" in the form of test scores on national norm-referenced tests and on locally developed criterion-referenced tests. Opinion data from surveys, parents, teachers, and students are also entered into the computer. The third component, "reducing the difference between what should be and what is," includes a framework of goal setting, planning, monitoring, and staff development. Users of the system are central office staff members and principals who are responsible not only for running the schools, but for managing the districtwide instructional improvement effort.

And a final example is a large urban district that routinely deploys its many evaluation staff members, who are based in the central office, out to local schools. Each of these local school evaluators uses the information system's output—in the form of a school profile made up of attendance figures, parent involvements, student transiency and dropout, teacher turnover, and parent, teacher, and student surveys—to assist principals and teachers in identifying school needs and in making plans to meet them.

SO, WHERE ARE WE?

It is possible that the signs indicating that Instructional Information Systems are coming are misleading. But we think not, given the social, technical, and school-related readiness factors just enumerated. We don't know, however, how they will come. It is possible that it will take longer than five years for them to emerge. They may, in fact, become widespread only when there are several ready-made models to choose from. Instead of the unique, customized IIS we see now in schools and districts, each laboriously created by inventors working alone, we may find that future Instructional Information Systems will be purchasable like hi-fi equipment—ready to be assembled and plugged in. It is also possible that Instructional Information

Systems, as a widespread innovation, could radically change learning, instruction, and school organization. Or alternatively, when they arrive we may find them to be more akin to the Xerox machine than to the light bulb—not revolutionary, but indispensable.

REFERENCES

Bank, A., & Williams, R. C. (1982, November). Linking testing and evaluation with school district instructional programs. *Evaluation Comment, 6*(3), 1–13.

Bank, A., & Williams, R. C. (1985). From program evaluation to instructional information systems. *Studies in Educational Evaluation, 11*, 159–82.

Burstein, L. (1983, April). *Using multilevel methods for local school improvement: A beginning conceptual synthesis* (Report to National Institute of Education, NIE-G-80-0112). Los Angeles: UCLA, Center for the Study of Evaluation.

Daft, R. L., & Becker, S. W. (1978). *The innovative organization: Innovation adoption in school organizations*. New York: Elsevier.

Levitan, K. B. (1982). Information resources management—IRM. In M. E. Williams (Ed.), *Annual review of information science and technology* (Vol. 17, pp. 227–66). White Plains, NY: Knowledge Industry Publications.

Millsap, M. A. (1985, January). *Evaluation and reform reconsidered: The impact of federal evaluation requirements on school districts*. Unpublished manuscript, Harvard Graduate School of Education.

Mitroff, I. I., Killman, R. H., & Barabba, V. P. (1979). Management information versus misinformation systems. In G. Zaltman (Ed.), *Management principles for non-profit agencies and organizations*. New York: American Management Association.

Rumberger, R. W. (1984, Summer). Computers. *IFG Policy Notes, 5*(3), 1–2.

Williams, R. C., & Bank, A. (1984). Assessing instructional information systems in two districts: The search for impact. *Educational Evaluation and Policy Analysis, 6*(3), 267–82.

Williams, R. C., & Bank, A. (1985). School districts in the information society: The emergence of instructional information systems. *Administrator's Notebook, 31*(6).

2
Instructional Information Systems: Dream or Nightmare?

MICHAEL QUINN PATTON

My task is to remind you of the things you know about information and the coming information age in order to establish a shared context for our deliberations on information systems in education. In so doing, we shall look forward and backward. As we strive to "invent the future," we shall talk about some of the nightmares we've experienced with data that did not provide us with either information or wisdom; we will renew our dreams and hopes for education in our society; and we will outline the role of information that might contribute to the improvement of education.

In times of fiscal contraint, budget cuts, and attacks on education from all sides, it's not always easy to renew our dreams and look to the future in a positive frame of mind. I recently saw a bumper sticker on the car ahead of me that said it all: THE FUTURE JUST ISN'T WHAT IT USED TO BE.

But one thing I want to remind you is how very recent are our systemwide efforts to provide excellence and equity in public education throughout the country. We hear so much in the news about reform, and so much change is occurring in public schools today that it is difficult, especially for those of us involved in education on a daily basis, to remember that, for example, the federal government has been actively involved in elementary and secondary education for only 20 years—a very brief time even in the short perspective of American history.

Indeed, we should take a longer-term historical perspective. It is worth remembering what the physical anthropologists tell us: that we have only been on this planet as a species somewhere between 3 and 5 million years, give or take a million—a relatively large standard error. During most of that period, we humans were organized in small hunting and gathering societies within specific territorial areas. The agricultural revolution that had us stay put on the land came next, and is only 10,000 years old. The industrial revolution which then replaced the agricultural society in some parts of the world is only 300 years old. And the information age—what some have called postindustrial society, and others the "third wave" (Toffler, 1980)—is only 20 to 30 years old. In short, we are still on the very beginning part of a learning curve—a steep upward slope—in figuring out how to use information effectively in the information age.

I believe that utilization of information is the key issue of the information age. The real challenge of our times is not in producing information or in sorting information, but rather, in getting people to transform information into knowledge. In the fields of medicine, nutrition, education, agriculture, and others, technological advances have far outstripped the willingness and ability of human beings to make new knowledge out of available information. It is people who use information. Computers and organizations generate data, but it is people who use information. The challenge for educational information systems is to point the way to the meaningful transformation of information into the knowledge of the future by students and educators.

There are really two parts to this information utilization issue:

1. What's *worth* knowing and why?
2. How can we get people to *use* information?

WHAT'S WORTH KNOWING AND WHY

The first question relates to the problem of focus in a time of information overload. One solution to the problem of focus has been not to focus but to trivialize. Unable to distinguish what's worth knowing, incapable of processing geometrically expanding data bases, unwilling to think hard about the relative merits of imperfect and conflicting knowledge, and resistant to the work of real knowledge utilization, some of us have turned to trivial pursuits. Our new national pastime—the pursuit of trivia—has become the best selling board game ever. Pursuing trivia solves the problem of figuring out what's worth knowing by making everything equally trivial. Winning the game rewards the recall of isolated facts and extols data storage and retrieval rather than focusing on the application and integration of information. I believe that many of the uses proposed for microcomputers in education border on the pursuit of trivia.

The game of *Trivial Pursuit*, then, is a manifestation of the information age at its most irrelevant level. By contrast, research-based, people-oriented, problem-focused educational information systems are examples of how the information age might enhance human potential.

Information systems are not ends in themselves. Indeed, information is not an end in itself. The computer and the media have made the acquisition of information easy and cheap. It's knowledge that is dear. I define knowledge as accurate, organized, and important information. Knowledge is power, but knowledge comes from knowing what information is worth having and knowing what to do with it. Information scientists tell us that 80 percent of what's worth knowing is contained in 20 percent of the facts (Anderson, 1980, p. 26). The challenge is figuring out what 20 percent is worth knowing, is worth focusing on, and is worth organizing, synthesizing, and using as knowledge.

Really taking seriously this challenge of focus—gathering only worthwhile and useful information—means an approach quite the opposite of what is usually done in designing information systems. The usual charge is to gather as much data as possible. The more appropriate charge, in my opinion, is: Gather the minimum necessary, not the maximum possible.

An information system out of control is one that produces volumes of statistics on virtually every aspect of educational programs, but the people who generate or review the data have no idea of what questions they are asking or how to arrange the outputs for use. This puts information system operators in a role similar to that of the Karnak character played by Johnny Carson on the "Tonight Show." Karnak the Magnificent, the all-knowing seer, sage, and soothsayer, provides the answers to unknown questions sealed in an envelope. After Karnak delivers the answer, the envelope is opened to discover the question. In the Karnak Approach, the information system generates answers and educators, given the answers, then try to figure out what were the questions. I recently spent several days working with a group of people in a county office helping them sort through their reams of statistics so as to figure out what questions they had answers to. When information systems are designed without specific questions in mind, the Karnak Approach to data interpretation may be the only way of using the data in the system. It certainly is not the most productive.

I suggest that information worth knowing exhibits several criteria:

1. It is problem-derived—that is, grounded in a real concern, need, or problem.
2. It is focused—that is, targeted at the articulated concern, need, or problem.
3. It is accurate.
4. Its context, boundaries, and origins are explicit.
5. It is understandable to those who must use it.
6. It is important to the knower because it provides insight or facilitates action.

HOW CAN WE GET PEOPLE TO USE INFORMATION?

Information utilization is inherently constrained because any one set of information is imperfect and incomplete. Information must always be interpreted and placed within a larger context. But having only imperfect or incomplete information should not keep us from planning and taking action. Recognizing the limits of information simply means that we should be realistic and modest in planning, and acknowledge the aphorism, "A good plan today is better than a perfect plan tomorrow."

Thus, inadequacies in information use stem not only from imperfections in the data themselves but also from the imperfections of human beings processing the information. We know that the information-processing capabilities of human beings are really quite limited. There are neurological limitations to human information-processing capabilities. The technical ability of computers to store information has far exceeded our mental ability to process and make sense out of information. Most of the time we act on biases, habits, rules of thumb, and "human heuristics" (see Patton, 1982, pp. 29–39), all of which distort the new information we take in and confound the new "knowledge" we generate. The good news, though, is that it is possible for us to become aware of our perceptual blinders and limiting habits. With that awareness we can become more conscious about our own information-processing mechanisms and can improve our knowledge-generating capabilities.

If computerized information systems that store, retrieve, and analyze data are to become genuinely useful to people, we'll need to apply to their development and operations what we currently understand about information utilization (see Patton, 1986). In capsule form, let me summarize some of the key things we've learned about how to get people to use information.

1. Since it is people who use information, information must be tailored to people.

2. Information only has meaning in terms of particular logics and values. The logic of research is not the only, or the dominant, way of processing information.

3. Information use requires getting the attention of users. Information competes for attention with other things people do and care about. Researchers and information system professionals need to learn a variety of attention-getting techniques.

4. Questions are as important as answers. Although we typically think of information systems as providing answers, the real challenge of the information age is asking the right questions. Figuring out the right questions makes it a lot easier to get useful answers. There is so much to know and so

much to do that it is easy to dissipate energy in trying to know and do everything. In a complex and rapidly changing world, where we can't know everything and we can't do everything, it is critical to ask the right questions that focus our efforts on gathering information to create knowledge worth having.

5. Information systems should be designed to be action- and decision-oriented. This means building in decision rules.

6. Information use is the responsibility of information providers. We can't blame those for whom the data are intended if they fail to use information we provide. For example, the ethical thrust of the *Standards for Evaluation* (Joint Committee on Standards for Educational Evaluation, 1981) makes evaluators responsible for providing data-based evaluations that are useful, practical, ethical, and accurate—and then for working with the evaluation users to ensure appropriate use. This point of view is also relevant to those who manage educational information systems.

In summary, I want to suggest that the future of information systems will be conditioned more by human factors than by technological or environmental factors. Human factors include both strengths and weaknesses. Our strengths are our abilities to reason, to reflect, to change, and to persevere in the face of difficult problems. Our weaknesses are our unconscious patterns, limited information-processing capabilities, biases, fears, and resistances to change.

Educational institutions are part of the cutting edge of the information age. We can help move ourselves and others towards meaningful transformation of information into knowledge. In this regard, the high technology of education is not machines and computers. It is, rather, a state of mind. A "high tech" state of mind in schools is one that helps people change information into knowledge so as to solve important problems and thereby create a better world.

REFERENCES

Anderson, B. F. (1980). *The complete thinker*. Englewood Cliffs, NJ: Prentice-Hall.
Joint Committee on Standards for Educational Evaluation. (1981). *Standards for evaluation*. New York: McGraw-Hill.
Patton, M. Q. (1982). *Creative evaluation*. Beverly Hills: Sage.
Patton, M. Q. (1986). *Utilization-focused evaluation*. Beverly Hills: Sage.
Toffler, A. (1980). *The third wave*. New York: Bantam Books.

3
What About Information Systems and Educational Improvement?

J. RICHARD HARSH

The title of this essay suggests an intriguing connection: through collecting, analyzing, reporting, and using accurate and appropriate information about students, classrooms, instruction, and support systems, we may be able to create a self-renewing and constantly improving learning environment.

Those who believe that such a connection exists encourage educational organizations to reconceptualize themselves so that the purpose of the educational enterprise will be clearly defined and understood by all concerned. Furthermore, in order to achieve these clearly defined institutional purposes, the believers insist that there be a set of explicitly defined objectives. Some of these, in turn, should be identified as essential student outcomes that should be tested and retaught to students if they do not pass the test. Many believers assert what they think is a self-evident corollary—that educational organizations should be run on a Management by Objectives (MBO) philosophy where resource allocation is linked to the priorities preassigned to various objectives. Management guidelines for school administration might even go so far as to specify that requests for additional funds, changes in staffing, replacement of materials, or introduction of new programs will be considered only when supported by documentation that includes data from the Instructional Information System.

All of the foregoing points are offered by supporters of this view of instructional improvement as common sense procedures that will produce more efficient and effective school operations. Believers argue that adherence to such a system will eliminate the ambiguity, controversy, and confusion that they see as contributory to the less-than-optimal levels of student attainment.

I am not a believer. It is my contention that the foregoing enthusiastic prescriptions for introducing and employing managerial and technological innovations in education have not paid adequate attention to the fact that education is a "people system." It seems to me that education's long history of strenuously resisting the introduction of methods and materials that appear to be effective in business or industrial production bears this out. (Even business has been led to question some of these methods: U.S. industry is recently discovering that the Japanese have prospered not by focusing on outcomes but by attending to the dynamics of the relationship between workers and the methods, schedules, and techniques they use for producing the product most efficiently.)

For example, the educational accountability movement, which borrowed from accountability notions developed in the defense industry, was hailed as an innovation that would force improved performance from all levels in the educational system. Of course, we all know that an idea has truly arrived when a state legislature mandates its adoption; thus, in California we knew accountability was here when the "Stull Bill" called for an objectives-appraisals-remediation cycle that administrators had to use with staff members (State of California, 1971). However, the nonimplementation of this attempt at accountability despite the passage of many years is eloquent testimony to how individuals in a people system develop effective defense mechanisms to protect themselves from unwanted and unhelpful external intrusions and pressures.

My reference to nonimplementation is based upon my observation that teachers who wish to be in compliance with the law state an objective for their classes, such as "40 percent of the children will go to the library once a month during the school year" or "the class will participate in all school assemblies and special events held on the school playground" or "75 percent of the pupils will be able to use the suffix 'ed.'" Such trivial objectives are not likely to be part of an orderly or prioritized instructional sequence. As an alternative subterfuge to writing trivial objectives, teachers write objectives that their students have already mastered. The anxiety and hostility expressed by some teachers and administrators towards writing required objectives reflects their attitude: "If you push us on this, we will find a way to comply that will not jeopardize or interfere with what we are doing."

It does not seem irrational, then, for me to suggest that introducing into schools and districts a comprehensive Instructional Information System that will probably require some organizational restructuring is not likely to lead to educational improvement. I suspect that an information system—even a good one—will not guarantee educational improvement. This declaration is based upon my experience during 18 years of consulting with the Educational Testing Service, and five additional years of evaluation studies, that teachers, administrators, students, parents, and board members do not agree about what constitutes educational improvement or contributes to it. Board members may seek efficiency and reduced costs, administrators may be looking for improved test scores, teachers may be looking for improved student motivation, and parents may want increased attention to the individual student.

With little agreement as to what it is that should be improved, I suggest that there is serious doubt that any information system will contribute to school improvement.

It is the case that the state of the art of automated data processing (entry, storage, retrieval, analyses, simulation, and so forth) clearly permits information about school facilities, student characteristics, teachers' personnel files, curriculum content, instructional procedures, assessments of attitudes, achievements, or interests to be entered, cross-referenced, and analyzed in more extensive ways than has been possible in the past. Moreover, we know that having extensive data bases makes possible some powerful and intriguing "what if" simulations. Without thinking further, some might conclude that educational improvement will inevitably result from an information system containing files that can be manipulated in that fashion. For me, such a conclusion seems unwarranted unless there are other conditions and events that shape information systems in the direction of educational improvement.

Permit me to talk about the contrast between the business uses of computerized information and the instructional uses of computerized information. The most straightforward application for information systems might be to deal with school facilities, supplies, transportation, and the like. Data about such things may be codified and analyzed in more complete and useful ways than was ever possible with manual methods. Indeed, up-to-date information may be presented on a screen in seconds. Purchasing decisions, for example, may be made in a fraction of the time required by manual systems.

There is no question that we have "speed"; we also have mountains of data representing "volume"; complex arrays of data may be integrated, separated, sectioned, or correlated in a matter of minutes. We can anticipate substantial savings in labor, time, and costs, as well as in bulky files, paper generation, paper distribution, and paper replies. Conducting inventories, handling acquisitions and replacements, and monitoring all these functions are facilitated by the new automated systems. Less manual effort, faster entry, communication, storage, retrieval, and analysis—they are all possible. These very substantial gains are appreciated by the staff working in the offices responsible for business, facilities, and operations. But would parents, faculty, or prospective employers acclaim these gains as evidence of educational improvement? I think not.

There is little doubt that it is the instructional program itself that most people would regard as the heart of education and therefore the focus of educational improvement. But instruction as it is delivered in classrooms has many facets that are highly resistant to change and to computerization.

For example, methods of organizing a classroom and preferences for instructional techniques are very personal and revered by the teacher using them. The teacher who has developed an excellent didactic presentation on a historical event will probably reject an itemized presentation transmitted by individually assigned learning packages covering the same material. Great efforts were expended to develop Diagnostic-Prescriptive-Individualized instruction for the educationally disadvantaged. Volumes of instructional materials were created and distributed but many teachers used them not at all or in many ways that were not individualized. This was due to many teachers' preference for their own instructional style, for their own ways of doing things.

Those who work with instructional programs are often skeptical of information that does not emerge from their own immediate classroom experience; they trust that which is recorded simply in their own grade book or in their own "memory file."

In spite of everything I have just said, I do believe that Instructional Information Systems do have some promise if we limit our expectations to what is realistic based on our past experience. A few historical events suggest some parallels. The radio was first thought to be an enormous benefit to education. It wasn't. And then TV came along and was to be a giant multisensory experience to motivate students and stimulate skill development. That didn't happen. Computers in the classroom are the most recent technical innovation. They were supposed to allow truly "individualized instruction" at a relevant level for each student. We all got excited; now, we thought, mastery learning would truly be possible because computer-assisted instruction would allow each student to progress at his or her own rate. We were told that desk top microcomputers were the answer to developing competencies in basic computation as well as logic and higher-order problem solving skills.

But evaluation of these technological additions to classroom activities reveals some remarkably similar patterns. At the outset we anticipated great improvement in both the motivation and achievement of students. The enthusiasm was shared by teachers, administrators, students, parents, and technicians. For example, initial small-scale demonstrations with computers in the classroom, and with video presentations, showed increased student motivation, positive attitudes, and spurts in achievement not previously attained. As larger populations were introduced to these innovations there was a strong tendency to offer them to all—and to deny them to no one. As a result, comparisons between treated and nontreated groups were difficult to arrange. Nonetheless, even using each group as its own control, the first semester of CAI or TV or video disks or desk computers showed positive attitudes and achievement gains. The magnitude of gain seemed to be highest at the primary grades, with a declining increment of gain through the upper elementary, junior high school, and high school years. But it seemed that there was a lack of "sustained effect" when students used the technology for the second or third years (Carter, 1984; Ragosta, 1981).

Short-term gains in academic achievement, increased student motivation, and teacher enthusiasm are fairly common results attributable to computer-assisted instruction during one or two years of the elementary grades. Sustained effects rest upon the ability of educators to integrate the CAI into a continuum of instruction rather than having it remain an add-on or on the periphery. This has happened only in some schools.

These experiences with technological innovations seem to me to provide some important cautions and suggestions for the implementation and management of information systems that are supposed to meet classroom needs.

1. Information systems must provide relevant support for the existing instructional system. Report formats must therefore be carefully tailored for different users. Irrelevant data may obscure the desired information; unclear formatting may make the reading of the report so laborious that it is rejected.

2. Educational improvement must be clearly defined with the input of many audiences. It may not be possible to get complete agreement on all details; even so, a description of desired improvements with statements of what would constitute evidence of improvement might suffice.

3. The design of instruction should be closely tied to the concepts and criteria for educational improvement.

4. Information systems should not be standardized. Rather, an IIS should be designed, developed, and used by the staff to satisfy their own interests, needs, dreams, or questions concerning instruction. Information systems need not be identical for all teachers but should be flexible enough for different cognitive teaching styles. Could we not figure out how to subdivide an Instructional Information System so that there might be different parts for the governing board, the community, the site administrator, the teachers, and other agencies? Once again, I believe that information systems must be designed to accommodate many different requests for specific data reports and a variety of analyses.

5. Every Instructional Information System should have a professional and technical support system to help in the "search for reality." Some persons have over-exuberant and unquestioning acceptance of numerical data, while others on the same staff will be irritated with such data and denounce their limitations. A system "counselor" could be a moderating influence and help with interpretation so that continuing participation of the staff is encouraged.

6. Information systems must be based upon trust, ownership, and control. One way to do this is to say that those affected by data should participate in the design of the data sets and be comfortable with uses that will be made of the data.

7. We must innoculate people against emotional appeals to stay up with the latest invention. We must stimulate a quest for reality testing. It is essential that security, satisfaction, and inquiry undergird the implementation of a new system. Moreover it is important that the system begin with where people are now—not where we may wish they were.

The foregoing suggestions for the development of an effective information system that will improve instruction stress the importance of (1) clear definitions of its content, use, and implication; (2) comprehensive understanding of the intent of the system by the many audiences affected by the system; and (3) a design for implementation that allows all participants and users of the system to suggest *en route* modifications that will increase the reliability, usability, and effectiveness of the system.

To be even modestly effective in supporting educational improvement, an IIS must be enthusiastically supported by the people who produce, report, and use the information.

REFERENCES

Carter, L. F. (1984, August/September). The sustaining effects study of compensatory and elementary education. *Educational Researcher*, 4–13.

Ragosta, M. (1981). *The study of computer assisted instruction*. Princeton, NJ: Educational Testing Service.

State of California. (1971). *California Assembly Bill 293*.

4

Some Lessons for Educators from Management Information Systems Literature

ADRIANNE BANK and ELAINE CRAIG

There is a growing literature in the field of Management Information Systems (MIS) that may have some transfer benefit for educators. While reviewing this literature from the perspective of the educator, it is important to think about the similarities and differences between business operations and schools' operations. Schools are not businesses; teachers, principals, and central office administrators are not managers; and students are not products. However, the adults who work in schools or districts and those who work in business organizations have common needs: among them, to have their jobs regarded as important; to have some amount of control over their daily activities; and to be consulted over changes that make their tasks easier, harder, or different in some way. So it appears that there may be some interesting organizational lessons that educators can learn from the business experience about introducing, developing, operating, and assessing information systems. At the very least, educators may be able to learn from business operations' mistakes. They can become aware of issues that need advance consideration at each stage in the life cycle of an Instructional Information System.

Before indicating more specifically what lessons we believe educators can infer from the MIS experience, we will characterize the MIS literature and describe one formulation of the MIS life cycle, using it to point to a few of the issues around which current discussion is organized. The journals that interested educators might peruse for current information about Management Information Systems include the *MIS Quarterly, Harvard Business Review, Management Science,* and *Sloan Business Review*.

CHARACTERISTICS OF THE MANAGEMENT INFORMATION SYSTEMS LITERATURE

The MIS literature of the past 15 years—which includes research studies, accounts of experience, and analytic articles—bears some resemblance to the evaluation literature of the same period. One resemblance is in the matter of definition. In the evaluation literature, there is no single accepted definition of evaluation; rather, there are alternative definitions connected either to evaluation models or to evaluation experts.

Within the management information field, there also appears to be little consensus on any single definition of its topic, Management Information Systems. Some authors discuss Management Information Systems as if they were information systems for managers; some write as if the field were concerned primarily with the systematic management of information. Frederick (1971) describes a Management Information System as "an interlocking coordinated set of management systems designed to optimize the planning, control and administration of specific processes operationally, tactically and strategically" (p. 9). Burdeau (1974) describes the major components of an MIS as the operating system, measuring system, reporting system, and management system. Holland, Kretlow, and Ligon (1974) describe MIS as "a communication process in which data are accumulated, processed, stored and transmitted to appropriate organizational personnel for the purpose of providing information on which to base management decisions" (p. 14).

A second similarity between the evaluation literature and the MIS literature is in the portrayal of changing concerns of the two fields. Much writing in the early days of educational evaluation dealt with the technical aspects of how to do evaluation—how to develop the appropriate tests or measures with which to collect data and how to develop the appropriate analyses with which to interpret the data. Hopes were high that with the solution of those technical problems, evaluation efforts would provide a way to compare programs, to monitor programs, or to manage programs so as to lead to greatly improved educational practice. More recently, the evaluation literature reflects evaluators' increasing concern that their work has not been used. The solutions to such nonuse seem to require new ways to match evaluation models with settings and with new techniques for integrating evaluation into organizational life (Bank & Williams, 1981).

Likewise, the MIS literature of 20 years ago reflects a preoccupation with technical problems, particularly data processing, and with forebodings as well as hopes that MIS would make significant changes in managerial decision making. During the 1960s and early 1970s there was academic speculation that the manager's workload would be increased due to the increase in quantity of detailed data (Diebold, 1969, p. 176); that the managerial work environment would change substantially and therefore that managers' behavior would be modified (Daniel, 1966); and that MIS would have a deleterious effect on managerial attributes, diminishing the value of such talents as accepting challenge, assuming responsibility, and making opportunities—in short, changing the type of people who would want to become managers (Anshen, 1960). However, by the late 1970s and early 1980s, after some experience with the actual impacts of Management Information Systems on their host organizations, there were more realistic, limited assessments of the amount of organizational and personal change, either for good or bad, that an MIS would introduce.

In an article entitled "Management in the 1980's Revisited," Hunt and Newell (1971) review several of the trends that had been predicted in the earlier literature. In particular, they discuss the prediction that computerizing information handling would centralize both information processing and decision making because time-sharing and fast transmission would make it more convenient and inexpensive to have a large centralized computer operation rather than a number of smaller decentralized operations. They note that, at the time, there was also the counterprediction that computerization of information would lead to decentralization, because of the assumption that businesses would rush to purchase personal computers for their managers. The authors conclude, based on reviews of the actual experience of businesses, that "the type of decision making is frequently determined not by the computer [itself] but by the personal preferences or philosophies of the chief executive" (p. 39). Kroeber (1982) corroborates this view, noting that it is management's attitude toward centralization that influences MIS structure, rather than MIS influencing the attitudes of management (pp. 130-31).

In terms of the predicted effect of computerized information systems on personnel, Hunt and Newell find that some of the earlier speculations about changes in managers' job descriptions have indeed occurred. "With the advent of computers, middle managers spent more time on such functions as communication, interpretation and counsel. . . . Repetitious, routine aspects of their jobs decreased or disappeared" (p. 40). However, the predicted takeover of the organization by the computer specialist apparently has not happened. "Evidence indicates that companies tend to put operating people in charge of the computer function rather than vice versa because it is easier to educate them in computers than to teach computer specialists about business" (pp. 40-41).

Whatever the experience of companies that actually use their computerized Management Information Systems, there appear to be many organizations where Management Information Systems have been installed but where the anticipated uses of the system have not occurred. Several major articles have started in ways similar to this: "Recently, researchers have suggested that a large number of information systems have failed and that many operations research models are never used. The problems of implementing information systems and operations research models must be solved if benefits from management science are to be realized" (Lucas, 1978, p. 39). From the number of papers dealing with MIS implementation issues, it is clear that information systems—like evaluation systems—are somewhat more likely themselves to be changed, subverted, or ignored by the host organization than they are to make drastic changes in the organization's structure, routines, and relationships.

Our brief review of the MIS literature, then, reveals the struggle of the writers to define what information systems are and do, their attempts to anticipate both negative and positive consequences of installing such systems, and their considerable dismay at the implementation difficulties encountered when new systems are introduced into old organizations.

Our review also reveals the growing interdisciplinary nature of the MIS field. Just as evaluation has become a diverse arena that now includes the contributions of anthropologists, sociologists, and economists as well as behavioral psychologists and psychometricians, so has the management information field expanded the range of experts on which it draws. The MBA brochure on computers and information systems at UCLA states that information processing to support management decision making "requires the contributions of a number of disciplines including accounting, economics, management theory, behavioral science, management science and computer science." Students pursue studies in "computer systems analysis, management of data processing activities, design of computer based management information systems, modeling and computer simulation, data base management systems and telecommunications and computer networks. The behavioral, organizational and economic aspects of information systems design also receive considerable attention" (University of California, 1983-84).

How do those interested in Management Information Systems deal with this interdisciplinary complexity? What organizing frameworks do they use that might assist educators who want to understand the research and experience in the business sector? We will here briefly describe the MIS life cycle, a convenient outline within which to discuss some major issues.

THE MIS LIFE CYCLE

It should be emphasized that the MIS life cycle appears to be laid out as a sequential and chronological approach to designing, installing, and using a computerized information system. The experience of those working with information systems indicates that despite the fact that the life cycle is a useful way to highlight issues occurring at each step, an administrator or designer would do well to understand the entire life cycle before beginning the first step. Additionally, many of the issues raised at one step must be addressed again at another, the process proceeding in spiral rather than in linear fashion. For example, the general problem of defining the organizational need for information systems may be raised and resolved during step

1, but statements of purpose may well have to be redefined and refined at a different level of specificity at step 5.

The concept of an MIS life cycle is widespread within the MIS literature. However, the steps in the life cycle—as well as the specifics within each step—have been given different names by different authors. Leavitt and Whisler (1958) label the stages as planning, purchasing, implementing, and utilizing. Lucas (1978) calls them inception, feasibility, analysis and design, and programming. We will use Kroeber's (1982) description of the cycle, paraphrasing his eight steps.

STEP 1: DETERMINING ORGANIZATIONAL NEEDS. A Management Information System can often satisfy needs that arise because of the complexity of operations in the organization, the volume of transactions performed, the interdependence of the operations, and the need to reduce errors and increase speed. Such needs might also include those of strategic planning and support for complex decision making.

STEP 2: FEASIBILITY STUDIES. To determine whether a Management Information System can be established, technical, economic, and behavioral feasibility studies should be performed. Technical studies include investigation of appropriate state-of-the-art hardware and software and of the technical constraints imposed by limits on storage space, access time, and so forth. Economic studies might include cost-benefit analyses in terms of both time and dollars. Behavioral feasibility studies answer the question, "Is this worth all of the trouble it is going to cause?" Areas for attention include analyzing the nature of the organizational resistance to Management Information Systems and likely options for dealing with it, staff training and retraining needs, and the possibilities of having to reorganize structure and staffing.

STEP 3: THE MASTER PLAN. At this point objectives, resources, and development strategy must be integrated into an overall plan. The decisions made at this time are critical and must therefore reflect input from a variety of stakeholders.

STEP 4: DEVELOPING THE MIS. Management Information Systems can be developed through a number of approaches: top down, bottom up, total systems, modular, and eclectic. Each of these development strategies has advantages and disadvantages. In the top-down approach, also referred to as an objectives-oriented approach, the MIS is designed to support the organization's goals and objectives as articulated by top management, thus gaining their commitment and support of the system. The bottom-up approach, on the other hand, first satisfies lower-level transaction-processing requirements, summarizes that data for first-line managers, reanalyzes that data for middle managers, and does so again for top-level managers. Bottom-up strategies attend primarily to the needs of middle managers, who are heavy users of Management Information Systems. If they are satisfied in handling the operations of the organization, so the argument goes, the satisfaction of overall organizational goals and objectives will follow. The total systems approach is a view that treats the entire organization as a single integrated operating unit to be served by a similarly integrated information system. The modular approach, by contrast, addresses each subsystem of the organization separately, only integrating the system at the end, if at all. Each subsystem may follow organization chart patterns, often along functional lines such as finance, accounting, production, and marketing. It is argued that the modular MIS is likely to be less disruptive to the organization than one designed in relation to the total system since it follows the existing divisions. The eclectic strategy says that features from any or all of the foregoing can be combined into whatever is appropriate for a given organization.

STEP 5: ANALYSIS AND DESIGN. Logical systems design requires defining the relationships between users, operators, equipment, input, output, and processing. Systems flowcharts are often prepared to integrate all elements.

In output design, the designer considers the content, form, frequency, and medium of output. Content of the data base may have been fairly well defined during earlier steps and may be only slightly revised or refined during this design step. Form design deals with such matters as column and row headings on reports, spacing, graphic displays, and so forth. Output frequency may be daily, weekly, monthly, on-call, or continuous.

The output requirements determine the input requirements. A weekly status report, for example, requires input on the type and frequency of some activity, or the hours of time expended, or what still remains to be done. Some of these data may be already collected routinely; others may have to be collected specifically for the purpose of the MIS.

In the process design stage, the designer determines the way in which input is converted to output. The design of the physical system means organizing and integrating personnel with facilities and hardware.

STEP 6: IMPLEMENTATION. The implementation phase is marked by four major activities: site preparation and installation of hardware, testing and debugging, training, and conversion to the new system. Site preparation and installation has to do with environmental requirements for the computers and actual installation. Testing and debugging means looking for syntax errors and logic errors in the programming. Training involves preparing personnel for the introduction of the MIS, assurances of job securities, solicitation of user support, and development of procedure manuals. Orientation and training sessions are usually needed.

STEP 7: THE OPERATIONS PHASE. Once the system is in place and working, several new considerations must be addressed. These include attending to the requirements for physical security (i.e., insurance against theft, fire, flood, and other natural disasters), making plans to deal with equipment and data losses, and the design of backup systems and of protection systems to guard against deliberate acts of sabotage.

Precautions must be taken to preserve the integrity of information. Some information may be confidential because it contains data of a personal or proprietary nature, such as personnel records or financial statements. All data must be guaranteed against computer crime and against serious errors that would result in losses to the organization.

Error detection can be done at various stages of processing. Verification is a means of detecting data preparation errors. Editing is a means of catching input errors, a reasonableness check can ensure that the data are within certain reasonable limits, a totals check prepares beginning and ending totals, and check digits guard against transmission errors when the data are moved from storage and back again.

STEP 8: THE CONTROL PHASE. Control really begins during planning and occurs during every phase of the MIS life cycle. During the planning period, control standards should be established and periodic evaluations should be scheduled. One type of evaluation, the progress review, should occur during the development phase. Another, the acceptance test, takes place during the implementation stage. Shortly after implementation—that is, early in the operating phase—a postinstallation review is conducted. Periodic audits are administered at regular intervals, usually six months or one year, for the life of the system.

Progress reviews measure actual activities against planned activities. The purpose of such a review is to bring to light the discrepancies between action and the master plan, and to redirect development efforts when that is required.

The acceptance test is the final activity before conversion to a new MIS. The acceptance test is a systems test to include user personnel, which must satisfy the MIS project management team that the MIS is ready for implementation. The acceptance test may be designed by MIS personnel but it should be conducted by an agency with less personal involvement. There must be clear, quantitative standards for acceptance or rejection. Error rates, turnaround time, and measures of accuracy provide unambiguous standards for comparison.

Postinstallation review occurs when the operation of the new system is technically satisfactory, but the system must be evaluated in behavioral terms. In brief, is the system accomplishing what it was intended to do? Several criteria can be applied at this stage: cost-benefit analysis, attitude surveys, and measures of impact that look at past performance.

Audits can be of three kinds: financial audits, operational audits, and management audits. Auditors may come from within the organization or from outside. The auditing of MIS operations may be facilitated by the use of performance monitors—that is, hardware monitors that keep track of active and idle time for various components such as the printer, and software monitors or computer programs that record processing time for application software.

LESSONS FOR EDUCATORS FROM MANAGEMENT INFORMATION SYSTEMS

Before we list some lessons, we should caution the reader that the "rules of thumb" we have selected from the MIS literature—based either on research studies or on reports of experience—are those that seem to us to be applicable in school settings. We know, for example, that businesses generally are perceived to have more control over the work life of their employees at all levels than appears to be the case in schools. We know that resource allocations in businesses are constrained by a different set of market, legal, and political forces than are resource allocations in schools. We know that the "payoff" for data processing systems is likely to be more easily identified, monitored, and described in cost-benefit terms in business settings than in school settings. We know that within educational settings today, in contrast to business settings, there are fewer outside or inside technical experts to provide assistance, fewer software programs written to accommodate educational information needs, and perhaps more technology phobia. Nonetheless, there appear to be a few generic lessons that might be useful for schools or districts interested in considering Instructional Information Systems for their organization.

DEFINING THE PURPOSE OF A COMPUTERIZED INFORMATION SYSTEM. The MIS literature assures us that the most important part of system design is defining the system's purpose. MIS authors make a number of observations about aspects of system purpose.

- The structure and management style of the organization affect the type of information system that is necessary (Tricker, 1977).

- Any information system must "solve the input problem," and so the question should be asked, "What are the classes of problems to which the system will restrict itself? Are they well known beforehand or unspecified? Fixed or changing?" (Mitroff, Kilmann, & Barabba, 1979).
- User Needs Analysis (UNA) is a process of problem identification, problem analysis, and presentation of alternative solutions that the system designer and the organizational leader should engage in to determine if the organization has problems that require information systems as a solution (Hall, 1979).
- The directions and goals of the organization should be considered in deciding what type of information will be required (Tharrington, 1985).

THE ROLE OF LEADERSHIP AT THE DISTRICT AND/OR SCHOOL LEVEL. All MIS authors are in agreement about the critically important role that top leadership plays in relation to developing and installing an information system.

- Managers should themselves be informed about the complexities of the entire process of creating an Instructional Information System so that the decisions about system purposes, software development, hardware purchase, installation, debugging, maintenance, required personnel changes, and training costs will not come as a surprise to them (Hiscox, 1984; Jones, 1984; Lucas, 1982).
- Management should support the development of the system with time, interest, and resources (Kling, 1977; Multinovich & Vlahovich, 1984).
- Management should understand the importance of "people issues" related to intangibles such as anxieties over changes in job responsibilities, job security, and status; fear of having to learn new skills; fear of computers; and worry about use of data for personnel monitoring and evaluating (Argyris, 1970; Multinovich & Vlahovich, 1984).
- Management should understand the political factors involving power, special interests, and the meaning of access that influence individual and group attitudes toward system design and system use (Robey & Markus, 1984).

THE ROLE OF TECHNICAL CONSULTANTS IN SYSTEM DESIGN. There have been some strong statements from MIS experts about the responsibilities of system designers. Some MIS writers advocate an expanded role for the designer, who should not only help the organization define the purpose for the system but also should stay around for the installation and implementation. This heavily involved designer is contrasted with what some observers have noted as a more restricted role for the designer—that is, the one who provides only technical software design services, while the organization itself defines the purposes of the system (Ginzberg, 1978).

Whether the role is expanded or restricted, however, selection of consultants who are compatible with the organization's philosophies and management style is essential. Often a team of consultants is needed, each with different technical or organizational skills.

- Kling (1977) suggests that the organization select its consultants based on their technical competence and the degree of congruence between the consultant's orientation in relation to the process of designing the system and the organization's. He then suggests that the organization provide continuing feedback to consultants about the organizational consequences of their behavior, about the extent of their responsibility for system success or failure, and about the level of management support and resources they can expect.
- System designers may require considerable time, encouragement, and perhaps even training to understand how to interact with users and to be committed to such a process (Ginzberg, 1978).

THE ROLE OF USERS IN SYSTEM DESIGN. As with other topics in the MIS literature, there is little consensus on how much the user should be directly involved in the definition and development of the system. A traditional approach suggests that user needs be initially specified and that the designer develop the product to meet the users' needs. Another approach suggests a continuing dialogue between users and designers, while some advocate a merging of roles where, at some point, the user becomes the system designer (Lucas, 1978; McLean, 1979).

- Understanding of user needs can be acquired by outside observation of their work styles and decision-making characteristics, by interviews, or by soliciting user participation on planning teams (Synnott & Gruber, 1981). Other strategies, such as vertically representative steering committees, encourage all users to appreciate the multiple roles to be served by the information system (Robey & Markus, 1984).
- Markus (1981) warns of two problems: pseudo-participation, where people are ostensibly asked to participate but feel they are manipulated into supporting solutions they may not really like; and user special interests, where people become concerned about their own needs to the exclusion or detriment of overall organizational uses.
- User involvement—however defined—in determining the needs for and the design of the information system often results in favorable attitudes

towards the system itself, towards the service it provides, and towards the system staff (Lucas, 1975).
- Potential users may require considerable time, encouragement, and perhaps more training to understand the need for a change in the way information is processed and distributed.

EVALUATING INSTRUCTIONAL INFORMATION SYSTEMS. There are some general guidelines about evaluating information systems that seem quite consistent with what we know about evaluating other activities.

- Formative evaluation should take place while the system is under development so as to speed up the design phase, detect early-appearing problems, and make corrective adjustments (Meals, 1977).
- Summative evaluation can compare the new system with the old and results against expected benefits (Meals, 1977).
- Cost-benefit analysis is not the only approach to evaluation. Rather, evaluation should start with a negotiated consensus on what constitutes success (Keen, 1975; Multinovich & Vlahovich, 1984).

The major inferences that educators should draw, then, from the Management Information Systems experience is that information systems are not simply technically improved ways of storing and accessing records. They are, in fact, complex and costly sociotechnical innovations that require extensive homework, planning, and evaluation. Each of these activities involves all levels, including top management, and each is ongoing throughout the life of the IIS.

REFERENCES

Anshen, M. (1960). The manager and the black box. *Harvard Business Review*, 38(6), 85–92.

Argyris, C. (1970). Resistance to rational management systems. *Innovation*, No. 10, 28–35.

Bank, A., & Williams, R. C. (Eds.). (1981). *Evaluation in school districts: An organizational perspective* (CSE Monograph No. 10). Los Angeles: Center for the Study of Evaluation, University of California.

Burdeau, H. B. (1974). Environmental approach to MIS. *Journal of Systems Management*, 25(4), 11–13.

Daniel, D. R. (1966, Nov/Dec). Reorganizing for results. *Harvard Business Review*, 44(6), 96–104.

Diebold, J. (1969, Jan/Feb). Bad decisions on computer use. *Harvard Business Review, 47*, 14-16, 27-28, 176.

Frederick, W. A. (1971). A manager's perspective of management information systems. *MSU Business Topics, 19*(2), 7-12.

Ginzberg, M. J. (1978, May). Steps toward more effective implementation of MS and MIS. *Interfaces, 8*(3), 57-63.

Hall, T. P. (1979, January). User need analysis. *Journal of Systems Management*, 12-13.

Hiscox, M. D. (1984, Summer). A planning guide for microcomputers in educational measurement. *Educational Measurement, 3*(2), 28-39.

Holland, W. E., Kretlow, W. J., & Ligon, J. C. (1974). Sociotechnical aspects of MIS. *Journal of Systems Management, 25*(2), 14-16.

Hunt, J. G., & Newell, P. F. (1971). Management in the 1980's revisited. *Personnel Journal, 50*(1), 35-43, 71.

Jones, R. (1984, November 1). *Microcomputing: An overview and response to common questions*. Los Angeles: Los Angeles County Office of Education, Regional Data Processing Center.

Keen, P. G. (1975). Computer-based decision aids: The evaluation problem. *Sloan Management Review, 16*(3), 17-29.

Kling, R. (1977, December). Organizational context of user-centered software designs. *MIS Quarterly, 1*(4), 41-52.

Kroeber, D. W. (1982). *Management information systems: A handbook for modern managers*. New York: The Free Press.

Leavitt, H. J., & Whisler, T. L. (1958). Management in the 1980's. *Harvard Business Review, 36*(6), 41-48.

Lucas, H. C. (1975). *Why information systems fail*. New York: Columbia University Press.

———. (1978, Winter). The evolution of an information system: From key-man to every person. *Sloan Management Review*, 39-52.

———. (1982). *Coping with computers: A manager's guide to controlling information processing*. New York: The Free Press.

Markus, M. L. (1981). Implementation politics: Top management support and user involvement. *Systems, Objectives, Solutions, 1*(4), 203-215.

McLean, E. R. (1979). *End users as application developers* (Information Systems Working Paper). University of California, Los Angeles, Graduate School of Management, Center for Information Studies.

Meals, D. W. (1977, July). Systems evaluation. *Journal of Systems Management*, 6-8.

Mitroff, I. I., Kilmann, R. H., & Barabba, V. P. (1979). Management information versus misinformation systems. In G. Zaltman (Ed.), *Management principles for non-profit agencies and organizations* (pp. 401-432). New York: American Management Association.

Multinovich, J. S., & Vlahovich, V. (1984, August). A strategy for a successful MIS/DDS implementation. *Journal of Systems Management, 35*, 8-15.

Robey, D., & Markus, M. C. (1984). Rituals in information system design. *MIS Quarterly, 8*(1), 5-15.

Synnott, W. R., & Gruber, W. H. (1981). *Information resource management: Opportunities and strategies for the 1980's*. New York: Wiley.

Tharrington, J. M. (1985, June). The science of MIS planning. *Infosystems, 32*, 52–53.
Tricker, R. I. (1977). The impact of information systems on organizational thinking. *IFP*, 213–221.
University of California. (1983–84). *Studies in Computers and Information Systems*. Los Angeles: University of California, Los Angeles, Graduate School of Management.

PART II

Alternative Types of Instructional Information Systems

Part II describes the variety of instructional information system models already being developed in districts and schools. These IIS models differ from one another in terms of purpose, underlying assumptions, scope, and development strategy. This is not surprising in view of the fact that each system was invented in response to the unique needs of the district as seen by an "idea champion" who was supported by technical and managerial skills from within the district or hired from outside. It is interesting to speculate as to whether future systems will continue to be developed autonomously, district by district, or whether a general development paradigm will emerge that will lower costs and considerably shorten the trial and error process.

Cannings and Polin report on their survey of 30 high schools, which investigated how computers were used by administrators. The authors conclude that computer use by principals is spotty and the need to provide orientation and training for them is great. However, in two high schools where an effort had been made to develop user-friendly data bases, principals, assistant principals, and counselors expressed enthusiasm for the computer's potential for spotting educational trends and identifying solvable problems.

Idstein describes the Christina, Delaware, Instructional Management System (CIMS), in which a computer network supports a comprehensive grade-by-grade testing program to track student progress through a basic skills curriculum. He traces the development of the system and discusses implementation problems related to logistics, equipment, training, data bases, multi-user systems, and adaptation to change. He also raises policy issues around promotion requirements, mastery learning, rights of privacy, equal protection, and due process. Speculating on what the future role of technology in education might be, Idstein looks forward to a world of empirical decision making based on dynamic data bases.

Blum and Butler furnish a description of a developmental effort by the Northwest Regional Educational Laboratory in which Centennial High School, Portland, Oregon, served as one of the early pilot sites. In this effort, called the "Onward to Excellence Program" (OTE), school staff members collectively make decisions about school improvement goals based on three types of student performance data: academic achievement, attitude, and social behavior. The profile development step in the OTE program is an information support system for communication among teachers, principals, and district administrators that provides the basis for determining school improvement goals related to student performance.

In "Developing an Elementary School Information System: The Computer-Assisted Professional," Cooley reviews the need for automated information systems and lists the goals, functions, and characteristics of effective systems. He comes out strongly for distributive systems that can be used for school improvement as well as central office research and record-keeping. He describes the prototype system developed by the Learning Research and Development Center in collaboration with a Pittsburgh public school. He explains the hardware and software and emphasizes that two kinds of expertise are needed to create effective systems: that of on-site educators and of research and data analysts. However, it is possible that the latter type of expertise can become a routine, built-in part of future systems.

Carey recounts his experiences in introducing into one elementary school a simple Apple IIe office management system to reduce clerk time spent on attendance record-keeping. He notes that this small change in the office management system created a ripple effect such that six schools are now participating in an enlarged system that includes a student file with achievement test data. Although the system has been easily learned by clerks, it has taken longer for principals to understand how it can be used to look at patterns and trends in student achievement. Carey stresses the need to expose principals to the potentials of the system, to urge them to ask questions of the system, and to encourage them to integrate the information coming out of an Instructional Information System with their own professional expertise and experience.

It is quite evident from the chapters in this section that even school districts and schools that have spent several years acquiring the computers, software, and data bases to get an Instructional Information System up and running are having to improvise as they go. Difficult as it may be to finance and initiate such a system, it seems even more difficult to administer it so that it runs smoothly and makes work easier and more productive. It is a complex task to create systems not only to increase efficiency on routine tasks but also to stimulate the new thinking and altered perceptions that will lead to problem seeking and solution finding.

Each of the systems presented in this section hints at what this new thinking or altered perception might involve. For example, Cooley points to trend spotting and problem identification that can be done easily by administrators if data analysis routines are built into the programs by skilled and sensitive technical experts. For Idstein, the IIS has raised ethical questions about individual rights as well as policy questions about how to structure student movement through the instructional system. For Blum and Butler, information aggregated in new formats provides opportunities for conversation among educators. Carey suggests that altered personnel policies and practices may be necessary because an IIS often affects school office management.

5

The Computer as an Administrative Tool: A Survey of 30 High Schools

TERENCE R. CANNINGS and LINDA POLIN

Since 1974, when the first personal computers appeared on the market, the microchip has changed working life for many of us; and its potential impact is probably even greater than its past impact. We believe that the likely effect on educational administration is particularly profound. With its ability to analyze vast amounts of information, the microcomputer will influence both the definition of educational issues and the decisions that are made about them by school administrators and classroom instructors. Says Nolan Estes, Coordinator of the Superintendent's Training Center at the University of Texas: "In the next two decades, microcomputer technology will revolutionize teaching and learning similar to the printing press, 500 years ago" (Estes, 1983).

But the U.S. school system is not known for the rapid adoption of changes. Reactive rather than proactive, it is often slow to respond to new ideas and make effective use of newly available resources, whether technological or human. The school principal is often a key figure in adopting innovation, not only because the principal makes the crucial decisions that determine a school's attitudes towards new ideas but also because the principal serves as a model to other school personnel. Therefore, it is important to understand the extent to which school principals, as well as other influential administrators in the school setting, are now using the new computer technologies as a basis for their own decision making and for performing other administrative functions. The study reported here was designed to provide that information.

We sampled 30 Southern California high schools—located in Los Angeles, Orange, and San Bernardino counties—selected from a list of those institutions that had installed a computer laboratory at least two years prior to our visit. During the winter and spring of 1985, we interviewed up to four administrators at each site, asking the following questions:

Where are the computers located?
Who has access to them?

Does the principal use a computer?
What is the most important use of computers administratively?
Given a hypothetical $250,000 to improve the use of technology in administering your school, what would you do with it?

We will give an overview of the survey results, describe two schools' computerized information systems, offer some general impressions, and summarize issues that emerged from our study.

OVERVIEW OF THE RESULTS

Location of Computers

The computer resources available at the 30 high schools can be grouped into four categories: (1) district mainframe with one or more terminals at each mainframe site, (2) microcomputers networked at the site, (3) individual microcomputers in the administration block or scattered throughout the school, and (4) indirect access via forms or requests sent to the district office for entry into the district data base.

Table 5.1 shows that the computers used for administrative purposes were located chiefly in the main administrative office or in associated offices. Relatively few terminals or microcomputers were located directly in the principal's office. Most of the principals interviewed felt that they did not need direct access to a computer; they delegated this responsibility to their secretary or an assistant principal. In most cases, library staff members did not have direct access to computers. Of more importance, neither did teachers, who usually had to go to the counseling office in order to use terminals or microcomputers.

The table confirms that microcomputers can be decentralized much more easily than can mainframe terminals. One school had a "terminal room," housing two terminals and available to two certified staff members.

Administrative Uses of Computers

As shown in Table 5.2, mainframe terminals were used more frequently than were microcomputers to record attendance, compile master schedules, and maintain and update student records, including each student's history and grades. Relatively few schools reported using computers for other administrative tasks. For instance, only nine used mainframe terminals, and only seven used microcomputers for word processing. Only one in four schools used the computer to order supplies directly from the warehouse.

TABLE 5.1. Location of Computer Used for Administrative Purposes in 30 High Schools

Location	Mainframe Terminals	Micros
General Administrative Staff Area	22	2
Attendance Office	10	4
Counseling Office	9	4
Registrar's Office	2	--
Assistant Vice Principal's Office	2	4
Principal's Office	1	2
Student Council Room	--	4
Library	--	2
"Terminal Room"	1	--

Computers were rarely used for site budgeting, since most school administrators do not have the authority to develop their own budgets; one administrator, however, did use the computer to find out what remaining funds were available to him. The term "curriculum organization" refers to the administrator's ability to group students with different needs into different subject areas; only one respondent mentioned this use.

Principals' Use of Computers

Very few principals reported that they themselves used a computer. Rather, they depended upon assistant principals, counselors, and clerks to provide them with readable copies of requested information.

At the four high schools where principals reported themselves as actively using the system, they all focused on the retrieval of information rather than on analysis. Two said they did "what if" experiments involving budget planning or monitored attendance problems in order to identify the need for

TABLE 5.2. Administrative Uses of Mainframe Terminals and Microcomputers in 30 High Schools

All Uses	Mainframe Terminals	Micros
Attendance	26	6
Scheduling	24	4
Student Records/Data	22	4
Word Processing	9	7
View District Budget	7	1
Report Cards/Grades	7	2
Supply Requisitions	7	--
Inventory	6	--
School-Home Reporting	4	4
Teacher Reporting	4	--
Facility Usage	4	--
Transcripts	3	--
Site Budgeting	1	2
Electronic Mail	1	--
Curriculum Organization	1	--
Student Activities Budget	--	9
Student Store Bookkeeping	--	5
Inventory	--	5
Tracking Student Work Experience Time	--	4
Plant Operations Energy Control	--	1
School Newsletter	--	1

parent conferencing. These principals were self-taught and had received little assistance from the district office. One active user did not even have a terminal in his office; he had to go to the attendance office to use the system.

In general, the principals' failure to make use of the computer for policy analysis comes not from avoidance of such decision making but rather from their preoccupation with daily monitoring tasks and their tendency to adjust policies or programs in response to immediate problems and needs.

Future Uses

To explore the direction that administrative computing may take in the near future, we asked our sample of administrators how they would spend a hypothetical $250,000 over the next three years. Table 5.3 lists their preferences. The most frequently mentioned desired expenditure was for hardware: Two-thirds of the sample said they would spend the money for additional terminals for on-site users, including central office clerks, counselors, assistant principals, career guidance counselors, registrar's office clerks, and librarians. Beyond this, there was little agreement among respondents about how they would spend their money. Responses can be grouped into three main categories: peripheral hardware (e.g., a system for networking on-site machines), software, and training.

Generally, administrators found it difficult to articulate specific expenditures. Rather, they spoke in terms of intended or desirable uses of data—for instance, the ability to generate textbook listings by course or the need to contact parents about their children. For the most part, their intended uses reflect their desire to automate current tasks rather than to accomplish new tasks.

Approximately one-fourth of the respondents said that more money should be channeled into instructional computing programs, either to start up or to expand various computer-based courses. Although the popularity of this option may be attributable to an inability to articulate other potential purchases, it seems more likely that the administrators in our sample saw classroom computing as a top priority not yet fully addressed by available funds.

The next section describes what we feel are two outstanding school examples of how computers can be used for administrative purposes. We selected these two high schools from the 30 we visited. They are by no means ideal models—in fact, one system had only been in operation for 12 months—but they give an indication of what can be achieved at the high school level.

TABLE 5.3. Future Uses

Desired Uses	# of Respondents Mentioning This Item (N = 75)
Provide terminals for all major users	50
Acquire computer-based ways of contacting parents about students: e.g., autodial for unexcused absences	17
Channel more money into instructional uses	17
Acquire on-site minicomputer with terminals in all important administrative offices/areas	15
Add scheduling software, or scan-tron attendance systems	13
Improve computerized inventory capability	13
Provide (more) terminals/micros for teachers' administrative uses: e.g., department chairs	13
Buy training time for personnel, buy consultant time	10
Acquire check-writing software for student accounts: e.g., student store	10
Add more personnel or increase personnel expenditures	10
Acquire "a system that will do my bidding"	8
Link up with district computer	5
Link buildings on campus via networking	1
Install security devices and systems	1
Add software capabilities: to print textbook listings for courses	1
Keep site maintenance records	1

MAYFAIR HIGH SCHOOL: A DECENTRALIZED INFORMATION SYSTEM

Mayfair High School is a leading user of technology in its instructional program. Computers are available in two labs for teaching word processing, data entry, and programming skills. Computers in a third lab offer computer-assisted instruction (CAI) programs for students requiring remedial work. The school and the district have been committed to computer literacy for several years. Staff members recognize the potential contribution that the computer can make to improving their own decision-making processes. Because the district wanted to increase the abilities of individuals at the school site to monitor students, Mayfair was one of several schools chosen to receive additional district funds for computer services.

Prior to this decision, the district office had a contract with three vendors (two neighboring school districts and a county office) to provide computing services. Under this arrangement, the costs of maintaining files on attendance, grades, and physical performance testing; for doing scheduling; and for CTBS test scoring, exceeded $100,000 per year. District officials felt that the contracted services were not meeting the district's needs: The system did not provide enough user stations, on-line access time was limited, and only a few types of reports could be generated.

Requirements for a Computerized Information System

Administrators and teachers wanted immediate access to data that would help them to place students in classes on the basis of previous academic performance and standardized test scores. Also needed was a system that would allow school administrators to monitor students' attendance. The system had to include a comprehensive student data base and had to provide immediate access to all information contained within the system.

The district's computer master plan (Bellflower Unified School District, 1984–85) states: "A comprehensive data base is vital to the principal and the staff that are making administrative and instructional decisions. The data base should be the basic foundation, remaining flexible enough to interface with all components of the system." Accordingly, it was decided that the system should be able to perform the following specific functions:

- Score minimum competency tests at individual schools, with quick turnaround for easy scheduling
- Correlate test instruments with curriculum
- Provide district scoring of CTBS, with quick turnaround and efficient dissemination of results to those who do scheduling and planning of learning activities

- Print the information needed, so as to eliminate wasted effort and expense
- Maintain accurate and easily accessible average daily attendance records, so that each student's attendance can be closely monitored with immediate parent contact
- Provide up-to-date printouts on individual students, including course history, competency test scores, progress toward fulfillment of graduation requirements, and other transcript analyses required by students, parents, school counselors, or instructional staff
- Maintain a grade reporting system that records academic achievement, citizenship, work habits, variable credit, and comments, and that provides mail-ready report cards as well as lists that allow teachers to verify the grades printed on report cards, analyses of grades awarded, and honors lists
- Provide a scheduling system that produces course tallies, student listings, lists of potential conflicts, prescheduling edits, class load analyses, and reject listings

It was also decided that all modules should be totally integrated, not only with the basic data file but with each other.

Selection of a System

In looking for their system, district personnel investigated the computer systems currently on the market as well as those in other districts across the nation. District administrators visited sites in Southern California and in two other states and attended conventions such as the National School Boards Association's national conference in Houston.

The business administration office concluded that the district's needs could best be met by decentralizing data processing through the installation of high-powered multi-user microcomputers. Cost was a major consideration. By selecting standardized equipment, the district felt it would be in a position to upgrade and enhance internal components based on emergent needs rather than having to replace entire systems. Each school would have its own microcomputer and its own data base. With such a system, "smart" user stations (that is, the computers located at each station could perform analyses) would be strategically placed throughout the school, so that qualified personnel would have immediate access to information and printed reports. The district's data processing department would also maintain master files in order to generate required state and federal reports, score and summarize fourth- through twelfth-grade CTBS tests, print district-wide reports, maintain and monitor attendance, and coordinate the entire program.

Several software systems capable of meeting current and future data processing needs were considered. The program that seemed best was the School Administrative Students Information System (SASI), published by Educational Timeshare Systems (ETS) of Fullerton, California. The hardware chosen to run the software program was the Digital Micro System, recommended by the Educational Testing Service. Other systems such as the IBM PC, Televideo, Kaypro, and IMS International were also available to run the program.

Advantages of the System

The district report (Bellflower Unified School District, 1984-85) listed the following advantages of a decentralized over a centralized system:

Infrequent "down time"
Less frequent repairs and less costly maintenance
Significantly more user stations
Increased flexibility in the physical placement of systems
Easier transfer and storage of data
No specialized or controlled environment required
Increased capability for upgrading and expanding data files
Multiple systems, to serve as "backups" for each other
No additional personnel required to operate systems
Increased accessibility and control at the school site
Significantly lower initial and ongoing costs

Installation of the System

One major benefit of this decentralized microcomputer system was that no additional permanent staff members had to be hired at the district level. Only about four weeks of additional clerk-typist time was required to input all new student data at Mayfair High School. At first, information gathered at the site level was transferred to the district office and other sites via floppy disks. Once modems were introduced, student files were then transferred electronically to appropriate sites.

The configuration at Mayfair consisted of one Digital Micro System computer with a 40-megabyte hard disk and two floppy disks, two high-speed printers, one letter-quality printer, scantron, modem, and stations. The total cost including installation was $55,510; the software package including all available modules cost $7,500. The district's total budget—for all three high school, six elementary school, and two district office systems—allows $4,000 per year for software updates and maintenance and $5,000 for hardware repairs.

The "smart" terminals at Mayfair were allocated as follows: one to the principal's secretary, one to the assistant principal, three to the vice principal, four to the counseling office, and three to the attendance office. Additional "smart" terminals were to be added in the nurse's office and in the library counseling clerk's office in the future.

All of Mayfair's administrators have access to the data base. The principal requests information through his secretary. The main users of the system are the attendance clerk, an assistant principal, and the counseling staff. Attendance is entered on a daily basis, and letters are sent to parents after three and six absences. Counselors can immediately access the records of any student needing to be interviewed.

The system facilitates positive contacts with students. For instance, the principal sends "reward" letters to outstanding students every 20 days. The letters are entered into the word-processing system, matched with addresses, and mailed out.

Mayfair's assistant principal demonstrated the "query" command to us. He asked for a list of all graduating senior girls living on a particular street. These data were displayed on the CRT within 10 seconds. All data for each student—grades, attendance, and history—could be contained on one screen. So impressed was the assistant principal with the new system that he expressed great frustration at not receiving additional terminals for other offices by the end of the school year.

According to the district computer coordinator, who visits each site frequently: "People can't say enough good things about the system." This comment was seconded by the administrators at Mayfair. Like any new system this one still has some bugs, but the current system offers greater efficiency for less money than did the previous system.

Problems with the System

The district computer coordinator and the assistant principal in charge of the system at Mayfair were asked to indicate what problems they had encountered during the first 12 months of the new system's operation.

TECHNICAL. These were minor and easily fixed. For instance, a twisted-pair cable linking all the terminals with the hard disk was replaced with a flat cable and a repeater every 1,000 feet. In addition, there were short-term problems with a nonfunctioning scanner and a nonoperational auto-dial telephone system. Finally, the use of the scanner during open access created some duplicated records.

PERSONNEL. Some employees were unhappy because the new system resulted in personnel reductions. Prior to installation of the system, four people had worked three or more hours a day to perform certain tasks. Now, only two people are required to perform the same tasks: one works eight hours per day and one works three hours per day.

ACCESS. Teachers did not have direct access to the terminals but had to channel requests for information through one of the counselors. Security presented no particular problem. To protect and check records, a backup copy was made of all files on a daily basis. These data were stored on seven floppy disks and kept in a security cabinet. Data were checked on a weekly basis.

The district staff expressed little concern over the inability to obtain day-to-day information. They seemed to be satisified with the weekly collection of data via floppy disks.

SOFTWARE. Wordstar was available on the system for word processing. As of May, Multiplan had yet to be added but was available on an Apple IIe.

Conclusion

Although the new system seems to be fulfilling its promise in the areas of attendance, student records, and scheduling, it has not yet contributed much to decision making. For instance, it has had only limited impact on teachers' decisions about what to teach or how to present material. Perhaps as more terminals are added, and as the ability to interact directly with the data increases, teachers will make greater use of the system to find out about individual students or about characteristics of their whole class. However, teachers may want to participate in the development of reporting forms if they start using the system on frequent basis. For example, noticing their students' areas of weakness on a standardized test should assist teachers in providing remediation. Administrators at both the district and the site levels could benefit greatly from the system's capacity to provide and analyze data.

FAIRFIELD HIGH SCHOOL: A CENTRALIZED INFORMATION SYSTEM

Rural Fairfield High School enrolls approximately 2,500 students, grades 10 through 12. In the backyards of some of the residences near the school are chickens and other livestock; a large poultry ranch is close by. Fairfield is located just a mile north of Interstate 10 and, despite its rural look, is the site of a large chemical plant and a train yard.

In contrast to Mayfair High School, Fairfield High School uses a centralized computerized information system. All administrative computing at this site is done on one of seven "dumb" terminals, which are directly connected to the district's Burroughs mainframe. Site administrators make use of the software developed by the district. All the elementary schools, as well as the junior and senior high schools, are "on-line" with this system. Early on, the district provided the schools with some funds for the purchase of equipment, and these funds have been augmented by site funds.

When the software for the system was being developed, school principals were invited to offer their own ideas and react to proposed developments. The principal of Fairfield High School took this invitation seriously and has been closely involved with the planning and implementation of software capabilities and displays. His involvement was facilitated by the school's close proximity to the district office and by his long tenure in the district.

The district has a small staff of programmers whose job is to develop and troubleshoot the system and its software. The district person in charge of the programmers and the computing system continues to solicit the involvement of site administrators in developing data base options and screen displays.

Data in the System

The mainframe offers an integrated software system comprising three main menu selections: a student menu, a personnel menu, and a business menu. Each of these selections includes a number of submenus.

THE STUDENT DATA BASE. The student menu allows the user to access "electronic cums," which include the entire school-related history of a given student: standardized and competency test scores (from seventh grade on), course grades and instructors, emergency information, extracurricular activities, attendance records (including referrals for truancy and tardiness), and sundry demographic data. In addition, the user can gain access to aggregated student data: for example, review the roster for a given class or the set of rosters for a given instructor, retrieve the records of all tenth-grade students, or obtain schedule or grade information for the current and preceding semester.

The student data base and menu options are used for scheduling, resolving schedule conflicts, parent conferencing, and monitoring student attendance and academic progress. The district is currently developing two additional record formats, both suggested by site administrators. The first is a "discipline screen" which will be used to monitor and record disciplinary actions taken against students. The second is an "awards screen" which will be used to track the special awards, prizes, and honors received by students and which should help the principal, assistant principal, and counselors when they are asked to write letters of recommendation for college admission or job placement purposes.

THE PERSONNEL DATA BASE. The personnel menu allows the user to access the records of individual instructors, aides, and clerks. These records include information on daily schedules and extracurricular duties, salary history, educational background (e.g., credits), in-service training, and demographic data.

The personnel data base and menu options are used to locate instructors at any period of the day, plan meetings during the instructors' free periods, allocate course loads or transfer individual students from one class to another, and identify instructors capable of teaching particular subjects. Although the principal did not say that the data base was used for teacher evaluation, the query procedure would make it easy to look at a teacher with respect to his or her students' test performance or to identify teachers whose backgrounds suggest expertise in a particular area (e.g., writing grant proposals).

THE BUSINESS DATA BASE. The business menu allows the user to access school budget information and to engage in spreadsheet "what-if" planning activities. In addition, the software provides breakdowns and modifications of line items. Thus, it can be used to transfer (and to track the transfer of) funds between categories, monitor expenditures of special-category funds, and track the billing of purchases. Any screen report can be printed, and this option is often used for purchase orders and follow-ups of purchase orders. Besides its obvious budgeting applications, the business data base contains information on staff salaries and benefits. A school equipment inventory can also be monitored through this data base system.

Use of the System

Users with appropriate password clearance can retrieve data in either query or report options. Teachers are not allowed to query the system directly; rather, they must submit requests for information to the principal, who then either retrieves the material for them or denies their request. Counselors, on the other hand, may directly access student records.

The principal of Fairfield has a terminal in his office, standing alongside his desk, with a wide-carriage dot-matrix printer located next to the terminal. At the time of our site visit, both the terminal and the printer were on; the terminal was standing ready, main menu displayed. The principal commented that one of the first things he does in the morning, when he gets to his office, is to turn on the terminal.

52 *Alternative Types of Instructional Information Systems*

Each of the school's four counselors has a terminal hookup on his or her desk, although no printers are available in the immediate area. Both the attendance office and the registrar's office have terminals located in a general work area for use by clerks; the registrar's office also has a printer.

At Fairfield High School, the computing system is used mainly for data and budget manipulations, with printer options for formatted reports. A rudimentary word-processing function is available. For the most part, however, secretaries continue to use IBM Selectric typewriters or Xerox Memory Writers and to maintain "hard-copy" chronological files.

Although neither the principal nor the assistant principal spontaneously mentioned research or policy analysis activities served by the on-line data bases, their remarks made it clear that they are alert to the policy implications of the data they retrieve. All those with direct access to the terminals use the system heavily. But teacher requests for information are infrequent and seem to be occasioned more by specific problems than by a motivation to plan or engage in self-assessment.

Wish Lists for the System

Speculating on what they would do if they had an additional $250,000 for computing, the principal and assistant principal said they did not need any more hardware. Rather, they mentioned the district's plans for developing further data base options and software such as a more sophisticated word-processing program. The principal wanted a second photocopying machine but added that he would spend most of the hypothetical money to acquire hardware and software for classroom computer use. He would also like each teacher (or at least each department head) to have a microcomputer and printer in order to carry out his or her own administrative and curricular monitoring and record-keeping responsibilities. Beyond that, the principal would increase the number of computer labs in the school. Generally, he was satisfied with the available on-line system and with the district's support and continuing development of the system.

IMPRESSIONS ABOUT ADMINISTRATIVE USE OF COMPUTERS

From the survey and case studies, we offer some general impressions about the use of computers as an administrative tool in the high school setting.

1. *On-site control of administrative functions is increasing.* In the past, most administrative procedures were channeled through the district office. But these days are gone. The issue of on-site versus district office control ap-

pears to fall more frequently in favor of local autonomy. What seems more important than location, however, is software that allows the administrative user to do what he or she requires. Local siting seems to make it easier for administrators to acquire the software relevant to site needs. The two school descriptions give some indication of the kind of hardware and software that administrators find useful at the building site.

2. *Administrators are still uncertain about how to use computers.* "I know what I want, but I don't know how to get it" was a comment frequently made by principals and assistant principals, reflecting their feelings of frustration and their lack of knowledge about how computers function. Many administrators still need extensive orientation in what computers can do and training in actual operation. Personnel at the district level must play an important role in the continuing training of school site personnel. It would seem that not enough attention has been given to the training and support of school personnel, especially in cases where administrative functions have been centralized.

3. *Training is essential for on-site use.* As suggested above, specific training programs must be put into place if school administrators are to understand and become familiar with the computer's capabilities. These training sessions should take place away from the school site; perhaps they could be organized with the assistance of county offices or local colleges.

4. *Instructional applications for computers are a top priority for many principals.* When asked how they would spend additional funds for administrative computing, most principals replied that they would prefer to use the funds in the classroom, to increase student access to computers. This response came not only from those who already had a "good" administrative computing capacity but also from those whose access to computers for administrative purposes was minimal. Our survey suggests that principals are conscious of the need for greater student access to computers.

5. *Word processing is a must for everyone.* All administrators, from the principal on down, should master word-processing skills. Those principals who had purchased their own microcomputers or had a micro in their offices reported that their use of the computer had increased significantly simply through word processing. In fact, one principal encouraged his senior students to compose letters, save them on disks, and turn them in to his office where he edited them before mailing.

6. *Assistant principals play a dominant role in facilitating the administrative use of computers.* Because many assistant principals have been assigned the task of computerizing the school, they themselves have had to become knowledgeable and proficient. Since these individuals will form the nucleus of future administrators skilled in using computers for administrative purposes, perhaps districts should focus their training efforts at this level.

7. *Most principals have very little hands-on experience with a terminal or a microcomputer.* Since most principals received their administrative training in an earlier, precomputer time, it is not surprising that they felt insecure with computers and hence delegated these tasks to their subordinates. As one principal put it: "We have entered into a new era in our society; I must learn the computer's capabilities and train my assistant principals." One of the reasons that the current assistant principal got an administrative appointment at this site was his willingness to learn programs such as Lotus 1-2-3.

8. *Teachers have little direct access to terminals and microcomputers.* The results of this survey indicate that the computer, when utilized for administrative purposes, becomes the property of the administrator, not the teacher. Perhaps this is a function of what information is contained in data bases, but it may also reflect the school district's unwillingness to give teachers direct access. We strongly recommend that future training programs include not only administrators but also classroom teachers. Microcomputers and terminals should be placed in staff common rooms and even in classrooms.

9. *Site administrators require information on new products.* Although most schools were using peripherals such as the "scantron" to facilitate data input, many administrators wanted to know about other ways of inputting and retrieving data. For example, a few schools in our sample had installed callback devices for informing parents of frequent student absences. Some of these devices perform more efficiently than others, and principals said that short reports and summaries of the advantages and disadvantages of these products would be helpful. Similarly, examples of the applications of software programs such as Lotus 1-2-3 should be circulated to school site administrators. No longer can administrators write their own programs for specific purposes; time and money limitations prohibit such development. Therefore, information about how to use generic software programs should be made available to them.

10. *In some districts, the goals of the district office are at odds with the realities at the school site.* All too often, the expectations of district office personnel far exceed the knowledge and expertise of school site personnel. Obviously, training programs must be developed, and school site personnel must be involved in district-wide planning committees.

SALIENT ISSUES

The results of this study suggest a number of issues that decision makers should consider as they try to increase the use of the computer as an administrative tool. The following questions should be asked and answered during the planning phase for a district-wide data base system, and should be repeated each year so as to determine needed changes in system components.

Issue 1: System Development
How might site administrators be involved so that they can influence the development of district data base systems, the acquisition of equipment, and other factors in system development?

Issue 2: Effective Decision Making
How can computer-generated information be used to make more effective decisions?
What administrative decisions should be preceded by queries of a data base?
How can (or do) principals use information from various data bases?
How can (or do) teachers use information from various data bases?

Issue 3: In-Service Training for Administrators
How should in-service training be conducted?
Where should in-service training be conducted?
Who should conduct in-service training? Should consultants from the district, the county, or local colleges play some role in training administrators to use computers?
Are principals hampered by the "can't type" syndrome that supposedly afflicts managers in the private sector?

Issue 4: Use and Misuse of Data Bases
Does frequent use of a data base system result in greater integration of data and a reduction in irrelevant data collection, or does it result in the collection of more irrelevant data?
Do administrators who use a computer system come to rely heavily upon the data bases for their perceptions of school problems and trends? Is this advantageous or disadvantageous? That is,
—Do they "get out and around" less often than previously?
—Do they consult fewer people face-to-face as they analyze problems or attempt to arrive at decisions?
—Do they make more administrative or instructional decisions?
What types of administrative tasks are or should be delegated to the staff?
What types of information are required by the district office? By site administrators?
What types of data help teachers make classroom decisions? Are such data readily available to them?

Issue 5: Frequency of Use

How many times each month do district administrators, school administrators, and classroom teachers access the data base?

To what extent does the type of computing system available—centralized or decentralized—influence the kind and frequency of computer use?

What types of information are required by the district office? By site administrators? Are there discrepancies?

What types of data help teachers make classroom decisions? Are such data readily available to them?

REFERENCES

Bellflower Unified School District. (1984–85). *Computer master plan*. Bellflower, CA: Bellflower Unified School District.

Estes, N. (1983, February). Keynote address to Association for Supervision and Curriculum Development, Dallas.

6

We'll Create the Future But Keep It Secret

PETER IDSTEIN

This chapter describes how one Mid-Atlantic school district is trying to get its information management act together. The title, facetious though it may be, describes how many data processing enterprises in school districts' central offices now operate. In most instances, such secrecy is not deliberate but comes from too much to do and too little time and too few resources with which to do it. People are too busy keeping their own heads above water to be conscientious about informing others of what they are doing. When you add the empire protecting, empire building, and empire assaulting that often accompany data processing operations, you have all the ingredients for "redundancy soup."

The Christina School District is a recently desegregated school district with a 22 percent minority population. By national standards, our 15,000 students, K–12, make us a small- to medium-sized district. In the State of Delaware, however, we are the largest school district and are looked to for leadership. Though we have a long-standing positive relationship with our local community, which has been extremely supportive over the years, our last two public referenda were defeated by wide margins and, as a result, we are operating under restrictive fiscal constraints.

Delaware is a comparatively small state and Christina is a relatively small district. All of our bureaucrats have faces, intra-agency personnel know each other, and citizens who are disenchanted with particular laws write new ones. Despite these seemingly small-town living and working arrangements, a student in the Christina School District has CTBS scores stored on a tape at CTB in Monterey, California, on a tape at the New Castle County Data Service Center, and on a disk at the State Educational Consortium's VAX; soon these same scores will be stored on another disk at our own LEA Microprocessor Network. How does this record-storage redundancy happen? It happens when well-intentioned people in a variety of locations try to be of service to school officials without checking to see if anybody else has been of service first. Sometimes there is a "Why do you need them when you have me?" mentality, and sometimes it is a matter of having resources available to solve what seems to be a problem even though no one has asked that the problem be solved. A sign that this is about to happen in the district office is when a data-processing person strolls by and asks innocently, "Why are you doing that by hand?"

THE CHRISTINA INSTRUCTIONAL MANAGEMENT SYSTEM (CIMS)

For the Christina School District, the need to develop the system described here was driven by several factors. First, our district uses a hodgepodge of texts and materials to teach the basic skills. Second, our recent desegregation and reorganization (which combined eleven independent school districts into one; then two years later split us into four new districts) left us with an even more fragmented self than our own tendency toward local school autonomy had produced. Finally, we had no special immunity from the generic educational ailment of inconsistency of assessments from teacher to teacher and school to school. Taken together, these factors made the CIMS project, or something like it, a necessity.

Purpose

The CIMS project was designed to address the following formal goals:

1. To provide consistent district-wide measures of a student's progress through the basic skills curriculum. (For districts that have district-wide text adoption this may be less of a need than it was for us. We had a hybrid of texts in all three basic skills areas.)
2. To assist teachers in determining the correct placement of students in September as well as in June when promotion decisions are made. (Student standing relative to state minimum performance requirements must also be available.)
3. To provide teachers with more instructional time by eliminating time-consuming record-keeping such as tracking student status objective-by-objective within subject matter strands.
4. To provide teachers and administrators with accurate, specific, timely information to evaluate student progress and instructional programs.
5. To provide a clear, unambiguous basis for communicating student progress to parents.

Curriculum Review and Test Development

More than 800 teachers represent the true strength of our district. As a group they are highly dedicated professionals who respond to efforts to improve instruction even if it means some initial inconvenience for them. Without their support, the program described in this chapter would never have been started.

During two summers approximately 150 teachers were involved in extensive curriculum review and test writing workshops. Their job was complex but they brought to it a willingness to work and a belief in what we were trying to accomplish.

We started with a commercial curriculum that we eventually restructured completely. We organized within and across grade level teams to make sure that the final curriculum would be fully articulated within and across grades. We restated objectives so that they could be used as item descriptors for our test construction efforts.

We used some preexisting items as they were, modified some, and wrote others from scratch. Teachers scrutinized and rewrote each item so that there could be no doubt that a given test item measured the objective for which it was written.

For skills that did not lend themselves to multiple-choice testing, such as paragraph writing and handwriting, two forms of teacher-evaluated tests were developed. These tests prescribed in detail what students were to do and what criteria teachers should employ in evaluating their products.

Artwork to accompany test items was done by the district's art teachers and is of professional quality. All tests were reproduced on district printing equipment. Annual summer workshops are planned to review teacher reactions on tests and make appropriate revisions. These summer workshops will also provide an opportunity to expand CIMS into subject areas beyond the basic skills.

Operations

The Christina Instructional Management System (CIMS) combines a comprehensive grade-by-grade testing program with a computer network designed to score, report, and store test results. There are 1,004 objectives in our basic skills curriculum along with 2,008 test items to measure them. When a teacher thinks a student has mastered a skill, a CIMS test is administered. Students mark their responses on an answer card. These cards are later run through a card reader attached to a computer in the school office. It takes less than 60 seconds to score and record 120 such tests. Teacher reports, including mastery versus nonmastery groups and item analysis, are also available in less than a minute. Student records are then transferred automatically to the central office, where school-level data are merged to provide district-level reports kept current on a daily basis. Parent reports are available to be sent home periodically as needed. Soon, we will be merging district test data with state testing data as well as with other relevant factors such as attendance, information on suspensions, dropouts, and student demographics.

Integration of Data Bases

Picture the farmer standing by his fence, a piece of grass dangling from his teeth while he scratches his chin in response to your request for directions. After careful deliberation he tells you that you can't get there from here. The scary thing is that he may be right.

Most of us who deal with information have at one time or another assumed that because a set of data was available on a computer "someplace" we could get it up on our computer and save a lot of hassle. To say the least, it ain't necessarily so. If data bases have not been predesigned to fit together, getting them from one place to another can range from a simple format conversion to "you can't get there from here."

At the start of our CIMS project integrated data bases, or relational data bases for microcomputers, were being discussed in the literature but had not yet found their way to market. Consequently, we had to develop our own. Although this had the advantage of giving us a fully customized program as the end product, it had the disadvantages of large development costs, frustrating tryouts and pilot testing, and time delays that have had significant negative public relations fallout.

After some three years, we are about 80 percent of the way toward achieving our goal of full data base integration. Our attendance programs, criterion-referenced testing program, and student enrollment programs complete with demographic data all share the same data base. A student who is enrolled in our system is automatically placed on a home room attendance list and entered into our CIMS data base. Forms showing changes in student information are automatically printed at the end of the day for mailing to our data service center. Soon these data changes will be transmitted electronically.

In addition, we have a communications network that allows us to send and receive files from each of our schools. We can also "take over" a school system from our central office system. This allows us to update programs and do troubleshooting from a remote site. Our file transfer capabilities will ultimately provide us with a functional electronic mail system. Further, the communications software allows us to communicate with systems outside the school district. One of the systems with which we interact frequently is our State Educational Computing Consortium. We have our CTBS files on disk on their VAX and can get group and individual data in any form that we wish. This facility has proven invaluable for answering individual questions raised by parents as well as doing needs assessment for Chapter I programs. Finally, our communications package enables us to be a part of the AERA:SIG teleconference on Microcomputer Applications in Education.

Getting to this point was not easy. The next section describes a host of problems we had to overcome during our pilot year. Some of these problems have been solved. Some are being solved; and some remain as the natural accompaniments of running an information management system.

Logistical Problems

In putting together a program as comprehensive as CIMS, it was inevitable that details would overwhelm us. For example, we printed 70 copies for each of 2,600 tests, put them in labeled hanging folders, boxed them and shipped them to the pilot schools, unpacked them when they arrived, and installed them in sequence in filing cabinets we had ordered for the schools. In this process, some tests were misprinted, some filing cabinets came unassembled, and some filing cabinets disappeared, having been "requisitioned" for other purposes. In processing the tests themselves, we found that some questions had incorrect answers in the answer key, some questions turned out to be ambiguous, and some were inappropriate for a given grade level.

After we began pilot testing we found out that several boxes of scan cards had timing marks printed too lightly for the card reader to pick up. Since this problem had not been anticipated, we had no error trapping system to catch faulty scan cards and the program crashed whenever such a card was encountered. There were times when a bad card was the 149th card in a stack of 150. The entire stack would then have to be rerun; we ourselves had to keep running to keep from being lynched.

A perennial testing problem is the crunch that comes at the end of the year. Even though we urge teachers to test students when it is instructionally appropriate to do so, it seems that for most teachers it is instructionally appropriate to do so the last two months of the year. This puts a tremendous burden on the teachers who need to run cards at peak times. It also strains relationships between instructional and clerical users of the system—that is, it often becomes CIMS versus attendance and word processing.

In an attempt to relieve these strains, we have restructured file maintenance backup procedures so that this function is more immediate and less time-consuming. This saves about an hour a day per site. In addition, we are providing student co-ops to run cards for teachers. These co-ops will use computers on a preestablished schedule for a limited amount of time, thus allowing more flexible scheduling for other clerical uses of the equipment in each building.

Equipment Problems

For reasons of economy and flexibility we chose to go with a generic S-100 bus configuration and a CP/M operating system. In 1981, at the time of our decision to do so, both were industry standards. Since that time it has become more likely that either Unix, MS/DOS, or some compromise between the two will become the industry standard. If we were purchasing today, we would probably opt for Unix, although we feel certain that CP/M will be supportable for the foreseeable future. Although the percentage of CP/M users is dwindling, the actual number of users remains large enough to guarantee support.

Specifically, our school configurations consist of an S-100 single-board computer. Mounted in a ten- or twenty-slot S-100 chassis are Teletek or Advanced Digital Z-80B boards running at 6 MHz, each board containing 64–128K of memory, a floppy drive controller, two serial ports, and one parallel port. This component becomes the service processor to coordinate slave processors when the system is expanded. We also have a 20-megabyte hard disk and an eight-inch floppy disk drive at each school site. Our terminals are Qume 102s, but the system will also support Hazeltine, Televideo, ADDS, DEC, and Beehive terminals, among others. The card reader is a Mountain 1100A with automatic feed. The printers are Data Products 80 or 132s. Finally, the modem is a Hayes 1200 Smart Modem. This basic system has proved reliable for us and with some notable exceptions we think our initial instincts were correct.

During our pilot year we learned a good deal about the trouble that internal and external power sources can cause. Power drops and surges played havoc with our systems and our data. Over a period of several months, highway construction in several areas caused intermittent drops or surges in power to the buildings. Some of these power fluctuations occurred during processing of data. Fuses or chips would blow and the system would crash, and data files would be lost or damaged. We eventually had to buy surge protectors for several sites.

In the middle of the pilot year we switched to hard disks only to find that the operating system would not run two floppy drives with the hard disk in place. Hence the configuration described above. We also learned that card readers were basically built by sadists. They would stick, skip, grind, crunch, and take on irksome personalities of their own. We also found that hard disk controller boards were monogamous creatures. Even though controller boards and hard disks are separate components, they must be calibrated together before they will function. Therefore, if either component fails, the replacement must once again be calibrated with its mate. On the other hand, the video terminals and printer technology proved to be fairly stable. None of our other equipment problems are generic enough to mention here.

Training Problems

Training teachers to use computer equipment and run an applications program is an illuminating experience. Most of our previous in-service activities had consisted of supplying information or demonstrating a technique where one-time-only feedback from the trainer to the teachers as learners was needed. This training was different. Teachers now were expected to learn, demonstrate their skill, and later implement what they had learned on a regular basis. Operating manuals would be lost, passwords would be forgotten, major red light warnings were ignored ("I got tired of waiting so I pushed the reset button"), and senility began showing up prematurely ("Oh yeah, I forgot you said that five minutes ago").

It was impossible to train teachers in large groups but we didn't have the time to set up duplicate training sessions for smaller groups. Instead, we used a training pyramid in which we thoroughly trained one or two key people in each school and then counted on a turnkey training operation to get the rest of the faculty trained. Where this process worked, it worked beautifully. Where it failed, it failed miserably. The difference between successful and unsuccessful training came down to a combination of individual abilities and building level leadership. Our experiences support the literature that cites the principal as the key ingredient in the successful school. It is no accident that CIMS has enjoyed the most acceptance and success at the schools where principals have recognized the potential of the system and taken responsibility. Conversely, when principals have been uninterested and unaware of the impact on staff and students, the system has foundered.

Data Base Problems

Our early problem of integrating our attendance data base and our CIMS data base would have been obviated if the relational data base management software now available had been available earlier. Even in our situation, integration would have been eased considerably had we been able to proceed simultaneously with the development of CIMS and our attendance package. As it was, the attendance program was up and running a full year before our

CIMS application was ready. By then, changes in the structure of the data base were costly.

Both the CIMS and attendance applications call for frequent sorting of the data base. To sort a major student file that contains all of the data elements necessary for both applications is extremely time consuming. It also exposes the critical data base to risk an inordinate number of times. In order to avoid the risk and cut down the sorting time, index files containing only vital records are created from the main file. These index files are then sorted. The structure of the index files accommodates both applications. Not knowing the space requirements of one application in advance either limits the utility of that application or requires a new index file structure.

We have recurring problems with data entry. Error trapping is a critical component of any management system, and a pilot effort is often not sufficient to uncover all of the mistakes that can occur. We found that the secretaries in our initial pilot schools were very careful about data entry, while those who came later were not. An example of error trapping that fell through the cracks was entering a student using a homeroom number that did not exist. If that particular student later changed homerooms, we could not withdraw him from his original homeroom because the computer could not handle withdrawing a student from a homeroom it could not find, and the program subsequently bombed. It is common knowledge that, unlike their human creators, computers know better than to take on impossible tasks.

"Hidden" characters—characters that show up in data files but do not appear on a screen or printout—continue to plague us. The problems are magnified because of the integration and consequent interdependence of data sets. It takes time and patience to work through the initial data base problems that one encounters in information management. It takes more of both to track down the continuing problems that inevitably occur when working with large, dynamic data bases.

We've described some of the problems we encountered during our pilot year, but this is not to say that successes did not outweigh failures. We eventually integrated our data bases successfully. Our middle school pilot tested all of its eighth-grade students on all of the critical objectives in the basic skills curriculum, and year-end reports for those students were generated automatically and sent to their respective high schools. Despite our training problems, over 75 teachers took part in the pilot effort and were enthusiastic enough about the program to recommend its full implementation.

Multi-User System Problems

Because of the success of the attendance programs and CIMS, and because of the demands on the word-processing component of our system, we have expanded our middle school systems and made them multi-user. Installing additional terminals and printers accessing all of the central components of the system through a common mother board within a school is an inevitable outgrowth of an information management network across schools. As users become more familiar with what is, they themselves begin to ask for what could be.

An important point to consider here is why one opts for an integrated multi-user approach in the first place. Adding a second user to a single-user component system requires the addition of a separate circuit board. This board, along with the terminal, is usually as expensive as buying a low-end personal computer. A second computer, however, would not give the shared access to the main data base. And in addition, third and fourth users are considerably less expensive on a multi-user system because the separate circuit board is only required once.

I mention this here because there are drawbacks to going multi-user. The main drawback is the mental set of the user that says, "Ah ha, I now have a second system. Now secretaries and teachers won't be getting in each other's way." While this may be true in terms of traffic patterns and space, it is not necessarily true of use of the system. Without going into a lot of detail, I'd like to point out that some shared functions can only be performed by one user at a time, even from separate locations. Two users cannot sort the same data base simultaneously, nor can two users query the same individual record at the same time.

Processes such as printing can be assigned to different peripheral locations, a decided strength of a multi-user system. However, once so assigned, a specific user might forget to reassign the process back to where it belongs, thus creating a problem for subsequent users. Another problem is in rebooting the system. Pushing the "reset" button in a multi-user system resets *all* users, even those who did not wish to be reset.

Learning to avoid such problems and think in terms of the whole system rather than in terms of one user or one isolated application requires people to become less ethnocentric. This is only one of the many personal and social ramifications that occur when one gets involved in an enterprise that affects so many diverse elements of an institution.

THE SOCIOLOGY OF CHANGE

In describing the implementation of an information management system it is impossible to overstate the importance of dealing with the human aspect of change. Though the considerations mentioned here apply to everyone involved in information management, my major focus will be on teachers who deal with computerized instructional management.

In trying to implement our system one of the first things we discovered was bifurcation. Our world was divided into those who were afraid of computers and those who were not. Those who were afraid of computers often mistrusted them, but mistrust was not the only ingredient in this fear.

I suggest that those who unabashedly fear the computer may also be conservative when it comes to change itself. In many, if not most, of our normal endeavors we can "fudge" our participation to the degree that we feel comfortable. We can attend an orientation but choose not to listen. We can appear to adopt a new teaching strategy but use only those components with which we are already familiar. We can nod our heads and smile but remain passive when being told what we should do to improve our classroom management; we can emerge unscathed and unchanged.

But the computer does not allow us to feign change. We have to learn the rules of its game and play by them or the computer won't play; and when the computer doesn't play it is a highly visible event. Some who have tarnished images of themselves as learners may be reluctant to engage in an activity that makes the learning act so public. Add to this very real threat the overall mystique surrounding computers and you have substantial cause for avoidance.

To overcome this fear on the part of our colleagues we called on what we knew about human behavior and the psychology of learning.

First, there were those extreme cases who were reluctant to push a single key on the keyboard. For them, we did an extremely detailed task analysis. "Push the #1 key. Push the RETURN key. Now look at the screen. What does it say?" We did this over and over again until the initial steps of entering a menu were routine. A combination of small steps, lots of repetition, and lots of encouragement worked wonders for many teachers who were afraid of computers.

Another principle of learning easy to overlook for everyone is learning by doing. There is no substitute for successful hands-on experience when it comes to running computer applications packages. When we ourselves act as teachers or as learning theorists, we have no problem accepting this principle. But when we function as trainers with limited resources, we often seek shortcuts. We get a small group of people together and talk them through the application and then demonstrate it. This usually works well at the sending end but comes up short on the receiving end. When we demonstrate, we don't usually make the same mistakes that a naive user makes. Fearful users have to learn for themselves that the sky doesn't fall when they mistype a direction or hit a wrong key. We have to keep in mind that we are doing more than teaching a lesson. We are asking adults to change the way they feel about computers and to change the way they think. The psychological and attitudinal changes involved for the very frightened, and perhaps even for the ordinary, teacher deserve a chapter of their own. My purpose here is merely to introduce the topic and give it some definition.

In many ways the changes experienced by those teachers who are comfortable with computers are even more deep and dramatic. Information management can cause widespread changes in organizations. Let's take this example.

It is common practice in schools to define the curriculum via curriculum guides. The printed curriculum guide is often pointed to in response to a visitor's question, "Do you have a district curriculum for drug education?" We answer, "Yes, here is our curriculum guide." And, depending on the quality of the product, the visitor leaves either impressed or shaking his head.

What if we build an operational definition of the curriculum around a domain-referenced testing program with a management system that closely monitors and reports student progress? We now have a functional curriculum that can be observed in practice in the classroom. We now have control over the curriculum. The significance of this possibility has become clear in our district. Suddenly, those who had been content to rubber-stamp previous curricular reforms when all that was meant was printing a new curriculum guide have become very interested in curricular issues of scope and sequence, test domains, articulation, course prerequisites, critical versus noncritical subjects, and so forth. An in-service day on mastery learning stopped being a time for reading the sports page or knitting. Suddenly, teachers are asking, "What do they mean, if twenty-five percent of my kids can learn it, ninety-five percent can learn it? Have they seen my kids?"

Policy issues have become more critical in our district because definitions of achievement now have criterion-referenced teeth.

POLICY ISSUES: HUMPTY DUMPTY

Perhaps you remember Alice's encounter with Humpty Dumpty in *Through the Looking Glass*—Humpty Dumpty sitting on the wall, witnessing to Alice that should he ever fall, the king himself had *promised* to send all of his horses and men to help. Well, I remember Humpty Dumpty for another significant quote: "When I use a word . . . it means just what I choose it to mean—neither more nor less" (Carroll, 1872/1936, p. 214).

Well, the white rabbit has been co-opted. With student achievement operationally defined and electronically documented, words are beginning to have the same meaning for everyone. Informed instructional decision making is now possible; and with that possibility has come the responsibility to take a hard look at what we want to decide to do as a district. The following nine policies are currently being debated in the Christina School District.

Promotion Requirements

There are no easy solutions to the problems raised by promotion requirements. Although it may be relatively easy to define what a kindergarten student must know and be able to do in order to be promoted to the first grade, even the most hard-nosed of empiricists may have doubts when confronting the tear-filled eyes of a six-year-old who has just been told he can't become a first grader. The psychometric issues in such a promotion decision abound. How do we know that the test measures what it purports to measure? What is an equitable and defensible method for determining a cut score? Are there factors equally as important for the promotion decision as test scores? What are they?

We don't yet have the answers to these questions, but I want to examine here the role that information management can play when dealing with promotion requirements. It certainly makes such requirements feasible. For example, instant feedback to teachers that profiles student performance on standardized tests documents a student's achievement and could give them a consistent basis on which to make promotion decisions. Having many test scores available for a child eliminates interpretation errors that might result from overreliance on a single test score. Easy access to longitudinal records should further facilitate our decision making.

Our overall instructional purpose is to provide timely information to those who need it in order to help children who are deficient. Our expectation is that if we give high-profile attention to these lagging students and to the particular skills they must acquire, the promise of mastery learning can be realized and promotion to the next grade will usually occur. There is a clear and present danger in the lack of sophistication of our existing skill and knowledge sequences. With the formalization of our program and the computerization of its logistics comes and undue legitimacy. Many users will be prematurely satisfied with the product. Still others will argue that nothing should be done until we are certain that the objectives and measurements are perfect. Though this latter approach would appear prudent, it is not feasible since it is the system itself that now is driving reform.

Mastery Learning: Will It Work?

The mastery learning literature is an interesting mix of skepticism, optimism, fuzzy-headed wishful thinking, and hard-headed empiricism. It is one of those wells from which half-full or half-empty buckets can be drawn at will.

In the Christina School District we are proceeding with optimistic empiricism. We have built our instructional management program to succeed, but we will proceed one grade at a time. We are starting with our current first graders. We insist that they must master 100 percent of a set of critical objectives. We are concentrating our reporting and remediation efforts on this group and will evaluate the results carefully before moving on to Grade 2 next year. Improved instructional efforts have to go hand-in-hand with our assessment program in order for us to avoid short-changing our students.

We will soon have very powerful tools for answering the question, "Is mastery learning working in the Christina School District?" We will know whether mastery learning is being implemented. We will know the objectives assessed in individual classrooms, the rate at which groups and individuals moved through the curriculum, trials to criterion, and so forth. We will also be able to pull matched control groups from the general population and co-vary on relevant variables. Further, these data will be generated in hours rather than weeks or months. Ultimately, we will be able to make curricular and instructional decisions based on inferences that have empirical support. It is this vision that drives us.

Rights of Privacy

Privacy issues in regard to access and use of data are inherent in all computer enterprises. We are concerned that our data base be protected. To guard student data, we have a three-tier password system that requires the entry of (1) a group I.D. (e.g., Teacher, Office, Manager), (2) an individual I.D. (user's name), and (3) a password. Access to specific files is restricted by group affiliation. Teachers as a group do not have access to student data files. Secretaries as a group do not have access to CIMS files. The question of access has surfaced particularly in regard to parent volunteers. Our tendency has been to approach the issue on a situation-by-situation basis; for example, a parent who pre-slugs names on printed scan cards for us and sees only student names and I.D. numbers does not pose a threat to privacy.

The possibility that our data base could be used to evaluate teachers is another issue that touches on the right to privacy and also threatens the life of the program. We have taken the position that teacher evaluation should be tied to CIMS only in that teachers are responsible for using the system. That is, a teacher should know where each student stands relative to the CIMS objectives and should be acting accordingly vis-à-vis instruction. However, accountability for student progress is a system-wide responsibility shared by teachers, administrators, students, and parents. Teachers, therefore, are not evaluated, even in part, on their students' progress.

We are in the process of forming standing committees to recommend guidelines for how CIMS data will be accessed and used and to adjudicate complaints about the perceived misuse of these data.

Equal Protection/Due Process

Although it was not designed for this purpose, CIMS enables us to pay proper attention to equal protection and due process concerns as defined by the Fourteenth Amendment. By standardizing the definition of learning and by assessing all students in the same manner we are providing a sound basis for equal protection guarantees.

Due process concerns are ameliorated, at least in part, by our management system. Parents are informed early and often regarding what is expected of their youngsters, how their children are progressing, and what is being done about it.

Acceleration

I was presenting our CIM program to a recent meeting of our district-level parents' group and some people became very excited about the possibility of using CIMS to identify and track students through an accelerated curriculum. (There seems to be no end to the issues that jump up and volunteer for attention when one starts down the road of computerized information.)

My response was that in its present state, the CIMS project is a long way from being able to supply the information necessary to make proper decisions about acceleration. Our current focus is on minimum standards; and these would not suffice for allowing a student to test out of a course of study. In building the CIMS curriculum we asked our teachers to identify the skills and knowledge that, collectively, they thought were necessary and sufficient in order for children to function successfully at the next grade level. By contrast, in addressing the notion of acceleration, we would have to ask curriculum developers to identify those objectives that, collectively, would constitute a thorough understanding of the respective courses of study. The accompanying assessment would have to be consequence-specific. I hope that someday our instructional management system can handle this kind of task.

Special Education and Gifted and Talented Students

Special education students are by definition special. Today the education of special education students is driven by the Education for the Handicapped Act (1975) and its I.E.P. (Individualized Educational Plan). Currently, CIMS has the capability of producing an I.E.P. for special education students and for generating the reports necessary for an I.P.R.D. (Identification, Placement, Review, Dismissal) meeting, as well as summary reports necessary for auditing purposes. We are currently looking into the feasibility of using CIMS for gifted and talented students. What we would really like is for the I.E.P. to be driven by CIMS. The thinking about this raises some interesting methodological, logistical, philosophical, and policy questions—for example, how do you structure a school around learning (i.e., empirically determined progress through an operationally defined curriculum) rather than administrative convenience (i.e., grade levels and classrooms). If the focus is on what students know, how restrictive need we be vis-à-vis how they obtain knowledge or skills? Are certified teachers the only people in the world allowed to take formal responsibility for facilitating learning?

Standardized Curriculum

When I get into a discussion of CIMS I often hear the question, "Aren't you standardizing the curriculum?" It is surprising to me that this question is raised usually as a criticism.

My answer is, "Yes, CIMS does standardize the curriculum." We are guilty! That was certainly our intent. We hope we have accomplished it. Our assumption is that there is a core of material common to every subject area and that we should be able to define that core at the district level. This definition should be common to all those who deal with the given subject matter. This viewpoint was not a hot issue when the definition of the curriculum was only a paper curriculum guide. Now that curriculum is also a testing program, however, it has become a very hot potato.

The issue gets even hotter when we talk about state curricula. Even those who agree that we should have a district curriculum balk at the notion of a state curriculum. Should you be crazy enough to mention a national curriculum, you could well find yourself very lonesome.

Again our position on this issue is simple; perhaps too simple. We don't believe you can logically or semantically have standards without standardization. The two are inexorably linked. The problem, I believe, comes less from the intention to draw that line than it does from deciding where to draw it.

Why have a standardized curriculum? We standardize our curriculum because we believe a third grader in one school should learn that same basic math skills as a third grader in any other school in the district. Fine. Usually no argument. Now, we ask rhetorically, what about a third grader in another district? Here we get an argument from our audience. That's different. Each district should set its own curriculum. But what if the third grader in the other district lives across the street from the third grader in our district, we ask? It doesn't matter, says our respondent.

The point is, it does matter. We have to ask ourselves, from the student's perspective, why two neighbors should be taught different basic skills or core subject matter. The question has to shift to that focus to do justice to the issue. Students today are not born, raised, and buried in the same geographical location. We live in an increasingly mobile society and the question of standards and consequently standardization is indeed a national concern.

Minima Versus Maxima

Discussions of instructional management systems inevitably raise the question of minimum requirements versus education for excellence. From a policy perspective it is important to note that it is just that—a policy concern. There is nothing inherent in instructional management in general, or the CIMS project in particular, that restricts anyone to either minimum requirements or upper-end curriculum objectives. Whether to choose one or the other or some combination is indeed an issue for discussion. The point is that discussion is independent of the decision to use a management system per se.

Personally, I have fallen into the trap of saying that CIMS deals with minimum performance objectives. What I should be saying is that our current use of CIMS is limited to minimum performance objectives. Without this distinction some people might think that we would need another system to deal with gifted students. This would be a costly misconception that might lead us to a number of fragmented systems, which would not only be more expensive but would sacrifice the flexibility of sharing data across programs. As stated previously, our purpose is to eventually have a comprehensive package that captures the full spectrum of student interaction with our entire curriculum.

If the day ever comes when this dream comes to fruition we will be in a position to deal seriously with the policy implication of the final item on our policy issues list.

Deschooling à la Illich

When Ivan Illich (1970) published a book called *Deschooling Society*, it received a lot of attention from the reform crowd. It has since slipped into relative obscurity. Instructional management systems in particular, and information management systems in general, are creating an environment in which a deschooling mentality can blossom. Briefly, Illich's thesis was that schooling as an institution was not very supportive of learning. He suggested that a better approach to learning would be to form natural groups of learners called learning webs. The only consideration for choosing a teacher for a given learning web is that the person have some knowledge or skill that children need and can teach it to them. Age, degrees, status, and formal schooling are all irrelevant.

At the time, one of the major criticisms (certainly not the only one) of this thesis was that there would be no way to assure that educational standards would be met. The concern was previously at the level of a higher-order social unit like the state or the nation. From a district perspective, we could see the time when it would be possible for a student to leave the classroom, join a learning web, and then come back to take a test on what was learned. The student then could get credit from us.

Today, many instructional management systems are already linked to computer-assisted instruction systems that provide branched instruction to students via interactive terminals. These systems are becoming more and more sophisticated, connecting microcomputer with videodisk technology. One of the first uses of such systems is for homebound instruction. The beauty of this first step is that it extends our system to those who can't be physically present. However, once this step is taken and taken successfully there should be nothing to keep healthy students from using it; nothing, that is, except district policy, which brings us full circle. Here again, our bottom line should be not what is possible but what we wish to accomplish. As we go further and further down the path of information management it would behoove us to start developing some policy-related road maps to keep us on track around the inevitable sharp curves ahead.

CONCLUSION: A STRATEGIC VISION

In *Megatrends*, John Naisbitt (1982) points out that in order to develop a cogent plan for the future one first needs a "strategic vision" of what that future would look like. So far in this chapter I have presented a description of what the Christina School District is in the process of doing to develop a comprehensive information management system. In this conclusion I would like to share with you a strategic vision of what this system will be able to do for us.

First, the district's information needs would be addressed in-house under the control of the district. Data processing functions, even if not physically carried out in the district, would nonetheless be directed by district staff. Our in-house network would be tied to regional and state computers to facilitate data transfer and share processing power and storage. Payroll, personnel, and business operations would all be processed using a common data base manager that would also drive instructional management functions.

CIMS would be expanded to become the comprehensive instructional management system alluded to earlier. Further, it would have as an integral component a sophisticated statistical package with built-in monitoring functions. These programs would periodically and without prompting, produce reports listing students who were in varying categories of academic risk. The programs would also produce lists, again automatically, of students making above-average (as measured against their own baseline) progress. These students would get superior achievement certificates or some similar recognition. The system would also be constantly running its own analyses of variance in search of generic main effects. These would be methods or curriculum packages that yielded significant gains in achievement but were not school- or teacher-specific.

Common-language menus would be available to curriculum supervisors and principals who might want answers about specific program effects. These menus would trigger control group selection, matching characteristics, and covariates, and define by the nature of the question the type of analysis to be run. Tests of specific model assumptions could be run automatically: If criteria were met, analysis would proceed; if not met, the user would be so informed and given the option to abandon the analysis or continue even though the statistical assumptions underlying the model had been violated.

Groups such as school boards, administrators, and departments of public instruction, who have reason to seek information from the system, would be educated over time to think in terms of data elements to be entered as well as reports to be extracted. The time to consider what information you want is not *after* but *before* data have been gathered. Further, we decision makers who have the inclination should have the option of getting original data in a readable format. Quality control of data would become everybody's business, and basing instructional and policy-level decisions on empirical data would become the norm for all constituencies.

Parents who might wish to check up on their children's progress could do so via modem and their own microcomputers at home. Access to CAI packages and homework might be available through the same technology.

On a larger scale, the district data base would be available to the State Department of Education for generating state-level reports automatically without bothering schools, teachers, or students. In turn, state resources such as item banks and CAI programs would be available to download to schools on some licensing basis. It is not inconceivable that data could be shared at the federal level as well. The National Assessment of Educational Progress might someday be sweeping local data bases to obtain its data rather than testing students directly.

In short, the information management system would be a fully integrated, totally responsive resource ready to facilitate decision making and also ready to link up with future technologies that today reside only in the heads of other dreamers. Against such promise, the mundane problems cited in this chapter pale in comparison.

REFERENCES

Carroll, L. (1936). *Through the looking glass*. In *The complete works of Lewis Carroll*. New York: Modern Library. (Original work published in 1872.)
Education for the Handicapped Act of 1975. P.L. 94-142, 94th Cong., 2d sess.
Illich, I. (1970). *Deschooling society*. New York: Harper & Row.
Naisbitt, J. (1982). *Megatrends*. New York: Warner.

7

The School Profile: An Information System for Managing School Improvement

ROBERT E. BLUM and JOCELYN A. BUTLER

The long-term improvement of student performance is a major priority in education today. Researchers and practitioners agree that a "quick-fix" approach is not the answer and that substantial, lasting educational change requires long-range vision, planning, and effort. Compiling accurate, comprehensive information about a school is an important first step in planning for change. Without thorough knowledge of students' achievement, and their social behaviors and attitudes, it is extremely difficult to change school practices so they will improve student performance.

The Goal Based Education Program at the Northwest Regional Educational Laboratory (NWREL) in Portland, Oregon, has developed a process called *profiling* that can gather accurate, useful information about student performance in any school. The results of profiling serve as the basis for planning and implementation of improvements.

The profiling process is an integral part of an overall school improvement program called "Onward to Excellence" (OTE). Development of this program took place during NWREL's involvement in the Alaska Effective Schooling Program. Researchers and practitioners worked together to create a flexible, widely applicable school improvement approach and training design. With funding from the National Institute of Education, NWREL adapted the Alaska design and piloted it with a number of schools in Oregon and Washington with good results.

In the OTE program, schools contract for training and technical assistance over a one-year period to learn how to implement an improvement process based on effective schooling research as synthesized by NWREL staff. Local schools move toward improvement by following these ten steps:

1. Form a leadership team (the school principal, staff teachers, and a central office representative) to introduce the program to staff members and set the stage for improvements
2. Study the effective schooling research and findings

3. Profile current levels of student performance—academic achievement, social behavior, and attitudes
4. Set a goal for improvement
5. Check current instructional practices
6. Develop a research-based prescription to meet the improvement goal
7. Prepare for implementation
8. Implement the prescription
9. Monitor implementation
10. Evaluate progress and renew efforts

Onward to Excellence provides a process whereby schools use data to set goals for improvement. All improvement efforts focus on student performance: The indicators of improvement in schools are changes in student achievement levels, behaviors, and attitudes. NWREL's experience has shown that team-based activities are effective in mobilizing the cooperative, school-wide efforts necessary to plan and implement lasting change. Starting with this process, local schools then develop their own resources for improvement. Thus, OTE becomes an ongoing way to manage local school improvement efforts.

THE PROCESS OF PROFILING A SCHOOL

School teams plan for and then introduce the profiling process to staff members. They next collect and summarize school-wide information that culminates in a written profile of the school. This profile is examined to identify strengths and weaknesses in student performance. Improvement priorities are set, goals are established, and profile results and goals are described to the school community. Plans and their implementation are based on profile contents. An overview of the entire process is shown in Figure 7.1.

Profile preparation requires: (1) collecting and summarizing information and (2) preparing a written version of findings—that is, creating the profile. Each of these tasks involves a number of steps managed through the assignment of specific tasks to participating team members. It is crucial that all staff members be informed of the profiling effort and that information collection be focused on creating a picture of the school as a whole rather than on monitoring the individual teacher's or student's performance.

Collecting and Summarizing Information

After the leadership team is formed and has familiarized itself with the overall thrust of the improvement program for the school, the team begins to plan for data collection. Team members discuss what types of informa-

78 *Alternative Types of Instructional Information Systems*

FIGURE 7.1. Profiling Overview

Step 3.

A Plan	→	B Introduce Effort	→	C Collect and Summarize Information	→	D Conduct Special Studies	→	E Prepare Profile
• Review steps • Write management • Assemble plans		**STRAND 1** • Introduce to staff • Collect staff feedback • Report back results		• Prepare and administer staff survey • Summarize results • Duplicate and distribute summaries		• Review each summary • Identify areas needing more depth • Plan and conduct special studies • Revise summaries		• Prepare narratives • Order summaries • Prepare report
				STRAND 2 • Select areas to profile • Collect and summarize information • Organize summaries				

Step 4.

A Review Profile	→	B Identify Strengths and Weaknesses	→	C Establish Priorities	→	D Set Goals	→	E Publicize Work
• Distribute profile to staff • Collect feedback • Report back results		• Evaluate narratives • List strengths and weaknesses		• Group weaknesses into problem areas • Select one area for improvement		• Restate problem as improvement goal • Set time-based target • Confirm priorities, goals, and targets		• Prepare report • Distribute report • Identify and problem solve concerns

tion they will collect by consulting a "profile contents menu" (Figure 7.2). There are three sections to the menu, each dealing with one area of student performance: academic achievement, student attitude, and social behavior. To achieve an overall view of students in the school, teams should collect at least one group of data in each of the three sections of the menu.

Using the menu as a worksheet, teams check off data sources already available to them. Results of achievement tests, attendance records, and student attitude surveys, for example, are readily available data sources in many schools. Team members then review the menu list and note areas where additional data would be useful. The team considers both existing and desired data and creates a firm list of items to be collected in the profile. The team members are assigned specific data-collection tasks.

With the management plan and selected data sources in hand, the team presents the improvement program, profiling process, and profiling areas to the entire staff. This action both introduces the effort to the staff and provides a means to collect staff feedback on the profiling process.

Preparing the Profile

Team members then decide how to display the data and who will make the displays. Each type of information is presented on a single sheet of paper in a form that can be used as a quick reference. Once data has been summarized and displayed appropriately, team members then write narratives describing each summary. Narratives contain simple, declarative statements and avoid educational or testing jargon. The narratives describe but do not evaluate the information contained in the data displays. They highlight the most important aspects of student performance using only a few short statements.

The result of these efforts is a series of one-page data display summaries with brief narrative descriptions pointing out data highlights (Figure 7.3). These data summaries become the profile of the school. Team members organize the one-page descriptions into a single document, prepare an introduction explaining both the process and the organization of material, make a cover, and then print and distribute copies to all staff for discussion purposes. By collecting, summarizing, and presenting data about several key areas the team draws a current picture of student performance on a school-wide basis.

USING THE PROFILES FOR GOAL SETTING

The completed profile becomes a tool for setting school-wide improvement goals, as the leadership team involves the whole staff directly in the process

FIGURE 7.2. Profile Contents Menu

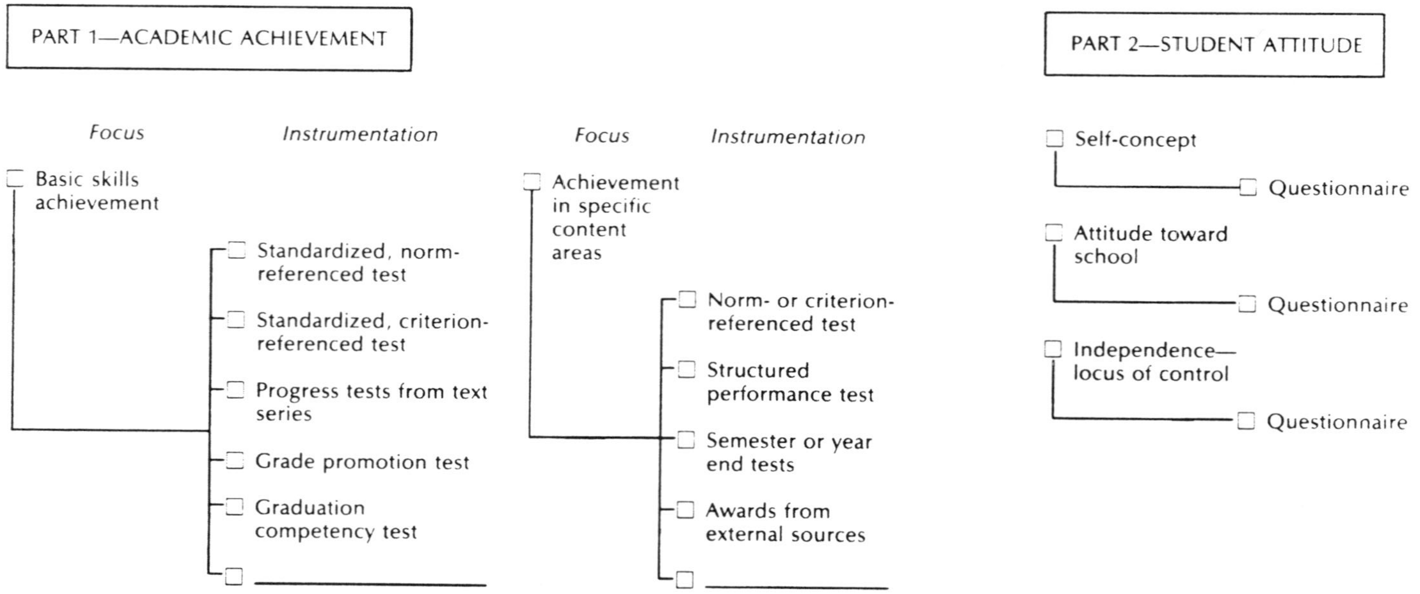

PART 1—ACADEMIC ACHIEVEMENT

Focus — *Instrumentation*

Basic skills achievement
- ☐ Standardized, norm-referenced test
- ☐ Standardized, criterion-referenced test
- ☐ Progress tests from text series
- ☐ Grade promotion test
- ☐ Graduation competency test
- ☐ _____

Achievement in specific content areas
- ☐ Norm- or criterion-referenced test
- ☐ Structured performance test
- ☐ Semester or year end tests
- ☐ Awards from external sources
- ☐ _____

PART 2—STUDENT ATTITUDE

- ☐ Self-concept — ☐ Questionnaire
- ☐ Attitude toward school — ☐ Questionnaire
- ☐ Independence—locus of control — ☐ Questionnaire
- ☐ _____ — ☐ Questionnaire

- Problem-solving proficiency ── □ Problem-solving test
- Life role proficiency ── □ Life skills test
- General intellectual attainments ── □ Standardized, norm-referenced test
- Generalized competence ── □ Follow up survey

PART 3—SOCIAL BEHAVIOR

- Attendance ── □ School records
- Tardiness ── □ School records/teacher logs
- Cumulative dropout rate ── □ School records
- Code of conduct violations ── □ School records
- Vandalism ── □ School/district records

FIGURE 7.3. Example of a Data Summary for Attendance: Percentage Absent per Class Period, Grading Period 3

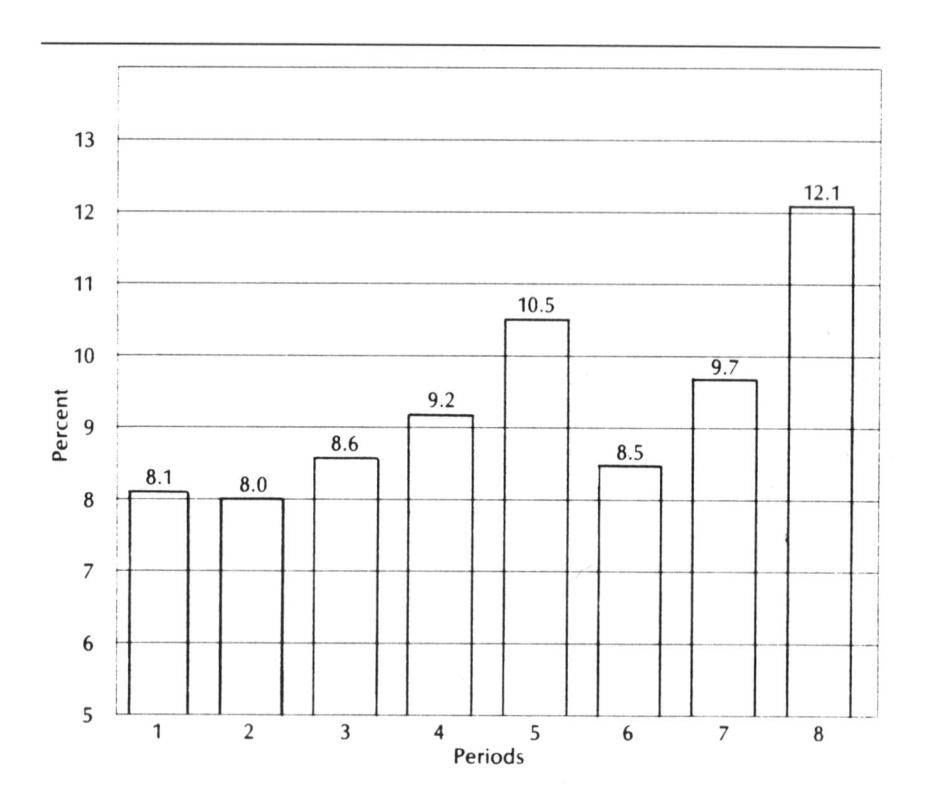

[Bar chart showing Percent absent by Periods 1–8: Period 1 = 8.1, Period 2 = 8.0, Period 3 = 8.6, Period 4 = 9.2, Period 5 = 10.5, Period 6 = 8.5, Period 7 = 9.7, Period 8 = 12.1]

Narratives

1. The highest number of absentees occurs in the final class period of the day.
2. There is a higher percentage of absentees in periods directly before and after lunch than in morning class periods.
3. Overall, more students are absent in the afternoon than in the morning.

of generating a school-improvement goal from the profile data already collected and compiled. Copies of the profile document are distributed to all staff members for consideration and evaluation in a final survey by the leadership team before the team makes improvement goal decisions.

The profile evaluation process solicits from all staff members feedback rating critical areas of concern about profile results. People are asked to individually fill out the "profile evaluation worksheet" (Figure 7.4) for compilation by team members as they prepare to set the school's improvement goal.

Staff members rate each narrative statement in all profile summaries on four factors:

1. *Degree of relative satisfaction* with the current picture of student performance. (A 10-point scale ranging from "−5" or "very dissatisfied with result, nearly all students need improvement" to "+5" or "very satisfied with result, nearly all student doing well in this area.")

2. *Relative importance for improvement* among areas with which staff members are dissatisfied. (A 5-point scale ranging from "1" or "low priority—a much less important area for student performance" to "5" or "high priority—a very important area for student performance.")

3. *Acceptable standard of performance* in areas of least satisfaction that would constitute "good" performance for students and result in a high satisfaction rating—a realistic standard to aim for in this area.

4. *A specific target for improvement*, selecting from among all identified areas for improvement a single short-term, time-based objective that is of high priority.

Using this feedback from the staff, the leadership team as a group then fills out a goal-setting worksheet (Figure 7.5), restating narratives on problem areas as improvement goals and establishing standards of performance for those areas. After assessing priorities, the team selects one area for improvement and a time-based target for improvement and reports the targeted improvement goal to the staff. In this way, the profiling data becomes a tool for setting an improvement goal. The leadership team then works through the rest of the Onward to Excellence program to plan a prescription for improvement, prepare for and implement the prescription, monitor implementation, and evaluate progress toward reaching improvement goals. Underlying all decisions is a firm knowledge of the baseline data about current student performance in the school.

Once the cycle of improvement is completed, schools can again profile the school, use new data to target another improvement goal, and follow the process through to plan for and monitor improvements. This cycle of improvement becomes a school-based method for managing improvements based on regular collection and analysis of data on student performance.

PROFILE CHECKLIST

The school profile can be a useful tool in any school improvement effort. It provides baseline data about student performance against which effects of

84 Alternative Types of Instructional Information Systems

FIGURE 7.4. Example of a Profile Evaluation Worksheet

AREA			NARRATIVE	Satisfaction Rating	Importance Rating	Acceptable Standard
Achievement	Behavior	Attitude				
			Overall, 9 percent of students are absent from one class period each day.			
			The highest number of absentees occurs in the final class period of the day.			
			There is a higher percentage of absentees directly before and after lunch than in morning class periods.			
			Overall, more students are absent in the afternoon than in the morning.			

FIGURE 7.5. Example of a Goal-Setting Worksheet

AREA			Goal and Target	Current Results and Standard	PRIORITY			Short-Term Target
Achievement	Behavior	Attitude			High Priority	Moderate Priority	Low Priority	
			Improve daily student attendance.	Currently, 91 percent of students attend all courses; the standard is 97 percent.				

school improvements can be measured. This information becomes a primary tool in the planning and managing of targeted school improvement efforts.

There are several important considerations in creating a profile of a school:

- The profile describes student performance on a school-wide basis.
- All students and all curriculum areas should be represented in the profile: the more comprehensive the profile, the more broad-based and complete a picture of the school that emerges.
- By creating a profile, it is possible to sharpen focus both on strengths and weaknesses in student performance.
- The profile is a "snapshot" of the school. It can become the first in a series that can be followed, perhaps annually, with updating and new improvement decisions.

Above all, the profile is a decision-making aid: knowing specific information about student performance facilitates targeting goals and planning for improvements in student achievement, behavior, and attitude.

8

Developing an Elementary School Information System: The Computer-Assisted Professional

WILLIAM COOLEY

During the school year 1984-85, staff members from the Learning Research and Development Center (LRDC) worked with the Pittsburgh Public Schools in the development of a prototype microcomputer system in an elementary school. The system is designed to help the principal become a more effective instructional leader; facilitate the implementation of two district innovations, Monitoring Achievement in Pittsburgh (MAP) and the School Improvement Program (SIP); encourage other professionals in the school to become more data-based in their planning and decision making; and make possible a more current and accurate district-wide data base. The intent was for the school-based microcomputer to complement the functions of the central computer system. This chapter describes the reasons for developing such a system, what it does, and how it is built.

THE NEED FOR AUTOMATED INFORMATION SYSTEMS

An analysis of the information requirements of school district policymakers and school managers clearly indicates that the same data are needed over and over again, with variations as to how the data are analyzed or what combinations of data are relevant to a particular kind of decision. In school districts a great deal of energy is expended in trying to pull together into one place the combination of data needed to shed light on a particular issue. In an extensive bureaucracy, such as a school district, different data are "owned" by different offices, be it personnel, compensatory education, transportation, or attendance accounting. These various data bases are often jealously protected by their various "owners" since ownership contributes to status and power in the enterprise. Because of the importance of timeliness, the recurring need to use the same data to shed light on different problems, and the critical requirement that data from different sources be brought together in one place, an educational enterprise needs to establish an automated information system (AIS).

People began discussing the potential use of computers to assist in the management of educational systems as soon as computers became available in the late 1950s and early 1960s. Since that time, all large school systems and even many of the smaller ones have developed computer support for central administrative functions. Sometimes these central systems include data on individual students, but student data tend to be restricted to those items needed for central administrative tasks, such as computing average daily membership for state subsidies or home socioeconomic status for federal compensatory education distributions.

Central systems tend to serve central functions, and they almost never get to considerations of how to help principals and teachers improve the effectiveness, pleasantness, and fairness of their educational environments. The demands of the central environment tend to overwhelm both the hardware and software development resources of the central computer system.

There have been many efforts to develop school-based computer-managed instruction systems (e.g., Cooley & Glaser, 1969). In the 1960s, when such systems were tried, the costs seemed too prohibitive to justify the effort, both in terms of the cost of the hardware and the cost of developing and maintaining such systems.

Several things have happened since 1973 that are encouraging a reconsideration of school-based automated information systems. The most obvious, of course, is the emergence of the powerful, relatively inexpensive microcomputer. Being able to purchase for less than $5,000 the computer power that would have cost hundreds of thousands of dollars in the 1960s is clearly a major factor in the renewed enthusiasm for developing school-based AIS.

Another important factor is the availability of software for establishing data base management systems. The new applications software makes it feasible to develop automated information systems for schools and do it in ways that make modification relatively easy and ad hoc inquiries possible (that is, not all possible retrieval requests need to be anticipated by the developers of the system).

Another invention that makes school-based computer systems feasible today is the desktop scanner, which facilitates a variety of data-entry tasks, including automatic scoring of student tests and scanning of attendance forms.

Finally, the existence of the inexpensive modem and the associated telecommunications software makes it possible to export summaries of school data to the central computer as well as import to the school computer data that are centrally available, or records of students who transfer from school to school. This recently emerging concept of distributed processing is contributing greatly to a reconceptualization of how school system information systems might be designed.

THE GOALS OF THE INFORMATION SYSTEM

As is usually the case, a consideration of the functions and characteristics of information systems should be preceded by a consideration of the goals for such a system. In general, the goals for an AIS in education are pretty much the same as the goals for the educational system. A possible difference is that when one takes on the task of defining an automated information system, it is much more important to be precise and explicit regarding goals, since these goals are to guide the development and implementation of such systems.

The general goals that have tended to guide our own work are: (1) improve student achievement, (2) enhance the quality of school life, and (3) provide equal opportunity to learn. To be useful in systems design, these very general goals need to be defined more explicitly. Then data relevant to the goals need to be specified, collected, and organized in ways that will facilitate knowing how well the educational system is progressing toward realizing those goals, and also guide in their realization. It is also important to recognize that a given data indicator may be relevant to more than one goal. For example, student attendance is a variable that is always part of such a student information system. Sometimes the fact that it is required by law insures its presence, but even if attendance data weren't required, such data can be assumed to be related to all three goals and therefore important to have in the system. That is, an absent student is engaged in less school learning than is a present student. A student who is unable to attend classes because of difficulties at home does not have the same opportunity to learn as a student whose home expectations are to be in school. Also, attendance data aggregated at the classroom or school level might signal the possibility that there are unpleasant school conditions that are being avoided. This might be the case if a classroom or school had unusually high rates of absenteeism.

One way of improving the quality of the school experience might be to reduce the rigidity with which schools tend to operate. Up until now, a major problem in breaking up the built-in rigidity of the school and its traditional format of classroom organization was the tremendous amount of information required by the more adaptive instructional systems. It is relatively simple for the traditional elementary school teacher to keep track of what happens each day with the 25 students in the classroom. Very little record-keeping is called for when all children progress through the same instructional materials at the same rate, varying only in how much they learn from those exposures. When all students are on page 38 in the arithmetic textbook, that single number defines where the class is. However, if this neat process were to be broken up and individual students were to be allowed to work at different objectives or toward the same objectives through different levels and rates, the teacher would have 25 times as much information to monitor for that same class. If students are also allowed to move toward different modes of instruction, the information-processing problem becomes even more severe. Back in 1967, McLuhan and Leonard were arguing:

> School computers can now help keep track of students as they move freely from one activity to another whenever moment by moment or year by year records of the students' progress are needed. This will wipe out even the administrative justification for schedules and regular periods, with all their anti-educational effects, and will free teachers to get on with the real business of education. (p. 23)

So in considering the goals of an AIS, it is important not to just "automate" the information requirements of the current system but to reconsider the broad aims of the educational system and seek ways to help realize some of the goals that have been more elusive, such as enhancing the quality of the school experience.

FUNCTIONS OF AUTOMATED INFORMATION SYSTEMS

There are many possible functions for an automated information system within a school. Probably the first and foremost is record-keeping. Schools must keep records of who is there, what students are doing, and how well they are doing. These records may be required by federal law, state code, or local board policy, and they are omnipresent. So, one function of an automated information system is to satisfy these needs for record-keeping, including updating the files as students come and go.

A second major function is report generation. A serious problem in schools is having information easily and quickly distributed to all who might need to know. For example, home information, including emergency phone numbers, which teachers might find useful as they attempt to strengthen school–home relationships, could easily be distributed to all teachers from school-based computer files. Once a school data base is up and running, it is amazing how many different applications there are for supplying various kinds of printouts to professionals in the building who have a need to know.

A third function is record retrieval. This is different from routine report generation, and involves searching for particular records or sets of records with specific features that might require special attention. For example, scanning for students who exhibit combinations of failing grades and high absenteeism can easily be done in such automated systems.

One turns to the computer for ease in record-keeping, report generating, and data retrieval, but the greater strength of the computer is its ability to do complex analyses quickly and easily. So a fourth function is data analysis. One of the challenges in developing such information systems today is to try to build into them the expertise of a data analyst so that the benefits of such analyses are available to people in the schools. That is, one should not expect all principals to know how to apply multiple contingency analyses to a set of data, but the questions that might be answered by such analyses can be anticipated by system developers and the results made available to users.

The fifth function of such automated information systems involves the application of the cybernetic model, which I call monitoring data and tailoring practices. Computer scientists refer to this as the process control application of automated information systems. The goal of this aspect of the system is to identify ways to tailor the school and its curriculum to the individual needs of the learner, rather than to make the individual learner adjust to the offerings of the typical classroom instruction. It is here that we need to build into the system the expertise of talented instructional leaders and learning psychologists so that options for dealing with observed trends can be made available to the users of the system.

CHARACTERISTICS OF EFFECTIVE INFORMATION SYSTEMS

Certainly one characteristic of an effective information system is that it contains data that are reasonably current and accurate. A major problem plaguing information systems is how to maintain current and accurate files. It is with respect to this type of dependability that central systems tend to fail. That is, if the focus is exclusively upon centralized data bases for district-wide planning and accountability, and data flow is only from the school to the central computer, there is no reason to believe the central files will be current and accurate. So one principle to be observed is that data be used as part of the operation of the local school. If data summaries that are to be transferred to the central system are also needed and used on a day-to-day basis within schools, it is much more likely that the centrally available data will be current and accurate.

A second principle to be observed is that the design of such systems include incentive systems for maintaining current and active files within the local school. For example, school site scoring of criterion-referenced tests can provide such incentives. When the Pittsburgh Public Schools launched its Monitoring Achievement in Pittsburgh (MAP) program, it was designed as a centrally scored achievement monitoring system. Even with the most heroic effort, the central system could only produce two-week turnaround on the test scoring and reporting. Insofar as such tests were designed to guide day-to-day instructional planning, a fortnightly turnaround was inadequate. With a scanner attached to the local school microcomputer, those tests could be scored on the day they were given, with reports going to students, teachers, and principals, as well as automatically updating the information system with student performance and pacing data.

The local scoring of tests not only illustrates one way of building in incentives for maintaining current files, it also shows how files can be more accurate. When scoring takes place and the results are viewed within a single day, errors that creep into testing systems can be easily found and corrected, and tabulations recalculated. An example of an error might be a teacher indicating the wrong form of the facing sheet that controls test processing for each homeroom. When a central system scores several thousand batches (one for each classroom), such clerical errors are usually not detectable and the inaccurate data become part of the centrally available file. Of course, when the printouts eventually reach the teacher, the teacher will notice the error and discard the results; but meanwhile, they have become part of the central system and are unlikely to be purged or corrected.

Another important point here is that locally used data files reduce the likelihood of the indicators becoming corrupted. That is, if data are collected and used within the local school to help in school planning and improvement, suspicious data (e.g., an overzealous teacher may have administered a test using nonstandard procedures) can be easily detected and corrected. Data produced exclusively for a centralized accountability system are far too easily corrupted by accident; and they may be intentionally corrupted if teachers and principals sense that those data are being used in unfair ways in their own evaluations. So shifting the emphasis towards data being used for local school improvement as opposed to central system accountability will result in a central data base that is sufficiently dependable for central planning and monitoring. The lesson here is that, in addition to building in incentives for keeping data files current and accurate, it is important that information systems build out incentives to corrupt the data. The move to distributed processing contributes to the solution of both those problems.

Another important requirement of AIS is to have built-in checks to catch out-of-range data. For hand-entered data, these checks should be part of the data-entry procedures. That is, as data are keyed into the computer, any out-of-range entries should be immediately detected and brought to the attention of the keyboard operator through audio and visual cues. Similarly, data captured in other ways, such as through scanners or files imported from other computers, should be screened for out-of-range data. Again, the advantages of distributed processing are obvious. Detecting out-of-range data centrally requires a more cumbersome set of procedures for correcting errors than if errors can be detected within the school where the correct values can be more easily established.

A further reason to go to school-based student information systems is to make it possible to examine a broad range of data in an integrated fashion. For example, school principals are often on the receiving end of a wide variety of computer printouts form different sources. They may get attendance reports from the central student accounting system, test results from the state assessment programs or the district's standardized test scoring service, listings of students eligible for compensatory education, report card grade summaries, or locally developed criterion-referenced test results. With a school-based student information system, such files can be input to the school computer so that relationships among these various indicators of student progress can be examined and inconsistencies noted and followed up. Effective information systems make it possible to examine a wide variety of student data in a correlated manner.

In addition to facilitating the examination of trends across domains of data, effective information systems make it possible to examine data over time. For example, longitudinal data can help to spot a student whose achievement growth seems to have leveled off, or one whose truancy rate has suddenly increased, or where grades have begun to decline. This type of "early warning system" can be built into such systems if longitudinal data are available.

Longitudinal data aggregated to the classroom level is a powerful analytic tool. For example, a principal who can study relationships between curriculum pacing and student achievement growth for all the classrooms in the school has a better chance of exerting instructional leadership than one who does not have access to that kind of data. An effective information system makes it possible to examine data at the student, classroom, and school levels. Longitudinal trends for the school as a whole are important in assessing how well the school is moving toward its goals.

One possible by-product of a school-based information system is an increase in the level of inquiry on the part of the professional staff in the school. When data are easily available and data displays are arranged in provocative combinations, serious professionals will tend to "browse" through those displays. Then when they encounter a surprising result, they will look to see if there are other incidences of that phenomenon or look for factors that may have brought it about. Inquiry can be a guiding force in school change, but the tools for conducting inquiry have to be available. An effective information system, which allows for ad hoc inquiries, is such a tool.

A school-based AIS should have the following technical features:

- An integrated software package that provides data management facilities and communication capabilities, making it possible to download relevant files from the district's central computer and send summaries of school-level data back to the district files at the level of detail the district needs for system-wide purposes.
- A scanner that provides test scoring services as well as updates the school-based student files with the latest achievement information.
- A menu driven program so that school personnel can use it easily. It should be capable of generating CRT displays as well as producing printouts that principals can share with other professional staff in the building.
- An easy-to-learn set of commands for making inquiries that were not anticipated in the menu options.
- A secure password system so that unauthorized users cannot have access to confidential data they have no right to see.

There are several currently available commercial systems that perform some of these functions, but none provides sufficient flexibility to adapt to local educational differences. Given the availability of sophisticated data base software, we think it is advantageous to develop and adapt these systems to local differences, relating to the types of criterion-referenced tests being used, ways in which student tracking and attendance accounting are managed, and types of special services available to students in the school. The new software also makes it easier to be adaptive to the existing central computer's file structures and methods of handling data.

DEVELOPMENT OF A PROTOTYPE

The staff at LRDC has been working on the design and development of such a system in one of Pittsburgh's elementary schools. We began by establishing an extensive data base for that school and then worked up displays of these data in ways that the principal and other professionals in the school found useful.

The M. L. King School is one of the participants in Pittsburgh's School Improvement Program (SIP). SIP had already been testing a "paper and pencil" instructional monitoring system in each of these schools (Venson, 1981). SIP staff had developed forms that monitor a student's reading progress, failing report card grades, failing teacher-made test grades, and the retesting of all failed tests including reading mastery tests. The SIP system was designed to help principals identify students in need of extra help. The SIP experience indicated that the principal had difficulty in "processing" all of this data and integrating the classroom information with achievement test scores and other data available in the school.

However, the SIP experience also indicated that decision making should be a prominent part of the principal's role as instructional leader, and that data are necessary for making informed decisions. The principal is involved in such decisions as the proper placement of students in the curriculum, deciding when a student needs extra compensatory services, or determining which classrooms should be the target of staff development efforts. As already noted, reports of other school improvement projects also mention the need to monitor student progress, but none has described precisely how that might be done. For example, how can the data be efficiently captured? What data should be monitored? At what level of detail? Displayed how?

The establishment of our initial data base in the M. L. King School took advantage of data already available in school district files. Thus, from the standardized test file we pulled off test data for the students in this school. Similarly, from the student tracking file we pulled student records relevant to this school. Data being collected from the classrooms for the SIP monitoring were hand-entered.

The system at M. L. King is currently operating on an IBM PC-XT microcomputer located in the school. The system has been implemented with a very flexible data base management software package called Knowledge Manager developed by Micro Data Base Systems. Its data-management language is much like natural-language programming. It uses free-form text similar to English sentences. Knowledge Manager is a relational data base management system that allows the user to combine data from different files within the data base and create tables and graphs of this information. It greatly simplifies the tasks of data retrieval and report generation.

We are now exploring alternative ways of displaying data, through tables, bar graphs, scatterplots, histograms, and so forth. Our objective is to develop displays that will signal various kinds of emerging achievement difficulties in ways that can suggest corrective action. For example, at a recent staff meeting the principal and supervisors were discussing a third-grade classroom in which reading progress seemed to be at a standstill. The lack of progress was noted in data from the monitoring system. Our next task was to work up data that might help the principal and supervisors plan an improvement strategy for that classroom. Analysis was guided by our own abilities to display and interpret data, but once we develop procedures that work with this type of question, they can become part of what automatically is done with these data when that type of question comes up in the school.

Our approach in working with this school is to make available to the principal the procedures that an expert data analyst would use to generate useful information from the school data base. Eventually this expertise will become available to the principal in the form of computer routines that will be automatically invoked when he or she asks particular questions. We do not expect principals to learn how to program computers, nor do we expect principals to learn different ways of analyzing and displaying data. What we are doing is building a menu into the software available to the principal that will make connections between different types of problems. The resulting data displays might help principals work toward solutions to those problems.

In addition to designing ways of being responsive to the types of questions that principals and staff are raising, we are also analyzing the data in order to surface possible instructional problems: We want to have a kind of early warning system. As particularly revealing displays are found, we are incorporating them into procedures that will become part of the principal's monitoring routines.

For example, monitoring only what is being taught in a class may be misleading. A principal may see that a teacher has covered 88 percent of the mathematics curriculum by midyear. At first glance, he or she might think that the teacher is doing very well, but if the principal examines how well the students are mastering the material, that might tell another story. The principal may find that even though a teacher claims that 88 percent of the curriculum has been taught, only 18 percent of the students have mastery of that material, as was noticed in one of our classrooms.

NEXT STEPS

What this project has accomplished during its first year of prototype development is to demonstrate the feasibility of a school-based information system. However, considerable work remains to be done if such systems are to operate without the day-to-day presence of a technical support team. What also remains is the very large job of building into the system the kind of expertise that will truly assist the professionals in each school.

Two major tasks lie ahead. One task is to carefully test out the notion that the system in the King School can be operated successfully by existing school personnel with no additional staff requirements. We are examining ways in which the computer system can produce required reports that now place a heavy load on the clerical staff. Automatically generating those reports will free up clerical time for data entry. We will study what happens as such a school information system becomes operational. We will learn how it is used, what kinds of problems occur, and how frequently technical assistance is needed to maintain an effective operating system. Therefore, we are placing the M. L. King system entirely in the hands of school personnel, providing them with whatever assistance is needed to do that, and studying what happens.

Our other major task is the implementation of the system in the Pittsburgh Elementary Model School (Brookline). This replication will be our first test of the problems involved in taking a system developed in one school and implementing it in another. Although we have intentionally tried to make the programs generic (that is, not specific to the characteristics of a particular school), there are no doubt adaptations that will have to be made to make the programs applicable in another school. We need to understand what they are.

In addition to testing the replicability of the system in another school, the model school setting will give us an opportunity to develop two kinds of expertise that we believe will increase the success of the system. One type of expertise is that possessed by talented and creative principals, supervisors, teachers, and other Pittsburgh staff members who are either resident at the model school or cycling through it as part of the school's staff development function.

We need to build into the system the kinds of things that such talented, creative school practitioners would think of doing when they encounter certain trends in the data. The system can make such options known to all users, so that the expertise can be available in all schools.

Another kind of expertise is that possessed by the LRDC staff. This includes the ability to analyze and display data in ways that can reveal student or classroom outliers needing special attention, or longitudinal trends in the data that need to be watched, and then linking such data to possible actions based on current research in learning and instruction.

Finally, it must be admitted that much remains to be done to solve the problems produced by distributed processing. The major one, of course, is to provide the training needed to operate such systems in each school. We are just beginning to appreciate just how difficult that task is.

REFERENCES

Cooley, W. W., & Bickel, W. B. (1986). *Decision-oriented educational research*. Boston: Kluwer-Nijoff.
Cooley, W. W., & Glaser, R. (1969). The computer and individualized instruction. *Science, 166*, 574–82.
McLuhan, M., & Leonard, G. B. (1967). The future of education. *Look, 31*, 23–25.
Venson, L. (1981). *School improvement program*. Unpublished manuscript, Pittsburgh Public Schools, Pittsburgh.

9
Reactions to an Elementary School's Computerized Office Management System

WILLIAM M. CAREY

This chapter describes our experience with a data base management system from its inception to its implementation in six elementary schools in a medium-sized California school district. The system operates on an Apple IIe computer with an 80-column card, two disk drives, and a printer. The main topics dealt with in this chapter are development, reactions, uses, and cautions regarding this type of management system.

During the spring of 1984 a colleague and I began to notice how the school office staff in the elementary school where we taught was conducting its day-to-day business. We saw that clerks were making repetitious entries on countless little cards with continual movement of paper. What they did was attendance reporting, test data management, and general record-keeping and correspondence. Having recently recovered from a bout of Pac Man fever, my friend and I were eager to find new outlets for our energies; computerizing some of these tasks seemed a reasonable endeavor. Although at this time we were both special education teachers working with blind and visually impaired students, we began pursuing this new project on our own in our small school.

DEVELOPMENT

We began looking at ways to computerize attendance record-keeping. We talked to clerks. Their first reaction was enthusiastic. Our system for attendance was clearly going to save them a tremendous amount of time. But this positive outcome was followed almost immediately by the next reaction: fear of job loss. In a school district like ours, which was experiencing declining enrollments and serious budget constraints, this was a very realistic fear. Rather than scrap our idea we decided to create a student file component in our system that would make use of the extra time the clerks would have available.

During our earlier observations in the school office we had often seen teachers and district specialists hunting for specific pieces of information in the office file cabinets at the request of one agency or another. We felt we could add a student file component to our computerized operation that would put all this information literally at the fingertips of the school clerk, thus freeing teachers and specialists to serve students. At this point we also decided to throw in a disaster-readiness component that would produce emergency information booklets. We also planned to include the district's stockbook so as to ease the paperwork involved in warehouse ordering. We thought we could add an off-the-shelf word-processing program, too.

Within a few weeks we found ourselves with a complete office management system operational in one small elementary school. The school principal's attitude throughout all of this was typical of a number of administrators we subsequently encountered: "Computers are great, let's use them, but please don't ask me personally to deal with them." The clerks, however, had no trouble at all jumping right in. They figured that we were making their jobs easier and more valuable to others in the school.

Since we now had this complete system working in one school, it seemed only right to take it on the road and trade it for cold hard cash. This now put us in the position of convincing the school district that two special education teachers could and should bring all the elementary school offices in the district into the computer age and be paid for it. Well, we did, and they did. After eight months, six of the district's nine elementary school offices were operating with varying degrees of success.

REACTIONS

There were, certainly, some noteworthy obstacles to overcome in this process. One reaction from the district's data processing supervisor was that these schools should have large, powerful systems that would link with a district-level mainframe, and our little Apples did not have that capability. From talking to personnel in other districts, we have decided that this seems to be a fairly typical syndrome of "we will do nothing until we do everything." We made the argument that we were providing an incremental introduction to technology for inexperienced office personnel, and we seem to have prevailed. As grassroots educators, our small-scale, step-by-step approach seemed obvious to us. School site clerical personnel seemed to be more welcoming of the small Apple computer system that they saw children using in classrooms than they would have been to an IBM terminal linking them to a large distant mainframe computer. We have written a simple manual on the operation of our system specifically for the office clerks. As a side benefit of learning our system, many of them have become proficient enough in using a data base and a computer so that their skills will transfer to any system.

We were very concerned about how to train people in the use of the system. We priced our system to include complete training and support and decided that we would sell it no other way; we had seen too many good products go unused due to lack of training and did not want that to happen to us. Our training was one-on-one beginning with the attendance portion of the package. The easiest part to start with was data entry, followed by updating records, and then generating reports. We anticipated the need for reports and made them available as simple menu choices. The manual itself was available, but more importantly, we ourselves were there in person on an on-call basis. Frequently, the requests following basic training began with "Is it possible to . . . ?" and we would come to the site to walk the individual through the process step by step.

USES OF THE SYSTEM

While the attendance record-keeping system is helpful to the office staff, it is the student file that has the potential for charting educational decisions, and for this reason the remainder of this chapter will talk about that portion of the system.

There are three specific components of the student file portion of the system: Student Data, Test Data I, and Test Data II. Student Data includes the basic information such as name, address, ethnicity, and grade; Test Data I has the CTBS (Comprehensive Test of Basic Skills) percentile scores for all years; and Test Data II has the CTBS grade equivalents for all years. Additionally, automatic calculations determine yearly growth, quartile 1, mean growth over the years, and GATE.

Early on, it became clear that only the school office clerk was going to master the student file system; and while a few principals initially expressed a desire to learn, none of them has. Therefore, we decided to meet regularly with the principals to help them realize the kinds of information they now have readily available. For example, there were many things that both principals and teachers were doing that the computer system could do faster and easier. A perfect case was the district's ethnic survey. Each teacher had to do a classroom survey and then the office staff had to tabulate it grade-by-grade for the entire school. Until we told them, it had not occurred to anyone that the new computer system would do this task (in 22 minutes, no less). The student file has a field for ethnicity and grade. This meant it was a simple matter of producing a report that sorted on these fields, giving the ethnic totals for each grade. The actual time spent by the user was probably less than five or six minutes, the rest of the time being spent by the computer grinding out the work.

In looking for the many other possible uses of our office management system, it is helpful to think about who might want to use the system, for instance: district administrators; clerks; other school personnel; we, as system developers; teachers; and, indeed last, principals. Perhaps the principals come last here because they are, so far, the most removed from the details of how the system operates and even of how the clerks do their jobs. For example, we observed one principal during the opening of school directing his clerk to input test data to the student file while the other clerk was typing and retyping class lists as changes in classes occurred. Had the principal realized how to use the attendance files in our system, he would have made sure that updated class lists were printed out quickly and easily after each change.

We have found that school clerks responding to informational requests from the district account for most of the actual use of the system now. Often this is at our urging; after we hear about a pending district request such as the ethnic survey, we show the clerks how to respond to it. Slowly, as teachers become aware of the system's capabilities, we hope they will request more reports from it. We think the same thing will happen for the principals.

Typical reports now being generated regularly include attendance, class lists, pupil counts, student movement lists, mailing labels, phone trees, and ethnic surveys. More specifically, teachers can request a list of phone numbers or mailing labels for very specific groups, such as Hispanic fifth-grade girls. Once a teacher sees this kind of request carried out in a matter of minutes, neatly printed, word gets around. These kinds of reports presently comprise the majority of uses, yet they tend to be primarily clerical in nature.

Here is a similar example at the principal level. One of the elementary schools in our system was designated for closure and its students were to be dispersed to three other schools. I waited for some time and received no requests from anyone regarding records for the students going to each school. The district had sent each school a list of the students it was to receive with only their address and high school graduation year. I took it upon myself to then produce a more extensive list for each school which gave student address and phone number broken out by grade and additionally indicated ethnicity and limited English proficiency. As a result of this, one of the principals has begun to realize what is now possible. He is presently requesting test scores and averages by various special groupings.

CAUTIONS

The most difficult part of introducing computer hardware and software into elementary school offices has not been in training people how to operate it, but rather in educating those who could benefit from it to the tremendous amounts of information now so quickly available. Of course, we get great satisfaction when principals timidly ask "Gee, do you think you could possibly get me this or that information?" and a few minutes later we see their surprise and amazement when we hand them a perfectly formatted, detailed report. It is definitely fun being the local wizard, but it is very important for people to come to independently realize the questions they can and should be asking of this kind of system.

The possibilities relating to the stored test data have yet to be realized, and while principals are aware of this, there is some uncertainty as to how to proceed. I stress that it be with caution. Tabulating test data on specific groups is an easy process and might help to spot trends or challenge assumptions, but to make broad or quick decisions solely on these results would be a mistake.

Using student test data in a variety of ways can show the real value of this type of management system. We have created student profiles to compare sample classes in two different schools. These profiles were done to graphically depict for principals the possibilities of what can be done. For instance, a principal can get an ethnic profile of each individual grade as well as the whole school, or can get a quick look at limited English proficient students throughout the school. We continue to stress, and hope that everyone understands, the dangers of misrepresentation. We emphasize that it is important to remember that whatever information we generate should be looked at in terms of seeking general trends and raising questions, rather than making immediate decisions. As with any single set of data, it is possible to misinterpret or draw false conclusions if there is not a careful weighing of many factors. It is our suggestion that conclusions reached using information from our data base be supplemented by discussions with a broad variety of participants.

CONCLUSIONS

As analyses of student characteristics and performance are extracted from this system, more and more interest is developing throughout our district regarding data base management. I am more convinced than ever, after developing and working with these systems, of the importance of raising everyone's consciousness with respect to the asking of questions. This is equally true for us as we go about designing these systems and for others as they think about actual uses for the systems.

As I look back to the original version of our program, I see that it has changed dramatically. Many of these changes occurred before it even arrived in the schools as a result of many different people reviewing it and offering suggestions. For example, one item we had not anticipated entering into the system was how many years a student had attended a given school. We now find this very useful, because it eliminates recent arrivals when we try to evaluate specific school programs over a number of years. We made other changes in the program after it started being used. When unforeseen needs arose, usually in the form of requested reports such as a monthly list of student transfers in and out of the school, people wanted them included as menu choices.

My other observation about this system is the great joy with which it has been received. This has been true not only for the clerical users, but also for teachers and principals and district people who are the end users of the information product.

What remains to be determined is the impact these systems can have on the education of children. One early positive outcome came as a result of our analysis of CTBS data, which revealed a large drop in scores during the summer months for Hispanic limited-English proficiency (LEP) students. While this may have been confirming the obvious, our documentation of this fact helped to move the district towards the creation of a summer program for these students. It will now be an expected and fairly routine operation to examine these students' scores and analyze the results of this summer program.

It is very exciting to be in education today, learning how to deal with this avalanche of technology. We must remind ourselves to use extreme caution with this new easy-to-access information. Although it is a given that these systems will help us work faster and easier, it is still uncertain whether we will work smarter. Certainly, calculations can be made accurate, but there remains the possibility of faulty understanding of easily codified data. Without doubt, important decisions should continue to be made based on human judgment assisted by many kinds of information.

PART III

The Technical Aspects of Instructional Information Systems

Any discussion of Instructional Information Systems necessarily involves consideration of the capabilities of computer technologies to run such systems. The chapters in Part III highlight some key technological issues related to the use of instructional information systems. Each author recognizes that technology is at present a "high-interest" topic for schools and districts, and each includes cautions for educational consumers.

The authors offer diverse responses to the emerging computer technologies. Responses range from suggestions about how to look at existing systems, to exhortations to jump aboard the technology bandwagon, to cautions about the hassles involved in adopting technology, to recommendations that educators reexamine their assumptions about technology and instruction.

Elaine Craig introduces the chapters of Part III by advising potential technology consumers to do their homework prior to purchasing both hardware and software. Craig suggests that a flexible, contingency-oriented plan will help educators anticipate likely implementation problems and react appropriately to those that cannot be anticipated. She concludes with a checklist of questions to ask prior to investing in a computer system.

Steve Frankel is clearly a high-energy commentator on the technology of the future. He is a believer in the power of the microchip to change the world of education, and he predicts that districts that do not keep up with technology will lose the battle when it comes to attracting students. Frankel's "Information Systems for School Improvement: What's Coming in the New Technologies?" provides a panorama of the state of technology—past, present, and future. He looks back over the last 10 years and then projects forward about another 10. For example, his projections are not limited to the new generation of computers but include other innovations such as cellular phones and satellite dishes. His view of the future is not limited to technology as it applies to Instructional Information Systems. Rather, his interest is with the range of possible changes that new developments in hardware and software will cause in the delivery of education in schools and other settings.

Interestingly, Frankel's chapter illustrates the difficulty of predicting the future in a field with a rapidly emerging and changing technology. Several developments that he had reason to believe were forthcoming have not materialized in expected ways. The chapter has not been revised to reflect these more recent changes but is included here as it was originally presented in February 1985. Nonetheless, Frankels' optimistic point of view merits careful consideration.

John King, on the other hand, warns his audience to be wary of predictions about what computers *will* do. Based on extensive experience with computer science at UC Irvine, his focus has "less to do with the promise of what can happen than with the probability of what will happen."

In his essay, "A Practical Assessment of Computerization in Schools," King acknowledges the exciting possibilities and the "entertainment value" that technology offers while warning about the "incredible hassles" that are involved once a commitment to install computer systems is made. King discusses motivations for using technology in terms of "supply–push" and "demand–pull." He describes how the very existence of a new technology motivates people to seek it. He also describes four different kinds of demand—endemic, institutional, affective, and fabricated demand. The last demand is one in which supply–push forces "succeed in convincing people that they have needs they do not in fact have."

King offers stories based on his computing experiences at UC Irvine. He describes narrowly avoiding a major mistake, rejecting a potentially costly "gift," and adopting "obsolete" technology because it could "do the job." He uses these stories as the basis for the suggestions he makes to educators considering computer technology.

In response to Frankel and King, and based on his own extensive experience with educational television, Saul Rockman, in "Technology and Assumptions: Let's Take Another Look," emphasizes the implied assumptions that educators themselves hold when they think about technology for their schools.

These range from the buyer's assumption that "technology will work" to the seller's assumption that "marketplace innovations will be adopted by schools effortlessly and painlessly." He questions the advocate's assumptions underlying Instructional Information Systems—that educators are seeking more data about student performance in order to improve learning, and that they will eagerly welcome information systems.

Rockman urges his audience to examine these assumptions before jumping on the technology bandwagon. He also recommends using what is known about the introduction of previous technical innovations, such as instructional television, to develop reasonable and feasible assumptions about the potentiality of computerized information systems.

10
Technological Issues Relating to Information Systems

ELAINE CRAIG

Advances in computer technology have been a prime factor in educators' recent interest in Instructional Information Systems. The concept of using information about students' test scores, backgrounds, and previous instructional experiences to guide decisions about instruction is not new. However, technological advances of the past few years have expanded educators' ideas of what they can do with information. The important feature of technology is not that it provides more information—since educators have more information than they can handle—but rather that it offers a new way of working with information, of selecting and combining data in ways not possible before easy access to computers.

Educators, intrigued by the possibilities of using technology for instructional management, are moving into uncharted waters. Their courses in administrative science didn't cover issues related to choosing, purchasing, and managing the technology of large information systems. Administrators' lack of knowledge in this area may contribute to what Williams, Bank, and Thomas (1984) have characterized as the "no-plan" phenomenon. Some administrators may refuse to deal with the uncertainties caused by hardware and software that "is constantly changing; is unfamiliar to many who would potentially benefit from its availability; and threatens some who think they don't want to or can't learn about it" (p. 37). Operating from relative ignorance, they buy into technology without a clear understanding of what is involved. Relatively naive users can be seduced by vendors' free or low-cost offers of hardware or software, not realizing that the district may become committed to a long-term relationship with the vendors and their products. Whatever the cause, when decision makers are not knowledgeable about technology, districts can end up with hardware and software systems in place before policy and implementation decisions regarding their use have been thought through.

Williams et al. (1984) reject the no-plan approach to technology management as well as the more systematic linear approach, which they consider unrealistic given the uncertainty and change associated with current use of computers. They favor, instead, a contingency approach to planning for district technology—that is, moving forward on (1) conducting a situation audit, (2) generating support within the district, (3) formulating a district-wide policy framework, and (4) developing an ongoing organizational plan. This type of planning requires that district administrators and their consultants become knowledgeable about many aspects of computers.

This emphasis on developing an organization-wide plan for acquisition and implementation of computer technology is found throughout the literature on information systems, as is the recommendation that administrators inform themselves about various aspects of technology (Hiscox, 1984; Jones, 1984; Lucas, 1982; Williams et al., 1984). A number of rational-thinking experts caution potential technology consumers to assess and identify organizational needs before selecting a computer system. Their idea is that once those needs have been specified, the consumer will then be able to select a computer system that can actually meet those needs. The logic of conducting a needs assessment prior to selecting a computerized system is quite compelling. However, the notion that one can specify organizational needs and then go find a system to meet them is overly simplistic. Certainly, one should have in mind some tentative problems that such a system could help to solve. However, most people will not know much about what they want from a somewhat mysterious technology until they see what it can actually do.

An example from the business world involves the earliest uses of computers. When they were first introduced, they were used primarily for accounting and record-keeping, tasks that had been done before computer technology was available. After experience with computers and their software capabilities, businesses are now using electronic spreadsheets, interactive data bases, and computer networks, all of which have markedly changed the ways businesses operate. The lesson for the educational community is that it is important to begin with some tentative notions of how computers can improve districts' functions and then to do extensive, ongoing research into their capabilities so that administrators can remain flexible in the ends to which they apply computer technology.

The main categories that administrators will have to research prior to purchasing computer systems include software, hardware, and implementation. Although the increasing capabilities of computers excite consumer interest, most experts caution first-time buyers to decide on the software that will meet their needs before purchasing the hardware to run it. Numerous examples have been cited of hardware purchases being made without any real consideration of what programs will run on the computer configuration selected, resulting in idle or under-used systems.

Actually, would-be computer consumers need to engage in a dialectical process of learning about what various types software can do and then checking on hardware capabilities to run the software. That is, before purchasing hardware, the buyer needs to know that useful, reliable software is available and compatible with that hardware. And before purchasing software, the buyer needs to know that the hardware to run it is available and affordable. In purchasing software and hardware, the buyer also needs to check a number of other features besides compatability that mesh with the institution's needs. These features are discussed below.

This introduction provides a brief overview of issues related to software, hardware, and implementation. These issues are also dealt with from various perspectives in the other chapters of Part III.

SOFTWARE

The importance of software to the success of any computer system cannot be overemphasized. All the technical wonders of the latest microcomputer innovation are worthless without programs that enable the computers to perform desired functions. There are four basic types of software to consider:

1. *Operating Systems*. Also known as system software, the operating system "manages the computer and its peripheral devices, allowing the user to run programs and to move data to and from the computer memory and peripheral devices" (Coburn et al., 1982, p. 256).

2. *Computer Languages*. Specialized languages are used to give instructions to the computer. They can be used to construct whole programs or to customize existing programs to user needs.

3. *General Application Software*. Designed originally for private-sector businesses, general-purpose software has been recently adopted in educational settings. The major categories of this type of software include word-processing programs, spreadsheets, and data base management systems.

4. *Specific Application Software*. This type of software is designed to perform one specific job. Examples of specific school applications include programs for attendance and enrollment, food service, transportation, state and federal reports, student test scores and analyses, class scheduling, and student records.

In acquiring an IIS, a school or district might look first at existing, commercially available software for specific applications, also called off-the-shelf software, to find a program designed for specific desired functions. If such a commercial program is not available, the school or district will have to consider customizing a program using either general application software, such as a data base management system, or a computer language such as Pascal or C. Both of these methods require technical expertise to generate the programs according to specifications. Using a computer language generally requires more time (and thus, more expense for technical expertise) but provides more power in terms of flexibility and control of the computer (P. B. Ender, personal communication, January 1986).

Because of the time and money involved in customizing software, a first step in acquiring an information system is to see if an off-the-shelf, commercial package is available that meets school or district needs. In selecting commercial software there are a number of factors to consider. The most obvious consideration is cost, and generally the better designed and tested software costs more. The consumer's task is to decide if the benefit the software provides justifies the cost. Another aspect of software selection is getting an understanding of what the software can do. This means going beyond manufacturer's claims, reading software reviews, testing the product, and talking to current users of the software.

Next to the performance of the software, the most important feature to check is the documentation, which refers to the instructions and explanations, most often in the form of manuals, that accompany the software. Software documentation is a notoriously weak aspect of many packages; yet comprehensive documentation is invaluable in helping the user initiate the software and use it effectively. Clear, helpful documentation is often an indication of a quality software application.

Other considerations in evaluating software include speed of data retrieval, error handling capabilities (does an unexpected response cause the program to crash?), and adequacy of the software for the scope of the job that needs to be done. Additionally, consumers are advised to watch out for "vaporware," that is, software that has been announced by a company but isn't actually available. It is important not to base any decisions on promises that may never materialize.

HARDWARE

The introduction of the relatively inexpensive and powerful microcomputer has put the power of computing within the reach of all educators. Even school districts with limited resources can now consider the advantage of computerized information systems. Not only are microcomputers inexpensive, but they are easy to use, require little space, allow users independence in program design and selection, and run a host of general-purpose and specific application software, including graphics. Their drawbacks, in comparison to mainframe computers and minicomputers, are their limitations in memory, storage capacity, and language sophistication. However, the technology is developing so rapidly that these differences will probably diminish in a very short time.

The major problem in buying a microcomputer or a system of microcomputers is in the vast number of choices the consumer has to make. Comparisons of different models and brands have to be made regarding the following features: processing speed, memory capacity, features of the operating system, languages built into the system, compatibility with other systems, display characteristics, keyboard functions, expansion slots, printer interfaces, disk storage ease and capacity, currently available software, communications capabilities, warranties, and service and support. Not only should the buyer compare competing systems on these features, but he or she should determine a match between these features and the anticipated needs of the software packages most likely to be used.

IMPLEMENTATION

The implementation of an information system is a continuous process; it does not end with the installation of the system. Ongoing formative evaluation should provide good information on how well the system is meeting district and/or school needs, how system users actually use the system, and users' reactions to the system and suggestions for improvement. Specific technological concerns related to system implementation include training, maintenance and repair, and backup. These concerns should be considered prior to the purchase of the computer package.

TRAINING. The introduction of a computerized information system will require training for those who will be using it and, quite likely, for those who may not use it directly but will want information from those who do. A number of sources of training are currently available, including:

Public sources, such as divisions of county offices of education, local colleges, and adult schools

Publications, especially manuals and books from the manufacturer, other books written by experts in the specific hardware or software application, and specialized magazines

Computer-assisted training or "tutorial" software, which is designed to provide instruction about a particular software application

Private training firms, which often provide comprehensive training but can be quite costly (summarized from Jones, 1984)

Before buying into a particular computer configuration, it would be wise to check on the effectiveness and cost of training available for the system, putting particular emphasis on the software applications.

MAINTENANCE AND REPAIR. It is important to find out before buying a computer system what the maintenance and repair options are. Choices commonly include "do-it-yourself," manufacturer service, dealer or distributor service, or third-party specialists (see Jones, 1984, for complete descriptions). The cost-effectiveness of a service contract should also be determined.

BACKUP. Because of the real threat of loss of data and programs through operator error or computer system problems, the procedures and expenses for regular backup are important to consider prior to purchasing a computer system. The time and money it will take to prepare backup copies of data and software on a regular basis must be included in an assessment of the utility and worth of installing the system.

School administrators considering investment in microcomputer systems to drive their information systems have numerous questions to ask:

- What software do we need? Should we buy commercial software or should we custom-design our own? Is there educational software available for school applications or will we have to adapt business software to our needs?
- What type of hardware should we buy? Can we find a system with the storage and memory capacity we need? Which product will best support the type of software we want to use?
- What difficulties with installation and implementation should be expected? Who will handle them? Who should be trained? In what skills? By whom? At what cost?
- How will new technology be an improvement on the current method we use? Will it be cost-effective? How can we convince the school board that it is worth the initial investment and the maintenance costs?
- Since the technology improves and prices come down every year, shouldn't we wait awhile—won't it be better to buy in a year or two? Is there any way for us to start using the power of the computer now and also upgrade in the future?

The answers to these questions are not readily available, but they are all technical questions that should be asked before a school or a district makes the decision to install an information system. The important task is to anticipate the questions and attempt to answer as many as possible before making a decision. This means becoming knowledgeable about the features of software and hardware and inquiring into the operations of districts that have already started information system implementation. It means reading journals and magazines, talking to vendors, attending conferences, and joining networks of other districts that are using similar technology. It also means going to experts who are familiar with Instructional Information Systems and with the technology that supports them. But current wisdom regarding purchase of technology is that there is no time like the present. Waiting until the next improvement is made, or until the price comes down, means waiting forever. Consumers are advised to make a decision on a system that will serve present needs and those of the near future.

REFERENCES

Coburn, P., Kelman, P., Roberts, N., Snyder, T., Watt, D., & Weiner, C. (1982). *Practical guide to computers in education*. Menlo Park, CA: Addison-Wesley.

Hiscox, M. D. (1984, Summer). A planning guide for microcomputers in educational measurement. *Educational Measurement, 3*(2), 28–39.

Jones, R. (1984, November). *Microcomputing: An overview and response to common questions*. Los Angeles: Los Angeles County Office of Education, Regional Data Processing Center.

Lucas, H. C., Jr. (1982). *Coping with computers: A manager's guide to controlling information processing*. New York: Free Press.

Williams, R. C., Bank, A., & Thomas, C. (1984, December). The school district role in introducing computers: A contingency planning approach. *Educational Technology, 24*(12), 37–42.

11

Information Systems for School Improvement: What's Coming in the New Technologies?

STEVEN M. FRANKEL

I want to give school administrators a peek into the near future, emphasizing the changes technology is apt to make in the way American schools operate. While I will focus on microcomputers, I will also discuss optical disks, cellular telephones, and satellite earth stations.

THE WORLD OF MICROCOMPUTERS

Shortly after the invention of microcomputers in the mid-1970s, the only microcomputer you could buy was the Altair. Manufactured by a company called MITS and about the size of a large microwave oven, the $397 Altair boasted 256 bytes of memory (about enough to save a paragraph of text in memory), a set of toggle switches by which it was programmed, lots of flashing lights, and not much more. Since it didn't have a keyboard to enter data, or a monitor upon which results could be displayed, or disk drives, or even a tape cassette upon which data could be stored, there wasn't very much you could do with it. In fact, one of the first projects of the nation's premiere computer club at the time, the Homebrew Computer Club of what is now Silicon Valley, was using the Altair to generate radio interference that in turn produced "computer music" on a table radio.

Yet the Altair spawned a host of computer enthusiasts, including Bill Gates of Microsoft and Seymore Rubinstein of MicroPro (the *Wordstar* word-processing folk). Only ten years later, that same $397 would buy quite a bit more. For instance, let's consider a machine that was introduced back in January 1985 at the Consumer Electronics Show in Las Vegas: Atari's ST-520, the so-called Jackintosh. A Macintosh look-alike for $399, the Jackintosh sported a full typewriter-size keyboard; 512K of memory (enough to store up to 200 pages of text); a 32-bit Motorola 68000 processor that could address 2 million bytes of memory, should anyone want to use that much;

a monochrome monitor of a better quality than the best TV set; and an operating system that would permit anyone to master most program applications in only a few minutes or hours and offered superb monochrome and color graphics.

Let's examine a few other examples of how rapidly things change. The first full-function microcomputers—such as the Radio Shack TRS-80, the Apple II, and the Commodore Pet—were all released in 1977. Selling for $795, the Pet came with 16K of memory (64 times that which the Altair offered only two years earlier), the keyboard and monitor that the Altair was missing, provisions for connecting the computer first to a tape cassette recorder and later to a disk drive, and a copy of the BASIC programming language which, together with the peripherals, meant that you could actually do something with the machine. However, at the time there was no software industry to speak of, and those who wanted to do something with a Pet, Apple, or "Trash 80" (the nickname affectionately given to the TRS-80) had to write the programs themselves.

Now, let's jump ahead to 1982, only five years after appearance of the Pet. The big hit that year was the Kaypro II. Using the same Intel 8080 microprocessor that the original Altair used, the Kaypro sold for $1,795 but came with 64K of memory (4 times that of the Pet and 250 times that of the Altair), a built-in monitor, two 200K disk drives, and most important—a rich software library. At first the software included "only" two versions of BASIC, a word processor, a spelling checker, a spreadsheet program, and a filing program; later, the software library grew to include a communications program and a true data base management system. The interesting thing about this development was that since the same software was selling in computer stores for close to $2,000, consumers were literally getting the computer for free; moreover, such a system could outperform dedicated word processors selling for up to $15,000, thus totally revolutionizing the way offices functioned.

COMPUTERS AND MANAGEMENT

This isn't mere verbiage. Twenty such Kaypros formed the backbone of the management system that the Montgomery County (Maryland) Public Schools Department of Educational Accountability installed; use of this system permitted us to literally triple our productivity while containing costs. Over a period of time, by using attrition to trade off clerical positions for microcomputers and giving those micros to the professionals doing the writing, the time needed to put a report through the usual six drafts dropped from three months to less than four weeks. Further, morale improved, since writers no longer had to worry about clerical turnaround time. In our shop, all staff members now have their own computers and are expected to use them to do nearly all their own typing and—increasingly—data analysis. Our clerks and secretaries are only expected to do final document formatting and type charts, and it is this change in job definitions that first permitted us to turn out about 60 major products a year with 17 full-time professionals, 15 part-time researchers, and 4 clerks and secretaries.

Today the picture is even brighter. Lately we've been buying IBM PCs, which we equip with a 10- or 20-megabyte hard disk and two 360K floppy disks (25 times the capacity of the Kaypro), 640K of memory (2500 times the memory capacity of the original Altairs), an ultra-high-resolution color monitor, a built-in modem for telecommunications, the 8087 high-speed math processor chip, a clock, and lots of other goodies. Although these units cost a bit more than the Kaypros, they permit us to take a good deal of our workload off the school system's huge mainframe computer, since we can now run SPSS at our own desks and do a host of other functions that would have been unthinkable only a short time ago.

For instance, over one Christmas vacation I used a data base management system called Dataease to develop a new budget-reporting system that the mainframe folk said would take at least two years to build. With my PC and Dataease, the job was done in about 40 hours. This is only one example of how we are exploiting the new technology, but it typifies our general approach, which is to use technology to permit our researchers to take over more and more of the tasks for which they previously had to rely on clerks, secretaries, research assistants, graphic artists, and programmers. In the near future even these capabilities will seem modest.

COMPUTERS AND LEARNING

Given the direction that technological developments seem to be taking, we may see some fundamental redefinitions in what schools do within the next decade. For, if a complete instructional system such as PLATO can be housed on a single optical disk, and if other optical disks with both data and audiovisual capabilities are also available, the time students spend in school being taught by certified teachers could be cut by at least 50 percent.

Yes, I know that we heard the same song and dance when educational films were big in the 1930s, when video was the rage in the 1950s, and when programmed instruction was king in the 1960s. But this time it might really happen.

Imagine a personal computer that combines the raw computing power of, say, an IBM PC-AT or Macintosh, coupled with an optical disk drive and a port that would allow it to be connected to an audiovideo system. With such a system a student could go through a series of lessons focusing on the Civil War in which the disks being used could include digitized versions of Matthew Brady's photographs, clips from *Gone with the Wind* broadcast in full color with stereo sound, the complete text of *Uncle Tom's Cabin*, and a data base management system that would permit that student to access portions of 50 or 60 other books and documents also included on the disk.

Impossible? Not on your life. In fact, all the components of such a system are probably available now or soon will be. And if the base price is in the $400 range that Atari predicted for its Jackintosh, the complete cost of all the components will be comfortably under $5,000. Further, when the optical disk drives that comprise about 50 percent of the cost drop down to about $100, as they might, and if the cost of 256K memory chips drops down to the cost of the present 64K memory chips, this same system would cost under $1,000, the most expensive component being the color monitor. Further, in mass market quantities, there is reason to believe that such systems will become available within several years at $500 or less. This means that families will be able to buy or lease such systems for somewhere around $25 a month.

At this point, if high-quality software becomes available—which I believe it will if there is truly a mass market for it—districts will have to consider distributing such systems to students for use either at home or in day care centers, or even in a section of the school staffed by less expensive paraprofessionals. Imagine, for instance, an arrangement under which systems of this type are provided to every student to use two hours a day, with their other three hours spent in classes that are half the size of those at present, or with teachers earning twice their present salary. Believe it or not, such a school could probably be run for no more than we are spending at present. It is my guess that it might produce significantly better results than the current operation. In fact, the economics are so persuasive that any district that is not beginning to think in these terms is probably going to be in a state of panic and have to play "catch-up" by the end of the decade.

After all, in this scenario, how will traditional districts be able to compete for teachers working in automated systems in which the average pay is over $60,000 in today's dollars; in which many seminar-type classes have no more than 15 students in the room; and in which teachers receive daily or weekly readouts showing each student's progress through the mediated portions of the curriculum?

Both the hardware and the software vendors seem to be going in this direction. Manufacturers are developing two-inch optical disks capable of storing 40 megabytes of data, enough for 26,000 pages of information. When perfected, these devices will probably be embedded in a so-called laptop portable computer weighing no more than 10 pounds and having its own power supply. Very powerful laptop portables, such as the new NEC PC8401A that I use to write with on airplanes, already cost less than $1,000. Even with the optical drive and the larger memories that will be needed, the cost of such machines can easily come under $500 within three to five years, and this reinforces the above scenario—except that in this case the computer used will be the size of a single book and will be designed to plug into any TV set.

OTHER TECHNOLOGICAL "GOODIES"

These are not "blue sky" fantasies; they are reasonable responses to cold-blooded market realities. Many forecasters of the computer industry are predicting that by 1990 the standard $1,500 home computer system will have two megabytes of internal memory and one megabyte of external read and write memory. Further, they predict that it will weigh no more than 15 pounds and be no larger than a Compaq or Kaypro is today. Such a system will have about twice the capacity of a DEC VAX 750 mainframe that now sells for about $80,000, and it should fill the role that mainframes have played to date.

As if all this isn't enough, I want to dwell on communications for a moment. Since I always like to be "firstest with the mostest," I installed a first-generation cellular telephone in my car in 1984, when the system first become available in the United States. That unit, also made by NEC, consists of a box the size of a stereo receiver in my trunk that contains a radio transmitter that is constantly connected to radio towers maintained by the cellular network, and a small handset next to the front seat. But that unit is already hopelessly out-of-date. NEC has eliminated the box in the trunk and replaced it with a box the size of a Sony Walkman that sits underneath the telephone cradle in the automobile cockpit. Further, this combined unit is fully portable and can be plugged into a small battery pack that takes up about one-third of the space in an ordinary attache case. This is why I am predicting that the newest status symbol on the beach some summer soon will be truly portable phones, capable of dialing anywhere in the world since they will be hooked into the cellular systems.

Now consider another innovation that is fast approaching: small—even portable—satellite earth stations. The new generation of communications satellites are sufficiently powerful that they can be received with a three-foot dish instead of the 10- to 12-foot models. With these new dishes, the cost of a so-called "earth station" is already dropping down to under $500 and could be half that amount in a few years.

Now let us combine the computer technologies about which we have been talking with those of the cellular and earth station technologies I have just mentioned. Put all of these together and it doesn't take much to imagine a combination cellular phone/laptop portable computer that fits in an attache case and also contains the satellite ground station electronics, and a small TV. And with decent design, maybe the cover of the attache case could become the satellite dish.

IMPLICATIONS FOR THE FUTURE

What you would then have is an instant portable school. For, not only could mediated instruction of the type earlier described occur for a fraction of the present hourly instructional cost, but such lessons could be beamed down from satellites to cover the entire nation. Two-way communications could be established via the cellular phone with instructional locations anywhere in the world, where instructors would be able to monitor students' work, question them verbally, and conduct group discussions with the "class" scattered over several continents.

Is this "blue sky"? Sure it is, but there is no reason to expect that systems of this kind will not be available by the turn of the century. The sheer economics of being able to reduce the labor and capital equipment costs associated with education by 30 to 70 percent, while being able to present much broader and more effective instruction, make these innovations inevitable.

Now, where does this leave us? What are the implications of these possible futures on the way we run schools today?

First, we have got to realize the nature of the technology that is almost here, and that will arrive, whether we like it or not, due to the forces of the marketplace. Consider educational software as an example. Many school people even today can be heard commenting that computers are going nowhere in school because the equipment or software "just isn't there." They are speaking out of ignorance. They don't realize that a program called Rocky's Boots, which has been on the software best-seller lists for some time now, has taught thousands of children—mostly of elementary school age—a great deal about digital electronics and circuit design without their even realizing that they were learning such advanced material. Educators also might not yet realize that millions of kids are now fairly good typists by the time they hit first grade.

Why don't we realize these things? Because we continue to insist that "real" education is what takes place in school. However, the computer software vendors have already made a conscious decision to bypass schools in their marketing activities and sell directly to parents. Thus, if schools decide not to buy into the possibilities offered by the new technologies, the marketers will decide that schools are irrelevant and market these vastly more sophisticated products directly to parents. In other words, I could imagine that the rumored IBM/Control Data joint effort to put PLATO on a single optical disk able to be read by an IBM PC may only be a precursor to these same corporations organizing private schools around these technologies.

Remember, computer firms have already made most of the technical investment needed to deliver these systems, and they will be looking for a way to amortize their costs over the widest possible market. And with the public's present disenchantment with much of the public education system, establishing "name brand" private schools may be one way for these corporations to go.

Could traditional public schools compete with such schools? Maybe, but I doubt it. We might lose many more of our middle and upper class students and could well end up with a network of "public" schools serving mainly poor children. I would argue that the survival of public education in the United States dictates that we actively investigate these new avenues of instruction and start pilot programs that will permit us to explore how they can best be exploited. I believe this needs to be done whether or not we can find external funding.

At the very least, we need to actively track these emerging technologies and form linkages with the firms and individuals who will be developing the software. By offering to serve as "beta sites" for testing such systems, we can experiment with different ways of restructuring schools as we know them, and influence future developments in what has, up until now, been largely our own exclusive domain.

12

A Practical Assessment of Computerization in Schools

JOHN LESLIE KING

There are now more computers used in schools than there used to be, and the chances are good that computer use will continue to grow. Promoters encourage this growth with promises of great improvements in the quality of education, in the cost-effectiveness of teaching, and so forth. Nevertheless, there are many reasons to be skeptical about this new movement. We should pause now, before schools are computerized, and take stock of what computerization is like as a practical matter. After the computers are installed and the excitement has diminished, somebody will have to take care of what has been created. This chapter provides some insights about what will be there to take care of and the challenges that school administrators and teachers will face as a result. The problems I relate here are on a scale considerably beyond what most public schools face at this time. But they are analogs of what is likely to come.

UPCLASSING AND THE RISE OF INFORMATION CONSCIOUSNESS

We often hear today that we are in or are entering the "Information Age," or that we are living in an "Information Economy." Our society, which at various times has been an Agrarian Society, an Industrial Society, a Postindustrial Society, a Narcissistic Society, and even a Great Society, is now becoming an Information Society. We are in the Information Revolution. If nothing else, this rhetoric has proved that the word "information" can be used as an adjective as well as a noun.

It is natural for people to wonder about those features of their own era that are unique and set them apart from those vast legions of people who have gone before. This fixation on classifying what we see about us is natural, but I have some concerns with the systematic bias that creeps into the prevailing rhetoric about our culture, and particularly when it begins with the word information. That bias I can best describe by the term "upclassing" as it is used in the advertising field. Upclassing is the deliberate casting of the average in the context of the above average. The television kitchen where Mrs. Olson pours coffee is a good deal nicer than the one most people have; the television bar where Michelob is poured is livelier and less depressing than most actual bars; and the new Nissan Stanza is driven home to a house most viewers would trade for their own, forgoing the Stanza if necessary.

Advertisers naturally portray products in a favorable light—no one would build a Michelob ad around a derelict in a gutter, even if derelicts could afford Michelob. But there is a certain kind of dishonesty that comes from upclassing, and upclassing in advertising can have some disturbing consequences. Three in particular stand out:

1. *Reification of reality*. Upclassing tends to strip away important features of the real world in which products are used. Beer ads ignore alcoholism, traffic fatalities from drunken driving, and streets and parks littered with beer cans and bottles; yet beer is in reality connected with these things, too. The world portrayed, however, is free of strife, full of smiles, and, in short, "looking good."

2. *Systematic devaluation of alternatives*. Although upclassing does not specifically denegrate the alternatives (with a few exceptions), it does suggest to people that they ought to aspire to the upclassed world being portrayed. Perhaps many people do aspire to that upclassed world, and advertisers simply exploit that aspiration. But people's aspirations are also influenced and to some extent created by the scenes portrayed in these ads.

3. *Discounting of what people are and what they already do*. Indeed, in the extreme cases this discounting is a wholesale effort to make people distrust their basic views and assumptions and join in with the "elite" being portrayed. It is not OK to be pedestrian, to be old, fat, poor, unhealthy, uneducated, or deprived in any way. It is OK to be slick, svelte, young, rich (or getting rich), and selfish. Most importantly, it is OK to "belong," and belonging is set by the context of the ads, regardless of how banal, hedonistic, and narcissistic that context is.

I believe that the problem is not in advertising per se. The classical economists correctly saw advertising as an appropriate and even essential mechanism for notifying potential buyers about products and their prices. But this notion of advertising always had the good grace to treat "demand" as the province of the buying public and not something to be cultivated, nurtured, or, when necessary, fabricated by clever psychoimagery. What we see in current advertising, and particularly in television and magazine advertising, is a great deal more than product information.

The hyperbole surrounding the Information Revolution, the Information Economy, the Information Age, and the Information Society bears the trappings of an elaborate advertising stunt to make people forget their better judgment and buy into an array of preposterous deceptions. The view of computing that is expounded lies on one of two poles of a continuum. At one extreme is the idea of "computers as poison." Here we learn about threats to privacy, the dastardly deeds of hackers who break into computerized records and cause havoc, and the accidental start of World War III. Here we do battle with the HAL 9000 somewhere out in deep space. But aside from occasional articles in the newspaper, endless congressional studies, and movies made in the 1960s, this end of the continuum does not have much of a forum these days.

At the other extreme is the "computers as the better way" view. Here we learn about the wonderful things computers are doing for us, and maybe more to the point, the wonderful things they will be doing for us soon. Computers make the Space Shuttle fly, they keep people in intensive care units alive, they protect us from our enemies, they teach Johnny to read, and most importantly for administrators, they save money and reduce staff. Here we are chumming around the galaxy with C3PO and R2D2, battling evil, and having fun. This extreme view is the prevailing one, at least at present.

We do not seem to hear much about the views that lie between these two extremes. Perhaps these are too boring to be taken seriously. But my research on the uses of computing in complex organizations has pushed me into this middle ground, and prompted me to make the following comments on the prospects of computing in the schools. The balance of this chapter, then, provides a brief commentary on ideologies we might bring to bear when thinking about computing in the schools. The issues I will focus on have less to do with the promise of what can happen, and more to do with the probability of what will happen.

A VIEW OF COMPUTING REALITY: COMPUTING IS AN ENTERTAINING HASSLE

I have repeatedly tried to come up with a catchy phrase to describe how I view computing. It has not been easy. In reviewing the upside and downside of my own experiences with computing—as a system builder, a user, and a manager of a fairly large computing enterprise—I finally found a phrase that suits: Computing is an entertaining hassle.

I will start with the adjective in this phrase, "entertaining," because it is critically important. Computing would never be a hassle at all if we did not engage in it. Why do we engage in it? There are a number of reasons, and I will get into them in a moment. But given the fact that many things are now wrapped up in computing trappings that do not have to be, I conclude that a primary motivator is pure entertainment value. Some people see entertainment as frivolous. This is ridiculous, and it flies in the face of human experience. Even people living in the most abject circumstances find ways to entertain themselves and each other. Entertainment is part of what being alive is all about. So I attribute much of the discretionary choice to adopt and use computing to entertainment, and I'm glad computers are so entertaining.

On a more serious note, however, it is important to answer with care the question of why we engage in computing. To do so, we have to look at basic motivations. I have found it convenient to divide motivations roughly into two categories: supply–push motivations, and demand–pull motivations. Supply–push motivations are those that come from the development of new ways of doing things. In simplistic terms, things are done because they can be done; we climb the mountain because it is there. If you look carefully, most models of how computing is adopted and used in organizations adopt supply–push views. Changes in computing use are tied to changes in computing technology. Obviously, without computers there would be no computing. And the supply side of computing is essential to what happens in computing. But I personally believe that the best explanations of what happens in computing use come from the demand–pull motivations. Without demand, the word supply has no meaning; yet we can name lots of demands for which there is no supply.

I break demand down into four types, each of which exerts a different kind of influence.

1. *Endemic demand*. This is what most administrators would see as legitimate demand. It refers to those standing needs in organizations to accomplish tasks, improve qualitative and quantitative performance, and expand into new promising areas. Computing technology helps us calculate and print things faster; it enables us to look up individual records from among vast records files quickly; and it enables us to do things we could not do before. If you will, organizations recover their computing costs by meeting endemic demand.

2. *Institutionalized demand*. This is a kind of demand that arises from trying to meet endemic demand. In other words, the very act of adopting computing technology to take care of endemic demands creates new demands solely around the computing activity. The best example here is the activity known in computing as "maintenance." Whether you are talking about hardware or software, what you have today is not necessarily what will work tomorrow. Equipment becomes obsolete, procedures become unworkable, and new ways of doing things supplant old ones. The most blatant case of this is when an organization is forced to upgrade its computing technology because the computer manufacturer will no longer provide support or

repairs for the equipment the organization owns. In short, institutionalized demand automatically follows efforts to meet endemic demand.

3. *Affective demand*. This is where entertainment comes in. Affective refers to those motivations to adopt and use computing that cannot be justified in rational management terms. People adopt computing for many different affective reasons: because they want to play with computers, because they want everyone to think that they are sophisticated and technically with-it, because parents call in and insist on having computers in their children's classrooms. There is nothing particularly wrong with affective demand—in fact, there probably would not be nearly as much truly useful computing activity going on without affective demand to spur it along. Most people will acknowledge the influence of affective demand if you get them out of earshot of their colleagues, and especially their bosses, but it isn't a very persuasive way to justify computer purchases.

4. *Fabricated demand*. This is the peculiar case of demand that is created by the supply–push forces when they succeed in making people believe that they need what they do not, in fact, need. It is extremely difficult to pinpoint when and how this happens, since motivations to adopt new technologies are convoluted and influenced by many things. But this is a real phenomenon. Take the example of personal computer magazines. One of the major magazines for PCs was the most successful new publication start-up in U.S. history. In its second month, it was in the black. This success was not due to subscriptions and newscounter sales; it was due to advertising. Certainly, much of that advertising was aimed at meeting what the advertiser felt was unmet demand. But many of the advertisers were quite interested in seeing whether they could generate demand. One of my graduate students did an interesting study in which he found out that a significant fraction of the personal computer software products advertised in personal computer magazines did not exist at the time the ads for them were placed. This so-called "vaporware," needless to say, creates considerable confusion in the computing marketplace.

To summarize the entertainment side of my catch-phrase about computing, whenever there is doubt about the practical justifications for engaging in computing and yet computing still emerges, one will usually find that the entertainment value of the technology is playing a major role. Entertainment as a powerful motivator should not be overlooked because it is essential to understanding why computing as a phenomenon is growing by leaps and bounds.[1]

Now we turn to the other key term, the "hassle" of computing. It is simplest to begin this discussion with a few explicit examples of life with computing. I have had the opportunity to experience life with computing from several perspectives in the Department of Information and Computer Science (ICS) at the University of California, Irvine (UCI). Like most research university departments, we have two fundamental missions: instruction and research. These are bound together by the administrative actions of the faculty and departmental leaders. One story in each domain—instructional, research, and administrative—will illustrate the kinds of things that can happen with computing. Bear in mind when considering these anecdotes that, as a computer science department, many people on our faculty and staff are experts in computer architecture, operating systems, software, and management. We also have colleagues and friends at other computer science departments who know things we do not know, and with whom we share information. In other words, these experiences took place in a sophisticated environment quite unlike the average organization with limited in-house expertise.

AN INSTRUCTIONAL COMPUTING STORY

The ICS Department handled computer instruction the same way for 20 years. Students used terminals connected to large time-sharing systems run by the campus computing facility. This caused a number of problems for students, including competition for terminals and slow response time. In 1980 we decided to move a large portion of our lower-division instruction onto dedicated microcomputers running UCSD-Pascal in the NCI-P system: a commercial package designed for instruction in computer science departments. The NCI system runs on machines using the 8088 processor, the best known of which is the IBM PC. IBM had not quite decided whether it would grant major discounts to universities (it subsequently did), and our budget was limited. We decided to buy IBM PC look-alike computers from a small company that offered excellent graphics capabilities as part of the basic package. We bought 60 of these and proceeded to set up our laboratory.

There were a remarkable number of hassles and costs involved in setting up a lab of 60 PCs. We had to run in additional power ($15,000), put in an alarm system ($4,000), order a large amount of furniture that really isn't useful for much else but a PC lab ($50,000), buy the PCs ($120,000), have them shipped (they came late), unpack them (what do you do with 200 cardboard boxes?), test them (five were DOA), and build the software support that would allow us to use them for the classes (this took a lot of faculty and graduate student time). We got the lab running about 15 nanoseconds before classes started in the fall quarter of 1981.

We immediately realized that we did not have enough PCs to meet demand. To do the assignments, students had to spend about 12 hours a week in labs. We had enough machines for 10 hours per student per week. We needed 15 more. We also discovered that these machines, which came with one floppy disk drive, were having lots of drive failures because the room was so dirty. Students would track in dirt, drop their disks on the floor, and then put them in the drives. So we had to institute a new cleaning schedule. We had to buy additional printers, and sacrifice some of our PCs to be printer drivers. And, of course, except for the purchase of additional PCs for which we did not then have the money, this all took place as the classes were going on.

In early 1983 we ordered 15 additional PCs from the same manufacturer. Here begins the story of a most interesting hassle. In late 1982 IBM sued three companies, including our supplier, on the grounds that they had infringed IBM's copyright on the software in the BIOS ROMs used in their machines. This is the software in the programmable read-only memory that controls, among other things, the graphics used by the machine. The three companies quickly settled out of court, and changed the software in the BIOS ROMs. One of the defendants went out of business as a result of lost sales; the other two, including our supplier, survived in a weakened state.

Our new PCs arrived, and we put them in the lab. Imagine our surprise when we discovered that the NCI-P system did not run on the new machines. After some investigation we found that the P system depends on IBM-BIOS software, and the new PCs no longer had that software. Our supplier was as blank as a brick wall when we brought up the subject: "What BIOS software?" they asked, with bovine stares. We were on our own with 15 machines that did not run. We called NCI and tried to get them to help. Their market is for about 20,000 IBM PCs and about 85 PCs of the kind we own. You can guess where helping UCI was on their priority list. Eventually we solved the problem by buying some PROM chips, soliciting the assistance of a friend from a PROM programmer, and burning a working version of the BIOS software onto those PROMS. We stuck them in the computers, and we were in business.

A RESEARCH COMPUTING STORY

Just prior to taking over most of our own instructional computing activity, we took in-house all of our research computing activity. We have an active research group in artificial intelligence that focuses on the subject of machine learning. This kind of research requires computers with sizeable amounts of computing power and main memory, as well as graphics disk storage capability. Advances in the technology have made stand-alone workstations available for this kind of research at a cost between $25,000 and $125,000 each. Our AI group recently decided that it needed five systems costing about $60,000 each for their work.

We initiated a search for the "right" system to purchase through a common method: asking likely vendors to show us their wares. Several vendor sales representatives came by, extolling the virtues of their systems and offering exceptional educational discounts. Eventually we chose one vendor, largely on the basis of what we had heard about the positive experience of another university's AI group in using such equipment. We signed a purchase order for approximately $200,000 worth of equipment, and waited for delivery.

Fortunately, immediately after signing the purchase order two lucky breaks saved us from a major mistake. First, a former faculty member with close experience with the machines we ordered visited us while passing through town. When he heard we were ordering these machines, he asked to see our configuration. He laughed when he saw it, and told us that it was the same configuration the salespeople had tried to sell him. It would not work for our needs. He also told us that the university on which we were basing our choice was abandoning this vendor's machines due to bad experiences. The vendor's equipment would do the job if we made major upgrades, but this would double the price of the configuration. We explored these comments with friends elsewhere, and discovered they were correct. Our second lucky break was the decision by the lawyers for the vendor to reject some aspect of the university's purchase order conditions, and request a modification. This permitted us to drop the purchase orders without cost to ourselves.

After considerable internal discussion, we reinitiated our search for equipment and eventually selected a much less expensive configuration with much greater power from another vendor. We had not known about this vendor before; our problems forced a wider search that revealed this previously unknown option. We placed our order with the new vendor, and after considerable delays, received the first machine. It ran for a week and then died. Several months later, we had all our machines installed, and since then they have been quite adequate for our needs. The elapsed time between first deciding to open a procurement for the AI machines and the final installation of the five workstations we did buy was nearly 15 months. In the 12 months following our purchases, new technological advancements caused us to reopen the prospect of obtaining replacement machines for the AI group and relegating the five existing machines for other purposes.

AN ADMINISTRATIVE COMPUTING STORY

Computer science is a popular area at UCI, and tax laws in recent years have made it worthwhile for corporations to donate equipment to computer science departments. We receive such gifts from time to time, and often they help us greatly. Occasionally, however, they cause a good deal of trouble. A couple of years ago we received a gift of about $100,000 worth of equipment from a major manufacturer. The manufacturer had solicited requests for gifts, and we responded with a proposal to receive two machines of a certain type for our instructional program. The manufacturer responded with an offer of several different machines that would not work for our instructional program or our research program. However, we thought we could put the systems to use in departmental administration. We accepted the machines, and put them in our basement storage area.

However, two years later those machines were still packed in their boxes in the basement. After detailed investigation of the appropriate possible uses for the machines, we found that we would have to spend approximately $45,000 on electrical upgrades and additional equipment to bring the systems into administrative use. Our needs were more easily and usefully met by spending $20,000 upgrading other equipment we already had running. This taught us an important lesson: look every gift horse in the mouth. Life with computing begins after the machines are delivered, and it is not a cheap life to lead. Not too long after this experience, the university was offered 350 powerful "advanced" microcomputers by a major manufacturer, worth a list price of $1 million. The university administration immediately assumed that our department would take delivery of most of these for use in instruction. With the boxes in the basement firmly in our minds, we responded that we wanted to look at these machines carefully before accepting any of them. It is a good thing we did so. It turned out that the microcomputer being offered did not and could not support the software systems around which our instructional program is based. They ran a strange hybrid operating system that all our technical staff agreed was a disaster, and that would be impossible to modify to fit our needs. We estimated that it would cost us about $150,000 to put these machines to work, and even then, we would be heading down a path with no future since the operating system was doomed to failure in the marketplace. We respectfully declined the offer, noting that for $150,000 we could probably buy exactly what we wanted off the shelves of other vendors. In retrospect, this proved to be a wise decision.

THE LESSONS TO BE LEARNED FROM THESE STORIES

The lessons from these stories can be summarized by a single axiom: Whatever hassles you think you will experience when you computerize pale when compared with what you will actually experience when you computerize. This can be said of many enterprises, but it is particularly true of computing. It is useful to focus in on why the management of computing is so fraught with problems.

Let us go back to the earlier discussion of supply-push and demand-pull. The supply side of computing is changing very rapidly, as technological capabilities improve and the price-performance ratios become more advantageous. There are two ways to understand this change and its effects. The first is marketing-driven change, which sees organizations and individuals as passive recipients of innovation. This is a common view of people who evaluate the implementation of computing, and it is typically articulated in terms of organizations "responding" to technical change as though such change is inevitable. The other perspective on the change takes the view that technical advancement affects organizational perceptions of opportunities, and thereby initiates the rearticulation of demand. Basically, this view holds that new opportunities affect perceptions of what is needed as well as what is possible. This latter view is more complex, since it requires some understanding of organizational behavior. But it also provides a much more powerful framework for explaining what happens as a result in changes on the supply side of computing.

This point can be illustrated by a long-standing concern of systems analysts who attempt to develop new computer applications for users. It is common to hear systems analysts complain that users who are asked to define their needs for computing systems do not know what they want. Why should this be the case? The problem is a version of the chicken-and-egg problem: People do not know exactly what they want until they have a good idea of what they can get. It is useless to explain to users of computing systems the technical advantages of this or that way of doing things unless the users can immediately relate the options to things they routinely do. In short, most people have to experience something before they know for sure whether they want it. The dilemma is obvious: Is it best to plan for what is needed and then acquire the ability to accomplish the plan; or is it best to acquire promising capabilities and then figure out what to do with them?

Most of the literature on the management of computing implementation says to plan first, and then act. This advice has a disturbing propensity to breed disaster. As seasoned military planners well know, no campaign plan ever survives contact with the enemy. The key to survival in computing is what I call "flexible response" capability. As one learns to deal with problems and opportunities, one's intuitive sense of how to anticipate problems and opportunities is honed. Eventually, individuals (not organizations) learn how to cope in a dynamic and turbulent world in which change is endemic in all facets of the enterprise: the environment, the organization, and the technology. The stories above reveal the steady (although often painful) learning experiences of the organization to which I belong: We solved the problems with the PCs and the AI workstations, and put the knowledge we gained to good use in evaluating subsequent challenges.

I have reserved one last example of our experience with computing to illustrate in detail the issue of flexible response. This example is an extension of my previous stories, and provides a reasonable analog to the issues facing most school administrators who try to cope with computing.

Not long ago, some friends from a major electronics manufacturing company called our department and offered us a discount price on a model of personal computer they had attempted to market but failed to sell in sufficient quantities. Each basic system came with a 13-inch RGB color graphics monitor, twin floppy disk drives, an RS 232C communications port, both parallel and serial printer ports, a high-quality keyboard, and all the necessary cables. With each system came a proprietary BASIC interpreter with excellent graphics and music primitives, as well as the CP/M operating system, C-BASIC, the *WordStar* word-processing package, and the *CalcStar* spreadsheet package. The machines were excellent in every respect but one: The central processor used was the Z-80, an 8-bit processor that is generally regarded as out of date. Since it is impossible to upgrade the processor, these systems were frozen out of the consumer market despite the other nice features they contained.

These little PCs are machines no self-respecting computer science department would admit to owning. But we bought 50 of them at the discount price of $500 each. We did so because we had learned from our past experience to evaluate the whole package surrounding every computing opportunity. Although the machines were low-powered microcomputers, they were perfect for instruction in a lower-division course for nonmajors. We had been running this course for over 1,000 students per year on a large minicomputer at a cost of about $13,000 per year for computing. These micros would more than meet our demand, and pay for themselves within two years. After that, we could throw them away and still be ahead. In fact, we anticipate that they will last us at least three years.

Here we have a most curious situation: Our department adopted obsolete technology to do a job, and even paid for it, while at the same time rejecting a gift of $1 million worth of technologically "advanced" computers. The reason we did so was simple: the obsolete technology did the job for us at a reasonable cost; the new technology did not.

Looking back on our discussion of demand, we can summarize our actions in relation to the obsolete microcomputers as follows:

- We focused on endemic demand. We concerned ourselves only with what we knew we had to do—deliver computing capability to a particular class, without worrying about other uses we might make of the equipment. The

new system actually proved to be an improvement over what we had been using.
- We avoided strong institutional demand forces. Our choice in this case locked us into a dead end. You cannot upgrade these microcomputers, so there would never be any argument to do so. We evaluated them strictly on the basis of their existing configuration. The low price for the systems made them not worth upgrading in any case.
- We discounted affective demand. We swallowed whatever pride we had and bought old technology that would work for as long as we could imagine needing it—two years on the inside, and four years on the outside.
- We avoided the fabrication of demand. The market had already spoken on these machines—it did not want them. Yet we took them. The reason we did so was we realized that the market, and many other sources of advice, are frequently right about the average case but often wrong about the specific case. In our specific case, market failure was the seedbed for our success.

THE REALITIES OF LIVING WITH COMPUTING

I see four conditions that must be met for managing computing successfully within a managerial rationalism framework. Briefly stated, these are:

1. Stability in the range of opportunities available to users
2. Clearly articulated and agreed-on goals for application of the technology
3. Readily available, comprehensible, and sensible guidance on how to manage under uncertainty
4. General agreement on what is to be accomplished in relation to the basic mission of the organization

Two of these conditions are immediately violated in public education: There is considerable disagreement over what is to be accomplished in relation to organizational mission (#4), and there is considerable controversy over how computing should be applied within that mission (#2). In the field of public education, there is a continuing and destabilizing sequence of changes in opportunities (#1), and a dearth of reasonable guidance on managing under uncertainty (#3). These conditions constitute ill omens for the rational management of computing.

All is not lost, however, since a rational view of the world is not the only reasonable view of the world. Returning for a moment to the discussion at the start of the chapter, we can now picture the challenge to the school administrator in charge of computing decisions as lying between two broad and seductive world views. On the one hand, there is the highly upclassed advertising characterization of the Information X, where X = Age, Society, Economy, Revolution, and so on. The other is the cool-headed world of rational management, evaluating opportunities, conducting cost-benefit assessments, and generally being conservative and smart. Most of us see without too much trouble the difficulties of the rational management view: If nothing else, we do not know enough about the details of the choices to feel comfortable with making decisions. But the alternative of adopting the upclassed vision of computing in the Information X is less than prudent. The predictions that stem from this view of the world tend to be logically flawed, empirically unjustified, historically absurd, and highly seductive. Those of us who have been living with computing for a long time know that computing is expensive, complicated, difficult to manage, and really entertaining.

SOME IDEAS WORTH CONSIDERING

Now that we have spent a long time considering how not to think about computers, it is only fair to devote a few lines to suggestions for thinking about computing. Here are four items of advice to keep in mind.

FACT VERSUS FAITH. Forget about making your computing-related decisions only on the facts. To a large extent, computing decisions are made on faith simply because they must be. Facts do matter, and it is prudent to collect all that are available and relevant. But where to find the facts is no small challenge, and an exhaustive search sometimes reveals that the facts are not available. The source of facts with high payoff is discussion with people who *are doing what you want to do*. Don't let them tell you what they are *going to do*; you can tell yourself the same story. But every bit of their genuine experience will dispel lots of your expectations. In the end, there will likely be many holes in the set of facts and you will still have to make a decision. It is here that you must recognize that living is risky, and that for many organizations the decision to computerize is an existential one made on faith that computerization is "good." And for many organizations, computerization *is good*. There is no reason to assume that, with a little foresight and care, computerization of your organization might not be good.

DEVELOP INSIDE EXPERTISE. If you decide to explore computerization seriously, it is essential to develop in-house expertise and have these internal experts check out *everything* about the planned changes. The architect Mies van der Rohe once said "God is in the details." He was right, and it is especially true in computing. There are very few activities where the want of a nail can truly result in the loss of a kingdom, but computing is one of them. There is no such thing as "almost good enough" in computing—it either works or it does not. Failure in the details can kill a project swiftly, surely, and without mercy. If the details cannot be managed, forget about the "big picture." Everything in computing is eventually bottom-up.

ESSENTIAL RESOURCES. There are two essential survival resources for computing in complex organizations: lots of discretionary cash and a big fire extinguisher. The cash is necessary to cope with the technical problems that will arise regardless of the best-laid plans. The fire extinguisher is shorthand for the flexible response capability provided by a seasoned person (or persons) in charge of computing. My general advice is to avoid starting—and if started eliminate as soon as possible—the computing "steering committee" that will oversee computerization. For the vast majority of organizations, computing needs a boss—a smart, knowledgeable boss with the power to take needed action. Users are generally much happier when they are given something that works and does the job they want done, without going through charades about their being involved in system design. And they would much rather have a computer system that does some things very well than one that does everything marginally.

THINK OF IT AS FUN. Computing is a hassle, but it is a fun hassle. Imagine what computing would be like if it were not only a hassle but painful as well. How is computing fun? Let me tell a short story that illustrates how. I recently had a discussion with a senior official of my university about the early days of the campus. Early on, UCI was supposed to become the "computerized" campus of the University of California. One day the regents of the university visited UCI for one of their periodic meetings, and were given a demonstration of the on-line geography course. Some of the regents sat down at old Teletype 33 consoles and took geography quizzes to see how the system worked. Everyone had a good time, and then left. Just after they left, a reporter from the school newspaper collected all the printouts from the terminals and the next day the newspaper featured a front-page article explaining in detail all the simple geography questions the regents of the University of California could not answer. How else but with computers could such a story arise? This is a wonderful feature of computing: It is engaging, entertaining, and interesting. This is one of its greatest assets, and it should be exploited by administrators. But it should be exploited with caution. After all, the objective is to get people engaged with computing in the interest of some larger goal, and care should be taken to avoid unrealistic expectations that cannot be met.

THE LARGER PICTURE

I will close with some observations that tie the practical aspects of computing management to the larger goals of the application domain of public education. As the foregoing discussion suggests, the future of computers in education is not tied to any extreme one can envision. Computing has something to offer, and certainly has a future in our schools. Computer use is and has been widespread for years in administrative data processing. In recent years, computing has entered the domain of instruction. Development will continue on both fronts. So there is no point in assuming that computing will make no difference. On the other hand, computing will not "revolutionize" our schools, at least for a decade or more. I have heard some of the visionaries of the "get on board or get left behind" point of view suggest that unless schools adopt computing in a big way, parents will pull their children out of school and educate them at home using PCs and laser-disks containing the encyclopedia. What planet have these visionaries been living on? Schooling should teach students how to read and write and do math, and perhaps the schools can improve at doing these important things. But schooling also has important socialization functions that are not likely to be handled well by personal computers, no matter what chips they contain.

Computing will fit somewhere within the structure of schooling, and if the experience of computing in other organizations is any example, it is the context of schooling that will shape computerization of the schools—not the other way around. As a result, we ought not to think about the computerization of the schools in terms of robot instructors, which after all represent a most extreme and unrealistic view of automation (and instruction). We ought instead to envision applications where both the substantive and affective characteristics of computing can be brought to bear in the educational context.

The substantive aspects of computing are fairly well understood, and are likely to be exploited as time goes on. These include computer-aided instruction as well as the analytical and monitoring functions computing might bring to tailoring instruction to the individualized needs of students. The affective side of computing has not received the attention it deserves, however, and it is here that I return to the theme of entertainment. If American public education adopts computing it will not be because educators are jumping on board so they will not be left behind. Computing use is growing and will continue to grow because computing brings something *new* to teaching, and new things reshape our views of what is possible. By "our views" I do not just mean the views of teachers and educational administrators and university professors; I mean as well the views of students and parents and the average citizen who supports the schools. Computing can unfreeze the existing order of things when computing capability is deployed in a sensible, reliable manner. Students who have not yet bought into the idea of getting an education sometimes find the prospect a good deal more attractive when they can play with a computer in the process. This does not work for everyone, but then, nothing works for everyone. And it does work for many students for whom nothing else has worked, and this is important.

The second-order, catalytic effects of computing are at once the least predictable and potentially the most important for public education. These effects are what is really behind the frenzy of interest in computing in the schools. A brief glance at the record certainly undercuts any argument that computing use results in improved learning. The few studies that have been done are so narrowly constructed that it is difficult to discriminate the effects of computing use from experimental effects. Are the students responding to the computers or to the intense attention they are receiving as part of the study? It does not matter as far as the promoters are concerned, and it does not bother the parents who insist that school districts buy and use computers in the classroom. For them, computerization in education represents something new and powerful, something exciting and promising. They are excited about computing because it means change, and the desire for change will have more to do with the reform of public education than all the computers we can ever hope to make.

I believe it is time for teachers and administrators to recalibrate their judgments about computing in the schools. They should recognize that computing in any quantity brings expense, trouble, hassles, and dependency. There is usually no going back after serious adoption of computing, even though the costs of continuing are often higher than anticipated. Yet computing is an exciting and potentially powerful tool in the arsenal of education because of its inherent flexibility and its raw appeal. This potential can and should be exploited, and in time, probably will be. The appeal of computing cuts both ways: It can lure the naive into serious and costly mistakes (though the mistakes can teach lessons), and it can be used as a lure in its own right to reorient students' thinking about subject matter and education generally. In the short run, the major task of educators who believe in computing will be to keep up community spirits when the inevitable disappointments and downturns in enthusiasm occur. We are due for several of these cycles during the next decade.

In the long run, the challenge is to integrate computing into the process of education so that eventually it will seem as natural as the use of books or calculators. The real opportunity that lies between the short term and the long run will come from exploiting the changes computing will make in people's thinking about what is possible in education.

NOTE

1. Another kind of demand that does not relate exactly to this discussion is tied up in the politics of internal resource allocation in organizations. This is demand arising from the "resource politics" of computing. Computing is expensive, and for all practical purposes unassailable as an expense category. Units that develop large computing enterprises find it quite easy to continue to justify their expenditure base for computing, and this, of course, makes them winners in the budgetary process. Sophisticated managers seem to know this.

13

Technology and Assumptions: Let's Take Another Look

SAUL ROCKMAN

As we face the current hype about technology's ability to help us manage instruction and provide information that will improve teaching, it is worthwhile examining seven assumptions that we may not know we make.

1. *We assume that our current technology will work.* Technology to support information systems is part of a far-from-perfect engineering and software development system. Although some schools may have accommodated to receiving their second semester's supply of books on graduation day, most prefer things that work out better than that. Educators want to be able to trust the description in the brochures. Our usual assumption is that what the brochures and the salesmen say will happen will actually happen. For hardware and software systems, however, what is ordered may arrive six months or a year after it was promised. And it may not work as specified.

2. *We assume that teachers want data about their students in order to do their jobs more effectively and efficiently.* What I believe teachers really want is to find what will excite their students; what will engage them in active, attentive learning; what will increase their motivation; what will reduce discipline problems. I am not confident that this information exists in a form that we can code and transmit to teachers via an information system.

3. *We assume that aggregated data are useful and that periodic reports that summarize information are needed.* What teachers and building-level administrators are likely to want is detailed information that provides specific feedback and can be used to make day-to-day activities more effective. We have learned from the research on computer-assisted instruction that feedback and coaching are key characteristics of instruction that improve learning. We should be able to use this finding to create Instructional Information Systems that help teachers learn better how to teach.

4. *We assume that we should introduce new technology by creating in-service programs to motivate and instruct the existing teaching staff in its advantages and attributes.* If the statistics from the State of California are accurate, and are similar to those from other states, then approximately 50 percent of the ex-

isting teaching staff will be replaced within the next five to eight years (Sykes & Devaney, 1984). Perhaps our in-service efforts would be better spent in designing new preservice courses for schools of education. We certainly need to put more energy into preservice education to affect the tens of thousands of new teachers entering the system. And since most of them will teach as they have been taught, perhaps we should also look at appropriate ways to use technology in postsecondary instruction on college campuses. How many faculty members now actually use computers to augment their own teaching or to aid in their work as administrators?

5. *We assume that gifts of computers for the schools are desirable.* We write proposals and encourage manufacturers through tax incentives to provide "free" computers for classrooms. California's "Apple Bill" resulted in more than 10,000 computers being given to schools, with an estimated value of close to $30 million (State of California, 1983). I calculate that over the two years following these gifts, state, district, and local education agencies have spent in the aggregate more than $100 million to take advantage of them (Grupe, 1984; Rockman, 1985). These costs are for new staff, staff development time, curriculum development, and additional equipment and software. All of these expenses are required because of a gift that has yet to demonstrate its effectiveness in moving us toward our stated instructional goals.

6. *We assume that schools are the exclusive providers of educational services in our society.* There are many existing competitive educational systems for postsecondary schooling (Eurich, 1985). I want to point out one of the many that exist for elementary and secondary education. About 100,000 students learn problem-solving and study skills each year through Stanley H. Kaplan Learning Centers (Toch, 1984). These learning centers may be more significant contributors to teaching children higher-order thinking skills than the public schools, even though public schools are presumably mandated by society to perform this function. The array of educational service providers is changing rapidly for more of us in public education as well as for those in business and industry.

7. *We assume that the adoption of innovations in the marketplace of education will occur rapidly and painlessly.* New developments in technology are, even now, well beyond the capacity of most businesses and consumers to absorb. Educational institutions are even further behind in their ability to use high technology effectively. I would like to present my own theory about how technology will get adopted in education. I call it the Panasonic Theory, recalling the electronics company's advertising slogan used to sell television sets and other technologies. It states that technology, or any other innovation, should be—like Panasonic products—just slightly ahead of its time. The implication is that an innovation too far in advance of current

practice will not find many adherents in schools, and one that is too similar to what is already in the school is likely not to be needed. Those innovations offering a clear opportunity to incrementally improve what schools do will be most easily adopted. We need to consider the value and timing of Instructional Information Systems with this in mind.

As teachers move from index cards and gradebooks to the district's computer printouts and commercial test reports, they will learn how to read and make sense of management information—if it is of help to them in their work. As teachers come to trust computers and as the software programs they buy give them back interesting information on student progress, then pieces of Instructional Information Systems will begin to appear. Once the first pieces are mastered, teachers will then move on to consider the more sophisticated possibilities.

Administrators, too, need to move incrementally, from one relatively safe and simple use of the computer to store and manage information—such as tracking attendance—to more complex tasks such as monitoring class-level progress across subject areas. Technologists find gradualism enormously frustrating, especially when they think they have an elegant and immediate solution to current problems. Educators are likely to skip over entire generations of machines as they progress slowly from simple to more complex tasks. Innovations take time to be integrated into the day-to-day school environment; technologists don't seem to have the time to wait and to encourage the laggards. Administrators need a support system that will permit them to make mistakes without being seen and to perfect their skills without doing damage to the existing data system. Although time may be compressed in today's increasingly rushed society, we have tried in the past to push innovations into the schoolhouse; and we have met with few successes.

We therefore need to take advantage of what we know of the past history of technical innovation in our current planning for computerized information systems. Our recent educational history is filled with good data and is, itself, good data. Over the years there have been a number of technologies that initially enchanted the public and the educational establishment. Let me for a moment review one that has had some initial success but that many people now call a failed effort.

Depending on how one views it, television in the schools can be seen as a failure or as a success. If early hype is used as a criterion of success, then television in the classroom must be counted as another of modern education's many failures. If, on the other hand, one considers the data—that more than one-third of our nation's students receive a regular part of their classroom instruction through television—then perhaps this technology should not be written off as a failure in the schools (Riccobono, 1985; Dirr & Pedone, 1979). Let's see if history provides any insights.

More than 25 years ago, television was proposed as the solution to education's problems. Most people believed then as now that schools were unsuccessful in preparing this nation's children for an increasingly technological society; there was a teacher storage—especially in science and math—and new curriculum efforts were being proposed. Television was touted as an economical means of providing high-quality instruction to overcrowded schools, making the best teachers in the nation available to every classroom. Given this expectation, a cottage industry grew up around the high-tech TV medium; in every "garage" or school-run television station, teachers were creating instructional materials—most of them mediocre (Cohen, 1964). Every station produced its own math series or language arts programs. The hardware manufacturers promised the world, but they offered little assistance in getting programs up and running. In the early days, when the technology was developing rapidly and without industry standards, recorded programs designed to play on one manufacturer's machine could not be played on another's (shades of VHS and Beta). Thus, materials created in one place couldn't be shared in the next community or even in the next school. Widely advertised educational television series rarely arrived in the school building on the date promised by the publisher—more vaporware. Piles of research studies and a series of foundation reports and federal task forces were generated (Advisory Council of National Organizations, 1975; Armsey & Dahl, 1973; Chu & Schramm, 1979; Commission on Instructional Technology, 1970; International Council for Educational Development, 1971; Rockman, 1976). Everyone ran around doing teacher in-service. Demonstration projects abounded. One demonstration project established a school in which portions of each and every basic course were provided by television (Stoddard, 1957).

It was some time before this initial flurry died down. Instructional television began to play a useful role in the classroom—doing important things well—and to find a significant audience for its contributions only when several agencies joined together to aggregate the resources needed for more-than-local instructional materials. When several organizations combined their fiscal and intellectual resources to create school television, they developed the strength to attack difficult curriculum areas and reach a level of production quality that, in some cases, rivaled the commercial networks. Sometimes it was federal dollars in combination with state or local efforts; often it was state money working with local talent. As successes were realized, interstate agreements were established and became integrated into the school television production system. Consortia were regularly formed to produce materials (Middleton, 1979; Rockman, 1977).

At their most successful, consortium projects combined the resources of 50 or more state, provincial (Canadian), and local agencies to develop television courses that each alone could never expect to produce. Under the direction of the Agency for Instructional Television (AIT, now Agency for Instructional Technology), a new consortium would be formed to create a particular television series. Each organization contributed money according to its population of potential viewers, and in turn received the rights to use the series without further lease or rental payments. AIT would then use the aggregated funds to define the appropriate use of television in the curriculum and create the materials at a high level of production quality. Regular meetings of the "sponsors" established common beliefs about the specifics of the television-based curriculum, and provided an opportunity to build dissemination and implementation strategies early in the product's development.

AIT, and other agencies as well, developed consortium arrangements to create substantive instruction in areas deemed important by educators, and did it creatively and with a concern for quality.

Given a product that did important things and did them well, teachers had a reason to contemplate the use of television in their classes. Television, accompanied by training from state department of education personnel or by the staff of public broadcasting stations, became a useful weapon in a teacher's arsenal. It was no longer touted as panacea for all of education's problems, but it could and did bring images and events into the classroom that would otherwise have been impossible to see and hear. Television was no longer promoted as a technology that would reduce the number of teachers or relieve them of the burden of teaching, but when used as part of a teacher-controlled and directed lesson, it showed itself to be effective. No one any longer proposed that all teachers use television to teach all subjects to all students, but TV could give teachers instructional alternatives they did not have before.

Now, low-cost half-inch videocassette recorders make instructional television a new technology. Teachers see the VCR as a consumer item transformed into an instructional device, freed from the restrictions of the broadcast schedule at school as well as at home. They can use their timer to record materials at home and bring the tape to school the next day. Each classroom teacher can stop and start the tape to make programs instructionally relevant for his or her students. The tape can be replayed to make sure all students understand the concepts. Television now becomes an appealing technology, well within the grasp of even fearful technophobes.

I do not contend that the parallels between television and computers are exact, nor that instructional information systems will follow the same implementation path as did school television. Nevertheless, the history of this earlier technology is worth considering in terms of what it directs us to do.

First, we should critically examine the assumptions we make about the relationships between school operations, computer technology, and Instructional Information Systems. What is the vision we have of education? How do we define and establish policies that support that vision? What are our underlying assumptions about data and how they can be used by teachers and administrators?

What information do we want in an Instructional Information System? Do we want teachers to define students by demographic or instructional data they will have available or do we want them to rely on their perception of the student in present time? How will the availability of certain kinds of data change the context and setting of instruction? How might it change teachers' day-to-day activities or their ability to plan?

Second, after we are clear that understanding and managing data is an important skill for teachers and administrators—and after we begin to train them in how to do it—then what do we do to keep them from jumping ship and obtaining a more lucrative employment deal from business and industry? What impact will our attempts to promote teacher professionalism through increased use of technology have on teachers and their vocational choices?

Third, I suggest that we turn to the variables that business and industry have been using in their research on management and productivity. We might start with the management research literature to generate the initial set of research issues to investigate in the educational setting. Among the issues to be considered are communication patterns and institutional rewards that promote the effective use of information to meet specific objectives, the professional status issues that affect how people elect to participate in data base activities, centralization versus decentralization, and security and the need to limit and control access.

We should be willing to adapt and learn from those who have already tried to use data base technologies for improvement. The problems in education are not likely to be very different. However, education can't as easily as business write off the costs of its technological mistakes. The computers we buy today will stay in schools well beyond their normal lifespan. That's why our schools have so many closets: to store all our discarded technologies. To keep computers and Instructional Information Systems out of the closet, we need to know not only how to operate them, but why we should want to.

REFERENCES

Advisory Council of National Organizations. (1975). *Public broadcasting and education: A report to the Corporation for Public Broadcasting*. Washington, DC: Corporation for Public Broadcasting.

Armsey, J. W., & Dahl, N. C. (1973). *An inquiry into the uses of instructional technology*. New York: Ford Foundation Report.

Chu, G. C., & Schramm, W. (1979). *Learning from television: What the research says* (4th ed.). Washington, DC: National Association of Educational Broadcasters.

Cohen, E. G. (1964). *The status of instructional television*. New York: National Instructional Television Library.

Commission on Instructional Technology. (1970). *To improve learning. A report to the President and Congress of the United States*. Washington, DC: U.S. Government Printing Office.

Dirr, P. J., & Pedone, R. J. (1979). *Use of television for instruction, 1976–1977*. Washington, DC: Corporation for Public Broadcasting and National Center for Education Statistics, Department of Education.

Eurich, N. P. (1985). *Corporate classrooms: A Carnegie Foundation special report*. Princeton, NJ: Carnegie Foundation for the Advancement of Teaching.

Grupe, F. (1984, December). *Computerworld, 18*(50), 62.

International Council for Educational Development. (1971). *Instructional broadcasting: A design for the future*. Washington, DC: Corporation for Public Broadcasting.

Middleton, J. (1979). *Cooperative school television and educational change*. Bloomington, IN: AIT.

Riccobono, J. A. (1985). *School utilization study: Availability, use, and support of instructional media* (1982–83 Final Report). Washington, DC: Corporation for Public Broadcasting.

Rockman, S. (1976). School television is alive and well. In D. Cater & M. Nyhan (Eds.), *The future of public broadcasting*. New York: Praeger.

———. (1977). The function of evaluation in cooperative projects. In T. Bates & J. Robinson (Eds.), *Evaluating educational television and radio*. Milton Keynes, England: The Open University Press.

———. (1985). *California computer donation impact study*. Sacramento: California State Department of Education, AB 803 Special Projects Grant, 03781-0316.

State of California. (1983). *Computer Contribution Act of 1983 (AB 3194)*. Sacramento.

Stoddard, A. J. (1957). *Schools for tomorrow: An educator's blueprint*. New York: Fund for the Advancement of Education.

Sykes, G., & Devaney, K. (1984). *A status report on the teaching profession*. Sacramento: California Commission on Teaching.

Toch, T. (1984, December). News firm to buy test-coaching centers. *Education Week, 4*(14), pp. 1, 15.

PART IV

Instructional Information Systems and Educational Realities

The first chapter of Part IV, "Realities and Scenarios: Instructional Information Systems in Classrooms of the Future," points out the importance of understanding the culture of educational organizations. Williams and Bank describe the limited power of administrators to command or supervise teachers, and suggest that administrators wanting teachers to use an IIS will have to exert their influence through communication. They note that teachers often view teaching as craft rather than as technique and are unlikely to find computer-generated data credible. Given such an orientation, the authors suggest that, if IISs are to become commonplace classroom tools, teachers must be persuaded to become a dedicated group of users. After offering several ideas on how to do this, they present three alternatives that describe a negative-impact, a limited-use, and a full-use scenario for the future of Instructional Information Systems.

The five other chapters of Part IV address these same issues from different perspectives. Hathaway is optimistic about technology's beneficial effects on education. He advocates a school district organizational revolution based on accurate, comprehensive information about students and their progress. Such information will then be a source of power and control. He hopes that the evolution of distributed data processing will move us along towards both decentralized decision making and better administrative and support services. More specifically, Hathaway makes a strong argument for a "bottom-up" approach not only to the design and operation of Instructional Information Systems but to the administration of districts. He sees the IIS of the future as providing needed information to individualize instruction, allocate services more efficiently, increase the productivity of programs, and contribute to basic research about how learning occurs. Although he is aware of possible IIS misuses, he is glad to "be along for the ride" towards a self-renewing learning society.

Stecher, in his chapter "Superintendents Don't Type—Advice for Those Setting Up Administrative IIS Training Programs for Administrators," points out one important area in which more work needs to be done before Instructional Information Systems will enjoy widespread use at the upper levels of the school or the district. He reviews the literatures on administrator preparation, evaluation utilization, educational change, and computer training, and finds in them relevant guidelines for setting up training programs. Such programs are needed to orient administrators as to how they might use computers to become more able instructional leaders. He concludes with a fable showing how the urgent concerns of information system experts may be merely tangential to the concerns of those people expected to use the systems.

In "Integrating Instructional Information Systems with Instructional Processes," Dussault points up another critical area where Instructional Information Systems and instruction could be incompatible. He suggests that an IIS, to be useful, must be consistent with the instructional philosophy of the school. He suggests that Instructional Information Systems are not only compatible with, but necessary for, a diagnostic–prescriptive approach to teaching, and can make possible the record-keeping, tracking of test scores, and analysis of relationships between instruction and learning that are necessary to operationalize such an instructional orientation. He gives examples of the difficulties, problems, and triumphs of a series of pilot tests in his own district.

In a suburban Los Angeles high school, Sirotnik and Burstein helped teachers to put selected data from a school-wide student attitude survey into their ongoing district-wide information system. Working closely with representatives of the high school staff, the authors developed three at-a-glance computer-generated formats to disseminate the key findings of the student survey. Their essay emphasizes the importance of having multiple sources of information included in an IIS data base as additions to the usual achievement test data. Sirotnik and Burstein point out that although teachers' clinical orientation to students makes many kinds of computer-generated reports irrelevant or redundant, some teachers do become interested in the process of examining data from a research perspective. The authors point to the competing epistomological paradigms underlying computerized information systems on the one hand, and the personal knowledge, experience, and intuition used by most teachers in their daily decision making on the other hand. They describe the array of tensions this created for them as they worked in their high school.

King forcefully represents what she sees as a prevailing teacher point of view towards IIS use. She addresses two points in her chapter: (1) the likely reactions of classroom teachers to installation of an IIS and (2) ways that administrators can increase the likelihood that teachers will take advantage of an IIS once installed. She describes three legitimate reasons for teachers' likely nonuse of an IIS, and then suggests activities that might encourage teacher participation. She strongly urges that teacher use of IIS information be an option rather than a requirement, and further suggests that care be taken not to erode or discredit teachers' clinical judgments.

14

Realities and Scenarios: Instructional Information Systems in Classrooms of the Future

RICHARD C. WILLIAMS and ADRIANNE BANK

Anyone acquainted with the history of educational innovation knows that the landscape is cluttered with the rusting hulks of seemingly promising new practices initiated with great fanfare but rather quickly discarded in favor of conventional practice. What does the future hold for the use of Instructional Information Systems in the nation's classrooms? Will teachers rid themselves of the informal information sources that have served them so long in favor of some new electronic wizardry? Or will they continue to rely on observations, hunches, reflections, and previous experience? Certainly, one can readily point to "lighthouse districts" in which Instructional Information Systems have clearly penetrated into the classrooms and expanded the teachers' sources of information. However, one has to remember that "a handful of lighthouse districts does not a national movement make." There are always pioneering districts, schools, and teachers that try out new practices. But spreading those innovations to other institutions, and indeed maintaining the innovations over an extended period—even in the originating lighthouse districts—is a formidable challenge. Regression to the mean has continued to be a powerful force in the history of American educational innovation and change.

In this chapter we will examine the probability that Instructional Information Systems will have a lasting and significant impact on the nation's classrooms. First, we will describe some selected realities that influence the implementability of this educational innovation. Next, we will present what we consider the critical factor in making these systems commonplace in our classrooms and schools. We will finally discuss some activities that should take place if this critical factor is to emerge. We conclude with three scenarios of what might result from the development or lack of development of these important activities.

SCHOOL REALITIES AFFECTING INSTRUCTIONAL INFORMATION SYSTEMS IN CLASSROOMS

A commonly observed characteristic of school systems is that they are disjointed or "loosely coupled." That is, there are only tenuous connections among the various organizational levels of school districts. Especially in instructional matters, the central administration, principal, and individual classrooms are not tightly linked to one another. The organizational ladder's lowest rung, namely the teacher, does not routinely respond to orders or suggestions from officials at higher rungs. Many are the disappointed school boards and superintendents who have ordered that a certain innovation be implemented, only to discover later that their order has been virtually ignored by, or not even communicated to, individual classroom teachers. The importance of this organizational reality for the use of Instructional Information Systems is that they are unlikely to be implemented solely by administrative order. Administrators wishing to install an IIS will have to use influence rather than power and carefully develop communication links between themselves and individuals at all levels of the system.

A second reality is that individual classroom teachers are generally shielded from direct administrative supervision. Schools simply do not have sufficient administrative personnel to insist and assure that a particular instructional practice is consistently carried out in a classroom. In addition, the culture of the school is such that teachers consider themselves quite autonomous in the classroom and administrators and supervisors do not feel comfortable visiting classrooms as a routine matter. To be sure, administrators may visit if they think a teacher is in need of help—but this is the exception, not the rule. The impact of this reality on the implementation of Instructional Information Systems is that there is no regular, accepted, available supervisory system to assure that an IIS will be used even if it is installed.

A third reality is that teaching is viewed and practiced by many teachers as a craft. Although they may have studied educational psychology and child development, and various pedagogical approaches, teachers have survived in the classroom by learning and refining their skills pretty much on their own. Early in their careers, they try out different approaches to solve classroom problems, and once they find a workable solution it is not likely that they will continue to explore or inquire into other approaches until their regular methods prove inadequate. Lessons learned on the job tend to be learned well and become deeply ingrained into one's occupational repertoire. New computerized printouts, no matter how useful in the abstract, will not be easily incorporated into a teacher's classroom routine. What is more, they will likely not be given much attention at all unless the teacher is convinced that this approach will better allow him or her to solve pressing, practical, pedagogical problems.

Thus, we see classroom teachers as working almost autonomously in their classrooms, quite immune to specific orders to change their teaching routines in any significant way, practicing a craft that has been learned largely on the job and in isolation, and not naturally seeking alternative ways of doing things as long as their present methods work to their satisfaction. Obviously, this summary overgeneralizes a bit. There are many individual teachers who are constantly looking for new and better ways, who regularly question their own methods and, when appropriate, change their classroom activities. But what is critical to this discussion is the fact that such teachers behave this way of their own volition. They function the way they do in spite of the school system, not because of it. Any school system wanting to install an IIS that will penetrate into the classroom and change teachers' pedagogical routines must face these realities and plan accordingly.

MAKING INSTRUCTIONAL INFORMATION SYSTEMS A REALITY IN CLASSROOMS

Clearly teachers, given their autonomy and their craft orientation, must be somehow convinced that Instructional Information Systems will help them better perform the difficult and demanding task of teaching students. They cannot be ordered to use an IIS; they will not naturally embrace it; it is not readily incorporated into traditional classroom practice. If they are to use information stored in and accessed through computers in the classroom, they must, as an economist might put it, "believe that the benefits of the system or approach outweigh the costs of learning and using the system." *Teachers must be developed into a dedicated group of users.*

Fortunately, information systems per se are not totally foreign to school systems. Central office administrators have been using such systems for years in performing various personnel, budgetary, and planning activities. Administrators use them not because they are required to do so but because they have increasingly come to realize the power computerized information systems have in helping to plan and perform administrative functions. And, of course, test scores are presently available in districts' computerized data base systems, but typically these scores are not regularly used by either administrators or teachers in making decisions about instructional activities.

REQUIREMENTS FOR MAKING TEACHERS
A DEDICATED USER GROUP

If classroom teachers are to become routine users of computerized information systems, the following four criteria must be met. First, teachers must become familiar with computers and overcome whatever computer phobia they might have. We predict that the presence and intensity of such phobias will eventually vanish, and indeed are diminishing even now. We are all increasingly exposed to computer systems in our daily lives as we interact with banks, telephone systems, and computerized billing systems. Also, more and more teachers have more and more students who have computers at home and like to play with them. Like it or not, computers are a new fact of life and teachers, like everyone else, will learn to use them.

Second, software and information systems that are directly responsive to the teachers' classroom needs will have to be developed. Such systems will have to be sufficiently flexible so that teachers can ask questions of the data base pertinent to their specific situation; and the data will have to be formatted in an easily understood manner.

Third, and perhaps most difficult, teachers and administrators will have to develop an inquiring mind set. They must begin to question their own assumptions about their teaching methods, the context within which they work, and the outcomes that they are achieving. This is a most difficult task for anyone, and especially for those who have learned their craft on the job. We have some limited hope that this will emerge because teaching is becoming increasingly more complex. With classrooms filled with students from a variety of cultural, racial, and socioeconomic groups, not to mention mainstreamed students with special educational needs, teachers have the very difficult task of keeping track of everyone's learning and trying to match learning activities and materials to the many variables that can affect individual needs. In short, teachers will likely need much more information than they now have about their students' abilities if they are to remain effective teachers. The human mind can only store so much data, and paper in filing drawers and storage boxes becomes confusing and time-consuming to use as there gets to be more and more of it. The computer not only neatly stores information but allows the merging of different data bases into a common instructionally relevant data base. Properly programmed, it can respond to specific inquiries from teachers about individual students. Teachers really cannot be blamed for not trying to locate pertinent information about students when such information is scattered in records all over the district.

Finally, arrangements will have to be made so teachers can see demonstrations of the ways in which an IIS can benefit them. It's likely that they will respond more readily to actual demonstrations of the system's usefulness in a real setting than to written descriptions, however sophisticated and well conceived. Moreover, they will likely respond favorably when they hear the practical ways in which this approach is more effective than the methods they are presently using.

In summary:

> If teachers can overcome their computer phobia;
> if software is developed that allows the data to be delivered in an understandable format responsive to individual teacher or school site needs;
> if teachers come to realize the importance of asking questions about student needs; and
> if methods can be developed that will demonstrate the power and effectiveness of instructional information systems to both teachers and administrators . . .
> then possibly a dedicated group of teacher users will emerge who will make information systems a commonplace in our nation's classrooms and school buildings.

THE IMPACT OF INSTRUCTIONAL INFORMATION SYSTEMS

Keeping in mind the need for developing this dedicated group of users, let us turn to three scenarios of what might emerge when comprehensive Instructional Information Systems are introduced into school districts.

A Negative-Impact Scenario

If information systems are simply introduced top-down into school districts without anyone attending to the developments and activities described above, we suspect the impact of an IIS will be largely negative, in a number of different ways. Data processing systems may produce considerable amounts of data that will be disregarded; or teachers and administrators might begin to suffer from "information overload" and sink into despair when confronted with mountains of unintelligible printouts, especially if they are expected to do anything with them. Or worse yet, educators may ascribe to computer-generated reports an unwarranted degree of credibility and make faulty decisions or take unwise actions on the basis of information that is inaccurate or misanalyzed. Flaws in the data are very likely to go undetected if the users of the system do not understand the system and the data it produces, or value it as a means for solving pressing problems.

A Limited-Use Scenario

If a usable information system were in place, but teachers and administrators remained uninterested and unmotivated, the system might, even under these circumstances, have some limited impact. For example, data storage and retrieval might be handled more efficiently by the data processing staff. They might be able to generate useful reports and respond to special requests. School administrators would probably be the greatest beneficiaries of such a system because they could then easily generate the routine reports required by district offices and state agencies. But actual use of the system by classroom teachers would not occur; the IIS and its output would be someone else's responsibility.

A Full-Use Scenario

If a district's Instructional Information System is developed in a way that includes the activities we described earlier in this chapter—with special attention to encouraging the teachers' understanding of the system and what it can do, appropriate demonstrations of practical applications, and adequate time for the teachers to learn the system and adjust it to their special needs—then there is a great likelihood that these systems will be implemented and utilized. By using such systems, teachers could develop teaching strategies and resources that have high probability payoff for given individuals or groups; principals could do better scheduling, grouping, developing, and deploying of staff; and central administrators would be able to pinpoint emerging staffing, building, or budgeting problems requiring immediate or long-term attention. New organizational structures and committees could emerge as Instructional Information Systems provide credible data in appropriate formats and within reasonable timeframes.

Likely all three of the above scenarios will coexist during the next decade in America's school districts. A major determinant of what will happen in any particular district will be the degree to which that district's leadership is aware of and values the potential contributions an Instructional Information System can make. But districts will need more than motivation; they will also require:

- Sufficient financial resources to purchase the equipment, and to provide administrators and teachers time for planning and learning the system
- Sufficient freedom to develop and implement such a system (A district that is beset by constant pressures to attend to immediate demands just to survive will not likely have the energy to explore this approach, even if

they might see ways in which such a system might help them out of their dilemma.)
- Sufficient patience to develop the system at a pace and in a manner that is consonant with the district's political, social, and economic realities
- Sufficient understanding of the realities of organizational and human change processes and the creativity to develop a strategy that reflects those understandings

For now, the really difficult and unanswerable question is not whether one district, one school, or one classroom can do it, but whether the lessons learned in successful districts will travel to other districts, thus increasing the pace and reducing the cost at which this innovation is disseminated across the land.

15

Hopes and Possibilities for Educational Information Systems

WALTER E. HATHAWAY

> When mankind has once realized that its first function is to penetrate, intellectually unify, and harness the energies which surround it, in order to still further understand and master them, there will no longer be any danger of running into an upper limit of its florescence.
> Pierre Teilhard de Chardin (1959, p. 280)

In the past, revolutions have started with someone riding or walking up to somebody else's city, palace, or church door and nailing up declarations of principle and action. Recently, acting in the same spirit, I put the message in Figure 15.1 on the CompuServe and Telenet electronic bulletin boards, which are well-used gateways to the electronically linked educational community.

I did this because I believe that within the education profession and in our society at large, we are on the verge of evolving comprehensive information systems that will capture, transform, and present back to us the information essential for the effective and efficient systems promised by the model of learning outlined in my message.

Three important factors supporting the emergence of information systems that will facilitate such major advances in scientific decision making in schools are (1) the development of low-cost information-processing and communication technology, (2) the emergence of increasingly sophisticated organizational units capable of utilizing new technology to support decentralized data-based decision making, and (3) the increasing availability of complex and comprehensive decision-making models and learning theories.

The main barriers to the development of such information systems, therefore, are found not in the lack of technical support or knowledge. Rather, they are due to deficiencies in the will, the wisdom, and the wherewithal to develop and use tools already within our grasp. All we need to do to make the hoped-for revolution happen is to turn our educational systems

FIGURE 15.1. Message to CompuServe and Telenet

We now know and have known for a long time what in theory we must do to help every child learn as much as he or she can as effectively and efficiently as possible, i.e.,

> The student's current, most pressing needs within a well planned curriculum must be identified.
>
> The student must be helped to set clear, relevant, attainable learning objectives to meet those needs.
>
> The student must be expected to succeed in attaining the learning objectives and must want to learn them.
>
> The student must receive individualized instruction directly related to the learning objectives designed to meet his or her current learning needs.
>
> The student must use the time allocated for instruction to work intently and seriously on the task of learning.
>
> The student must know when he or she has succeeded and when not and must experience a reinforcing sense of accomplishment and achievement as a result of knowledge of success.
>
> The student must receive and return a sense of caring, personal concern, interest, respect and commitment which provides the psychological support necessary to want to learn and to work to learn; and finally
>
> The student must receive and accept parental and community support and encouragement for success in learning.

The main barrier to our putting this proven theory of effective instruction into practice is <u>lack of information</u> about:

> Students' individual learning needs;
>
> What learning activities and experiences are matched to diagnosed student needs and established learning objectives;
>
> When the student has mastered the objectives and is ready to move on; and,
>
> The degree of overall success of staff and programs at each level in supporting student learning.

upside-down, unleashing all the energy and power now submerged at the bottom of the present educational hierarchy where teachers and kids live.

Contrasted with this view is the current anachronistic educational reform movement, which is full of nostalgia for an earlier, simpler era. It has been characterized by futurist Alvin Toffler (1980) as the dying throes of a dinosaur-like system. George Leonard (1984, p. 49) has chided up for taking a horse and buggy system, repainting the buggy, paying the driver more, keeping the passengers in it longer, and foolishly expecting it to go faster and better. Such criticisms are not surprising. The key learning notion trumpeted from the state capitols is "back to basics." The central management focus is on more and more control from places further and further away from the classroom. These emphases fly in the face of almost everything we know about achieving human excellence in organizations, as summarized by commentators such as Peters and Waterman (1982) in their book, *In Search of Excellence*, where they point out that decentralized control and decision making along with trust and support are the mainstays of excellence in human enterprises.

As I think about where we are and where we could be with educational information systems, my hope is that we will seize the opportunity created by the possibilities of distributed, multilevel information systems to delegate to the lowest level of the educational organization as much of the control and of the decision making as possible, leaving to the next highest level only those decisions that are absolutely necessary for the collective good.

Learners should be back in control of their own learning, and teachers back in control of their own teaching, although there needs to be an information loop to the "top" so that administrators and policymakers can properly do their job of adjusting resources and providing other forms of support, including feedback to the grassroots about overall educational success and failure.

A second step in the coming educational revolution is a structural one in which the walls of today's educational system will come tumbling down. Among the barriers to be razed are those of place and time. In the long run, information systems can offer each of us the possibility of being tutored by the best minds in the world, in any area we wish to learn, when and where we want to learn, and to receive credit and certification for our newly mastered skills. Also, most of the information riches of the world can be at our fingertips. When these things come to pass, teaching and learning will belong as much to homes and highways as to schools, and to the old as well as the young.

Unfortunately, today we are still a long way from realizing this revolution. Education is one of the few major areas in our national life where choices that consume our resources on a prodigious scale and that have personal importance for each of us continue to be based to a large extent on tradition, personal bias, and benevolent guesswork. It is ironic that, in this fourth decade of the age of scientific management and quantitative decision making, decisions about the educational process—a process that supposedly teaches us how to make rational decisions—continue to be made in such unstructured and intuitive ways.

But I think that we have made at least some promising beginnings. For many years, enlightened school system administrators and teachers have been laboring to create, maintain, and use information systems for both instructional and management purposes. Their goal has been to apply those ideas of data-based decision making born in the turmoil of the Second World War to the important task of creating more magic learning moments for individual students. Driving these efforts has been the hope that by collecting, analyzing, reporting, and acting upon accurate and appropriate information about individual learners, as well as about classrooms, schools, and districts, we can create self-renewing, effective, and efficient learning communities.

We have met a variety of obstacles along the way. It has been far easier to commit resources for generating data related to the "business" part of school operations than to find money for generating instructionally relevant data. The shortcomings of extant hardware and software systems have discouraged all but the bravest and most technically proficient from moving full speed ahead. These shortcomings are in part due to the lack of causal models of learning and to our uncertainty about how best to support learning. So it has been difficult to translate our hopes for technologically based instructional improvements into reality. But most important of all has been the difficulty of enlisting the sustained commitment of overworked school teaching and administrative staff in the continuing task of gathering and maintaining data bases for their own purposes as well as for reporting "upward" that which is needed to support decision making at higher levels in the educational hierarchy. We have not yet removed this obstacle, one that has hampered us from the beginning—namely, the perception of data irrelevance by the all-important data originators. We have only occasionally and temporarily surmounted it by force of authority and resources. We have, however, been fighting a battle we cannot win and one we need not wage, since there is a path we can walk together to quality data and informed, satisfying, efficient, and effective decision making at all levels of the educational enterprise.

The easy part is already happening. Information subsystems have been developed for classroom instructional applications, as in computer-assisted and managed instruction; for local as well as central administrative record-keeping related to student background, characteristics, academic performance, attendance, and behavior; and for monitoring of personnel, programs, and financial records. Gradually, through a combination of commitment and technological advances, we have begun to weld these subsystems together at the central district, school building, and classroom levels to create the beginnings of the comprehensive information systems we now can envision and so desperately need.

The wedding of new conceptualizations of educational information systems with new technologies permits us to think about the hard part—the turning of school management topsy-turvy. We can imagine real reform led by easy-to-maintain, comprehensive student and classroom information systems filtering up-to-date, accurate data "downward" to their servants in administrative and support systems offices.

This wedding can be arranged by a new phenomenon—distributed data processing—where classroom-based networks of micro- and miniprocessors are linked to one another, to the school office system, and to the district's central processor. With this new arrangement, teachers, principals, and school office staff members would not be asked to fill out endless and to them useless forms for "the hill" or for "downtown." Nor would they have to capture and store data, for example, on student mastery of objectives, for school and classroom decision making in such clumsy and difficult ways that falling back onto intuition or old habits becomes irresistible. Rather, nearby computers could store and analyze data to make teachers' jobs of teaching and school administrators' jobs of administering easier and more effective. Through careful planning, linking, and scheduling, the data necessary for program, policy, evaluation, research, and resource allocation decisions "further down the line" could be painlessly skimmed off.

We can imagine many uses to which such emergent information systems could be put.

- Collecting and analyzing information about the needs, abilities, readiness, and learning styles of individual students either so that instruction can be individualized or so that students can be grouped most effectively for the task at hand
- Collecting and analyzing information about resources and how they are utilized so that classrooms, buildings, and central office functions can be better managed
- Collecting and analyzing information about program costs and program benefits to increase educational productivity
- Collecting and analyzing information about long-term demographic trends to make more accurate budget predictions and building and staffing plans
- Collecting and analyzing data that will monitor policy implementation and stimulate options for new policies

- Collecting and analyzing information to increase basic knowledge of how learning occurs at specific developmental stages and for specific categories of learners

Let me say a special word about this last point on the research potential of information systems. Right now in our district, the Portland (Oregon) Public Schools, besides doing 50 or so major program evaluations and policy analyses we are conducting at least 10 research efforts through our comprehensive test, student, and system data base. For example, in collaboration with a university researcher, we are combing through six years of twice-a-year basic skills achievement measures searching for curves that might describe and predict the pace at which subject learning occurs in relation to developmental indices. In this study we are searching for learning patterns by ability, age, ethnic background, sex, and so forth. The result may provide major contributions to the science of learning. Based upon experiences such as this, I believe that the data analysis for dissertations and publication-quality research that once required months or even years to do can now be done in less than a week at one of the 10 terminals in my office. This is a tremendous resource that we are only beginning to learn how to use wisely.

It goes without saying that we will also have to learn how to identify and deal with the potential misuses of comprehensive information systems as they emerge. Among them are the authorization of "fishing trips" through data instead of the well-thought-out and planned research and policy formulation that we need; the invasion of individual and institutional privacy; the emergence of "data junkies"—people who become afraid to move ahead without all possible data and endlessly massage their data bases; the overestimation of the accuracy of existing data; and premature satisfaction with the quality, quantity, and appropriateness of existing data. All of this would constitute an inappropriate pushing of the educational pendulum in the direction of science at the expense of craft.

In summary, let me note that our need for a decentralized and scientific approach to educational decision making has come from a transformation of the scale on which education takes place within our nation. As long as each school was an isolated institution in a small, homogeneous community, instruction and teaching could be personalized. Intuition and tradition were satisfactory underpinnings for instructional decisions. But as schools and the communities that they serve have become larger, more diverse, and more complex, we must teach large numbers of students who bring an astonishing range of needs and experiences to the task of acquiring the skills they need to function in the social and economic environment of the future. To help them to do this effectively and efficiently, education must operate as an integrated whole system while encouraging the individual autonomy of both students and teachers. Daily decision making in the classroom must be guided by policy and by information rather than simply by tradition and intuition. And in turn, policymaking at the district level must be shaped by deep understanding of human, organizational, and educational needs on the one hand, and by the availability of human and financial resources on the other.

I believe that distributed computerized information systems will allow us to harness the energies in school buildings and classrooms. We are now about to unhitch the good but tired old horse, put a powerful engine in the educational buggy, turn the drive loose, and ride off swiftly toward meeting our goal of helping every child become everything he or she can and wants to be. I, for one, am pleased and excited to be along for the ride on this historic leg of the educational journey.

REFERENCES

Leonard, G. (1984). The great school reform hoax. *Esquire, 101*, pp. 47–52.
Peters, T. J., & Waterman, R. H., Jr. (1982). *In search of excellence*. New York: Harper & Row.
Teilhard de Chardin, P. (1959). *The phenomenon of man*. New York: Harper & Row.
Toffler, A. (1980). *The third wave*. New York: Morrow.

16

Superintendents Don't Type—Advice for Those Setting Up IIS Training Programs for Administrators

BRIAN STECHER

Though the title of this chapter is light-hearted, the problem alluded to is serious. The future of computer-based educational tools depends upon our ability to train administrators to use these systems effectively. Not being able to type—or choosing not to type—is a major impediment to the practical use of a computer-based information system. Concern about seemingly small problems such as these is essential if computerized systems are ever going to have the desired impacts on education.

The topic of this chapter is training. However, what we must think about in designing training programs to support Instructional Information Systems extends far beyond teaching administrators the proper way to log on to the computer and run the desired piece of software. An effective training program should also prepare the participant to understand the relevance of the IIS for educational planning and instructional decision making and to want to use it for these purposes. To be effective, training must address all of the anticipated problems and impediments to IIS utilization. Consequently, the real purpose of a training program should be more comprehensive than skill development. With this in mind, an alternative title for this chapter might be "Issues in Utilization-Oriented Training."

What are these likely impediments to administrative use of an IIS? Since we are still inventing the future, we cannot know for sure. Yet there are a number of existing research efforts that may provide us with relevant guidelines. By extrapolating from them, we can identify factors likely to be important in training administrators to use an innovative, computer-based planning and information system.

We believe such a user focus is appropriate not only for training but for examining IIS design and implementation. Guidelines for system design and implementation as well as for training can be derived from the specific needs of potential users and from extrapolations of educational research. For example, knowing that superintendents don't type suggests, at a minimum, that

159

an IIS should separate data entry functions from data access functions and should offer a user-friendly access strategy such as a touch screen or mouse. However, we will not deal with hardware and software issues. The remarks that follow will be confined to training issues.

SOURCES FOR ADVICE

Four bodies of literature are relevant to the problem of training administrators to use an IIS: administrator preparation, evaluation/information utilization, educational innovation/change, and computer education/training. In fact, the present topic lies at the point where these four realms of inquiry meet. Although not much has been written about this topic directly, much can be learned from examining the four areas that surround it.

The literature about the preparation of school administrators encourages us to be optimistic about the overall value of Instructional Information Systems for administrators. For example, the American Association of School Administrators (1983) recommended that administrative training be designed so that participants become competent in the "use of computers and other instructional technologies as instructional aids" (p. 8) and the "application of computer management to the instructional program" (p. 9). Instructional Information Systems represent just such an application. In discussing the implications of these guidelines Hoyle (1985) emphasized, in addition, the importance of knowledge about the application of technology to evaluation. He said, "Computer applications to curriculum development, sequencing and evaluation are required skills for today's and tomorrow's successful administrators" (p. 80).

The literature also offers practical advice concerning what not to do in administrative training programs. Farquhar and Piele (1972) reviewed the research and found that school superintendents appear not to be receptive to training programs that stress theory but ignore the practical reality of school operation. Similarly, in a survey of superintendents' attitudes toward continuing education, Goldhammer and associates (1967) concluded that "Few, if any, of the programs are based upon a realistic perception of the needs of administrators in the field" (p. 157). Others have noted also that training programs typically tend to be too brief and narrowly focused (Albright, 1962).

Recommendations for what to do in training programs for educators include addressing informational and personal needs before outcome concerns, providing frequent expressions of support and encouragement, comparing current practices with new expectations, and encouraging expanded communication with other administrators (Rutherford, Hord, & Thurber, 1984).

The literature on evaluation utilization offers us some suggestions on how to increase the utility of testing and evaluation data for school planning. The factors that contribute to increased evaluation use may be relevant to increasing IIS utilization as well. Administrators in training programs should be told about them. For example, Patton (1978) emphasized the importance of the "personal factor," the role played by committed individuals who champion particular research or evaluation activities. We know that key individuals will have to be interested in and excited about the information provided by an IIS for such a system to make an impact on the organization. The training program should therefore be motivational. It should be designed to generate this interest and commitment on the part of high-level administrators.

Alkin, Daillak, and White (1979) proposed a framework that included seven clusters of factors that affected the use of evaluation information. For example, they suggested that increased utilization was related to organizational factors such as the quality of the relationship between the school and district and the structure of the on-site organizational arrangements. Effective administrator training for an IIS should recognize the importance of such elements and provide guidance for administrators on how to deal with them.

In a broad sense, an IIS represents an educational innovation. We therefore might regard the developers of the IIS and the trainers as change agents. The literature on educational change offers many suggestions about how to promote change and increase the implementation of innovations. Although these suggestions are based on the study of classroom-based instructional innovations, they offer useful ideas that administrators should be apprised of in their training sessions. For example, Fullan (1982) reviewed the literature on change and emphasized that the role of the principal is key to successful change and innovation. Berman and associates (1975) found the implementation strategies that were most effective were "adaptive planning, staff training keyed to the local setting, and local materials development" (p. 6). Thus, effective training of administrators should recognize their need to adapt the IIS to their own local situations, and not subscribe to rigid, fixed solutions or approaches. Hall and associates (1975) characterized the levels of use of an innovation, and pointed out that educators increase their level of use by proceeding through stages. "Strategies must then be developed that deal with a user's present [level of use] and facilitate growth" (p. 56). Hall (1979) classified six stages of concern that typify the users of innovations, and he suggested actions that are effective to address the users' concerns at each stage. What this implies, as we have noted earlier, is that training should not begin with a focus on desired outcomes, but should focus first on the individual's personal and informational needs concerning the innovation (Rutherford and associates, 1984).

Finally, there is a growing body of literature about the problems of training educators to use computers. Most of this writing is addressed to the training of teachers, but many of the concerns are equally relevant to training administrators to use a computerized system for the first time. Computer scientists and computer educators have suggested curriculums for training programs (Bitter & Camuse, 1984; Taffe & Weissmann, 1982; Taylor, Poirot, & Powell, 1980) and have reported the results of individual inservice activities (Anderson & Smith, 1984; Carroll & Johnson, 1981). These studies recommend an emphasis on hands-on activities, the use of extended time for interaction with the computer, and opportunities for individualization. Stecher (1984) has identified a number of factors relating to facilities and equipment, personal characteristics, and program activities that affect computer training success.

SUGGESTIONS FOR ADMINISTRATOR TRAINING

Training administrators to use an IIS requires that trainers be sensitive to, and increase administrators' sensitivities to, each of the four research areas just discussed.

With these in mind, I will offer a number of suggestions for organizing administrator training programs. These are my translations from and adaptation of principles derived from the research, as well as my own observations and the experience of others. They are provided as a first step in "inventing the future" for Instructional Information Systems. There is little doubt that this list will be modified and expanded as that future becomes clearer.

The following are offered as planning guidelines for administrator training programs.

1. Select as trainers people who have adequate knowledge of Instructional Information Systems, experience in school administration, and proven ability to communicate with administrators. Instructors should understand computer operations and the role of computers in educational administration. Instructors should be familiar with the needs and problems of school administrators on a practical, day-to-day level. Instructors should be able to communicate technical subjects to novices without being condescending, and should demonstrate genuine respect for the knowledge and abilities of the participants.

2. Provide an appropriate setting that has adequate facilities and minimum distractions. There should be sufficient hardware to allow all participants to have access to computers. Training sessions should be insulated from interruptions and work-related distractions. Attention to participants' comfort and convenience enhances the effectiveness of training.

3. Lecture as little as possible. Introduce interactive computer activities as quickly as possible.

4. Organize activities to provide large blocks of time for extensive hands-on experience. Interactive learning about computers usually needs two-hour blocks of time or longer.

5. Emphasize integration of the IIS into school planning and decision making. Illustrate how one might use data for instructional decisions. Demonstrate useful administrative applications as soon as possible. Avoid extensive discussions of related but not directly applicable computer topics such as programming, computer-assisted instruction, and so forth. Examine existing administrative goals and suggest new goals relating to instructional decision making.

6. Convey clear goals and objectives for the training sessions. Structure the lessons with adequate introductions and guided practice. Novices are often frustrated by unstructured, "discovery" approaches to computers.

7. Encourage peer interaction and continuous sharing of information. Plan activities that foster interaction among participants. Try to establish patterns of communication that will last after the training is completed.

8. Avoid "one-shot" training programs; plan for continuing contact or ongoing support in one form or another.

9. Be prepared to address people's resistance to computer use—for example, their fears about depersonalization, fears of failure. Illustrate the potential payoffs and personal rewards of computer use.

10. Be sensitive to psychological and organizational differences among potential users. Restrict initial training sessions to homogeneous peer groups. Do not include superintendents, staff assistants, and clerical personnel in the same workshops.

11. Address the potential need for organizational changes. Examine organizational links between the planning, evaluation, data processing, and decision-making functions of the organization. Explore ways to provide more efficient communication among organization units that might be involved in IIS implementation.

12. Stress the use of the IIS as a tool for solving local problems, and recognize the likelihood of mutual adaptations of the model to local conditions.

13. Examine the potential costs and benefits of the IIS. Costs include training, data entry, and maintenance of the data base, as well as expenditures for hardware and software. Provide realistic assessments of the likely

payoffs and investments. Frankly examine questions about whether the value of the additional information justifies the resources that are needed to develop and implement the system.

This list of recommendations is designed to ensure that IIS training activities will be as effective as possible. The key to effective training in this realm, as in most others, is sensitivity. If the training program is sensitive to the needs of the participants, the potential of the system, and the constraints of the workplace, then it is likely to have greater impact. If guidelines such as these are followed to introduce administrators to an IIS, then there is greater likelihood that the system will achieve its full potential. If training is taken for granted, this might not be the case.

However, no training approach will succeed unless the IIS itself proves to be a useful tool for educational planning or decision making and provides answers to questions that educators believe are important. The following fable emphasizes the importance of this issue.

AN INFORMATION SYSTEM USE FABLE

Once upon a time there was a wise physician who treated the sick and infirm to the best of her ability. However, hers was a frustrating job because the medical knowledge of the time about how to cure people was incomplete. Consequently, she could not heal many of the sick people who sought her help. She worked in one of the best clinics in the country with other doctors who had the same frustrations.

One day a team of evaluators and information systems experts came to the clinic. They visited the wise doctor as she was looking in on one of her patients.

"What's wrong?" they asked.

"Well, as you can see," she replied, "he is feverish, and he is pale. Moreover, he cannot keep any food in his stomach and he has been coughing up blood. And, despite my efforts, he does not seem to be getting any better."

"We think we can help," they said, "if you will give us a chance."

"Certainly," she replied, and allowed the team to examine the patient.

The evaluators and information systems experts reached into their bags and took out their specialized instruments with which they examined the patient. They took a few minutes to analyze the results of their tests, and then announced their findings to the doctor.

"The patient's white blood cell count is elevated, far above normal limits. In addition, he seems to be suffering from severe anemia. His blood sugar level is reduced; yet, his respiration is normal and his blood gas level is at the mean for a person of his age."

They continued with great pride to relate more of their detailed findings. When they were finished, the doctor thanked them warmly for the information and wished them well.

The next day the team returned to look in on the patient. They were surprised to discover that his condition was no better than before. They sought out the wise doctor and asked her why her patient had not improved.

"Well," she said, "I listened to all the information you gave me, but it did not tell me what I could do to treat him other than what I am already doing. And that, clearly, is not enough."

Frustrated with the doctor who wanted prescriptions rather than diagnosis, the team went to see the administrator of the clinic. Certainly, they thought, more information could improve his administrative understanding and help him help the doctors make sick people well. They explained to the administrator that they could provide the clinic with an almost magical assortment of sophisticated information management tools that had taken them years to develop. With these tools, the administrator could know almost instantly the problem with every patient in the hospital, could chart the day-to-day progress of symptoms and monitor the success rates of the doctors, and could compare patients this year with patients last year.

The administrator sat quietly through their presentation. He nodded appreciatively at the charts and graphs and agreed that they did, indeed, capture trends and relationships very vividly. Yet, when they asked if he would like the system in his clinic, he said no.

"Why not?" they asked. "Isn't this wonderful information?"

"Sure," he replied, "I might find it useful. But it would take a lot of time and work to install it. Frankly, I'd rather have a couple of hundred doses of penicillin and some expensive new drugs."

The team of evaluators and information systems experts left the clinic in silence. They would not return. To this day no one knows what they learned about the proper ratio between diagnosis and treatment.

The moral of this fable: Not all information is power; not all tools are equally valuable. An IIS may provide a great deal of information; its value for school improvement depends upon whether such information can help administrators help teachers help students to learn.

REFERENCES

Albright, A. D. (1962). An administrative staff college for education. In J. A. Culbertson and S. P. Hencley (Eds.), *Preparing administrators: New perspectives*. Columbus, OH: University Council for Educational Administration.

Alkin, M. C., Daillak, R. H., & White, P. (1979). *Using evaluation: Does evaluation make a difference?* Beverly Hills: Sage Publications.

American Association of School Administrators. (1983). *Guidelines for the preparation of school administrators* (2nd Ed.). Arlington, VA: Author.

Anderson, C., & Smith, R. L. (1984). Instructional computing in Texas schools: Implications for teacher training. *AEDS Journal, 18*(1), 1–16.

Berman, P., Greenwood, P. W., McLaughlin, M. W., & Pincus, J. (1975). *Federal programs supporting educational change, Vol. IV: A summary of the findings* (R-1589/4-HEW). Santa Monica, CA: Rand Corporation.

Bitter, G., & Camuse, R. A. (1984). *Using a microcomputer in the classroom*. Reston, VA: Reston Publishing.

Carroll, T., & Johnson, N. (1981). Educating urban elementary school teachers in computer science. In D. Harris & L. Nelson-Heem (Eds.), *Proceedings of the National Educational Computing Conference* (pp. 302–8). Iowa City: University of Iowa.

Farquhar, R. H., & Piele, P. K. (1972). *Preparing educational leaders: A review of recent literature* (UCEA monograph series, No. 1). Columbus, OH: University Council for Educational Administration.

Fullan, M. (1982). *The meaning of educational change*. Toronto: OISE Press.

Goldhammer, K., Suttle, J. E., Becker, G. L., & Aldridge, W. D. (1967). *Issues and problems in contemporary educational administration*. Eugene: University of Oregon, Center for the Advanced Study of Educational Administration.

Hall, G. E. (1979). The concerns-based approach to facilitating change. *Educational Horizons, 57*(4), 202–8.

Hall, G. E., Loucks, S. F., Rutherford, W. L., & Newlove, B. W. (1975). Levels of use of the innovation: A framework for analyzing innovation adoption. *Journal of Teacher Education, 26*(1), 52–56.

Hoyle, J. R. (1985, Winter). Programs in education administration and the AASA preparation guidelines. *Educational Administration Quarterly, 21*(1), 71–93.

Leithwood, K. A., Stanley, K., & Montgomery, K. J. (1984, November). Training principals for school improvement. *Education and Urban Society, 17*(1), 49–71.

Patton, M. Q. (1978). *Utilization focused evaluation*. Beverly Hills: Sage Publications.

Rutherford, W. L., Hord, S. M., & Thurber, J. C. (1984, November). Preparing principals for leadership roles in school improvement. *Education and Urban Society, 17*(1), 29–48.

Stecher, B. (1984). Improving computer inservice education for teachers. *AEDS Journal, 18*(2), 95–105.

Taffe, W. J., & Weissmann, S. (1982). A teacher's introduction to computers. In J. Smith & G. S. Moum (Eds.), *Proceedings of the National Educational Computing Conference* (pp. 359–63). Columbia: University of Missouri.

Taylor, R. P., Poirot, J. L., & Powell, J. D. (1980). Computing competencies for school teachers. In D. Harris & B. Collison (Eds.), *Proceedings of the National Educational Computing Conference* (pp. 130–36). Iowa City: University of Iowa.

17
Integrating Instructional Information Systems with Instructional Processes

NICHOLAS F. DUSSAULT

In recent years, three major trends have influenced educational management and have made us optimistic that new information technologies can give us tools to improve student achievement. Those trends are (1) the availability of more powerful and less expensive computing equipment, (2) the development of criterion-referenced achievement tests, and (3) increased knowledge of the factors that contribute to effective instruction.

This chapter will explore issues in building Instructional Information Systems and the potential of such systems for increasing student achievement by improving instruction. My view is that Instructional Information Systems can help teachers in many ways, provided that the collection, storage, manipulation, and reporting of the information is convenient to them and consonant with their instructional processes. Information systems must be able to provide flexible, usable, timely, and reliable data to teachers upon demand.

My major premise is that in order to improve student achievement, Instructional Information Systems must be coordinated with routine classroom processes. Although there is no evidence that Instructional Information Systems by themselves can improve student achievement, we do know of particular instructional techniques that have demonstrated ability to improve student learning. We think that the combined impact of Instructional Information Systems and these effective classroom techniques can make powerful differences in student learning.

This chapter will first describe some instructional management needs that could be met through Instructional Information Systems. Second, it will suggest the stages that are logical for schools to follow in developing an IIS. Third, it will present work done in the Sheboygan (Wisconsin) Area School District in developing such an Instructional Information System.

NEEDS FOR AN INFORMATION SYSTEM INTEGRATED WITH INSTRUCTION

An Instructional Information System is a method by which instructionally relevant information can be collected, stored, processed, and reported to various users in a timely manner. Such information, stored on a computer, can be updated, shared, and used by several persons. The major goal of our Sheboygan Area Instructional Information System is to provide better, more precise, and timely information to support and manage the instructional system at the classroom, building, and district levels.

Our IIS is to be an integral part of the instructional system available to classroom teachers. We believe that Instructional Information Systems are intermediary Management Information Systems, but they should not be only for district- or building-level managers. An IIS may ultimately serve district-level management functions, but we think that it must first serve teachers' needs. Teachers are "managers" in that they must manage the teaching of their students in their own classrooms and as members of a school-wide team. Thus, we must abandon the notion that Instructional Information Systems are solely for higher-level managers. The accent must be on instruction, and the system must be built up from the instructional process. When central office or building-level managers need to make management decisions based upon instructional data, they should use whatever information is developed as a normal part of the instructional process, not create an additional burden upon it.

We have tried to do this in our district. In the Sheboygan Area School District most of these policy and management functions fall under the heading of program evaluation. Our program evaluation is directed toward (1) determining whether or not students are learning the skills, behaviors, knowledge, and attitudes specified in the curriculum; (2) reporting information about district performance to the board of education, the public, and other interested constituents; (3) using that information to determine needs for instructional improvements; and (4) helping to plan for those needs. The data we use in the district for program evaluation are the same as those that teachers use for instructional management.

Teachers' General Need for Information

I have said that in order to improve instruction and student learning, Instructional Information Systems must provide useful information to teachers. Thus, it is important to know what teachers' information needs are and how Instructional Information Systems can meet those needs. It is helpful to know how information needs of teachers change under different methods of instructional organization. This section will review teachers' information needs.

Most of the information teachers use in the classroom for instructional decision making is based upon personal observations and intuition (Shavelson & Borko, 1979, pp. 184–85). Teachers make hundreds of instructional decisions a day and have no time to go through a formal, prolonged information-gathering and analysis process. In the classroom, students need immediate attention and decisions about dealing with them must be made on the spot (Jackson, 1968, p. 144).

Nevertheless, information about test scores can be of help to teachers in learning more about their students. Calfee and Juel (1977) report four needs of teachers relative to student test information: (1) test data that relate directly and appropriately to teaching strategies, (2) a pattern of data that highlights relative strengths and weaknesses, (3) information that will enable a teacher to determine the conditions that enhance or inhibit performance on specific tasks, and (4) information that is easily available and cheap to access.

The first three needs describe how test information should be presented to teachers so that it easily leads to decisions about how to teach. The fourth refers to the manner in which teachers get the data. Altogether, they describe key components of a useful IIS.

Information Supporting Specific Types of Teaching Strategies

Several innovations in instruction have great potential to improve student learning outcomes. Instructional Information Systems can support each of these teaching approaches in particular ways.

ADAPTIVE INSTRUCTION. Instructional Information Systems are needed to undergird that type of instruction called clinical teaching (Rudman and associates, 1980, pp. 46–50), adaptive instruction (Wang, 1980, p. 2), or prescriptive teaching (Bloom, 1976; Glaser, 1977; Rosenshine, 1979). For the purposes of this essay, all three of these approaches will be called adaptive instruction. This instructional approach is welcomed because it makes optimum use of school resources, including student and teacher time, and organizes classrooms to focus on individual student learning needs (Wang & Walberg, 1983, pp. 350–51).

This approach requires that instructional objectives be defined and that objective-referenced diagnostic tests be created. The basic assumption underlying adaptive teaching is that, with good and timely data about student performance, a teacher can accurately diagnose achievement deficiencies and, based upon the curriculum, formulate a plan (prescribe) to remediate deficient skills (Block & Burns, 1976; Bloom, Hastings, & Madaus, 1971; Frieder, 1970; Goodson & Okey, 1978; Hickey & Hoffman, 1973; Keller, 1968; Yeany, Dost, & Matthews, 1979). Information on those skills that students have mastered and on those skills that students have yet to master allows for better lesson planning and more purposeful grouping of students (Educational Research Service, 1983, p. 41; Spartz and associates, 1977, pp. 20–21).

The "effective schools" literature supports this form of teaching and concludes that measuring and analyzing children's extent and rate of learning, and adapting subsequent instruction to their present status, is an effective way to improve the achievement of all children. Such cycles of diagnosis, evaluation, and feedback were found to be essential components of effective schools.

There is evidence, then, that classroom techniques, classroom management arrangements, and instructional planning can increase student achievement. Wang, Gennari, and Waxman (1984) have found that, other than students' level of prior achievement, instructional planning and classroom management variables had the most effect on achievement. In their view, instructional planning and classroom management meant such activities as creating and maintaining a file of instructional materials, using diagnostic testing, monitoring and diagnosing, prescribing, and record-keeping (p. 38).

Benjamin Bloom (1984) has also cited classroom practices that have, he says, resulted in improved student achievement. Bloom, citing the research of Walberg (1984), systematically compared the effect of alterable variables on student achievement. The most effective of the learner-as-object variables is the feedback-corrective approach. This approach enhances student achievement by "providing students with cognitive and affective prerequisites for each new learning task" (Bloom, 1984, p. 7). Prerequisites are those skills, knowledge, or attitudes that prepare students to efficiently learn a new skill.

When the teacher is ready to teach a new skill, the records of a large number of students can be searched to determine their readiness to learn, based upon their achievement of cognitive prerequisites. Students can then be grouped on any of several factors (depending upon what is stored in the IIS), such as reading ability, prior learning (as well as rates of prior learning), facility with study skills, the need to use certain methods or materials, aptitudes, and handicaps. Instructional groups can be created based upon the recommendations of the Instructional Information System for the purposes of reteaching skills that were not learned, reviewing material taught in the past, or enriching the experiences of students who have quickly mastered the material in curriculum. This approach could be applied to any course of study that has a sequence of learning tasks.

DIAGNOSIS AND MONITORING OF STUDENT LEARNING PROCESS. Wang (1980) recognizes that changes are needed in schools in order that they may implement adaptive instructional concepts.

> While the potential value of providing adaptive instruction is widely recognized, practical problems in implementing adaptive instruction in classroom settings do exist. Adapting instruction to student differences places considerable strain on the teacher's time, as well as the teacher's skills in diagnosing and making curricular decisions, reorganizing and restructuring the classroom environment, and managing the classroom processes. Therefore, effective implementation of adaptive instruction will require some fundamental changes, not only in the nature and the structure of the curricular materials, but also in school organizational patterns, the teaching and learning processes, and in teacher and student roles. (pp. 3–4)

Computerized information systems can be used to support adaptive instruction and relieve some of the strain on teachers' time. They can provide information to help in diagnosing student deficits, organizing and linking school resources to student needs, monitoring rates of learning, and generating individual and group reports on student achievement.

Specifically, in terms of monitoring student achievement, an IIS can store and report on students' achievement of skills in the curriculum and give teachers and principals "snapshots" of student performance at a single point in time, or a "movie" of their progress over time. Printouts can list skills mastered or not mastered in any course of study, show the distribution of students as they progress through the skills in a particular curriculum, recommend how groups might be optimally formed for instruction, and provide reports to parents. Teachers will be able to identify the individuals who have failed to demonstrate mastery of a skill. Principals will be able to identify those subject areas that need either more or less instructional time.

Instructional Information Systems also have the capability of indexing objectives to an instructional resource file. A student who failed to master a particular skill could be given a computer-generated list of remedial materials to work on. A more sophisticated IIS would eventually have a more fine-grained error analysis component to diagnose learning problems from the incorrect distractors students select on multiple-choice exams, and then present an individualized remedial sequence.

MULTI-AGE GROUPING. Wang (1980) argues that teaching diverse groups of children requires the organizational flexibility that is possible within a multi-age grouping or ungraded classroom setup. This arrangement allows students to progress at their own rates without a feeling of failure. A multi-age group is most useful if it is considered a temporary group. With this form of grouping, no child is stigmatized by being permanently placed in a low ability or remedial group. In a temporary multi-age group, especially one that is relatively homogeneous in terms of skill level, no student is in a group for a long period—since achievement rates vary, children move out of the group at different times. Other advantages to multi-age grouping pointed out by Wang (1980) are the more efficient use of teacher time and the increments to learning added by peer modeling and peer tutoring (p. 10). (See also Allen, 1976, and Lippit, 1976.)

An IIS can handle many of the logistical problems associated with short-term grouping and regrouping. In addition to assisting teachers in the formation of groups, it can keep group rosters updated and can track the distribution of materials and room schedules.

TEAM TEACHING. Team teaching is another valuable organizational arrangement for improving learning. When compared with self-contained classrooms, team teaching increases the amount of time spent on learning tasks (Cohen, 1976; Schmuck, Paddock, & Packard, 1977). Wang (1980) indicates that team teaching presents several benefits to teachers, such as greater collegiality and an increased sense of autonomy in making decisions about classroom matters. "It also allows for a wider range of instructional styles and provides flexibility in scheduling" (p. 11). Team teaching permits individual teachers to specialize or to change emphasis from year to year. Other observers claim that team teaching promotes closer student–teacher relationships (Adams, 1962; Cohen & Bredo, 1975; Cohen, Deal, Meyer, & Scott, 1976; Dawson & Lunstrom, 1974).

Team teaching requires shared information on which to make collegial decisions. When a teacher works alone in a self-contained classroom, all of the information needed to manage the classroom is in that teacher's head, supplemented by the gradebook. However, when teachers work as a team, they must share information with one another. Record-keeping needs to be easily transferable and flexible in format so as to fit different teachers' styles.

In a one-teacher classroom, the most effective way for a teacher to store and retrieve information is to do so in an informal class record book, accompanied by personal notes. Since no one else has to have that information (except for required student behavior reports), there is little need for formalized record-keeping systems. For example, a teacher might add a note mentioning that John and Sue both seem to need more time to do their library report and may need some individual help next week. That informal note is enough to jog the teacher's memory.

However, if three grades are being team-taught by four teachers who must meet and distribute the students among themselves, a lot of information needs to be exchanged. Generally, the greater the number of persons involved, and the more information to be exchanged, the more formal and regularized that information base must become. If a team of teachers groups students for a library report lesson, they might decide to form heterogeneous groups based upon reading levels, or knowledge of reference materials, or past experience in writing research reports. If all of this background information has been previously entered into an IIS, then the students could be ranked on these skills and several groups created with relatively similar levels of skills, abilities, and prior experiences, regardless of their grade placement. Additionally, materials in libraries and classrooms, pages in textbooks and supplementary materials, computer software, and other resources could be catalogued and cross-referenced to curriculum objectives, skill levels, learning styles, and other characteristics.

STAGES OF IIS DEVELOPMENT

Instructional Information Systems are not at a point in their development where the average school district can acquire them ready-made. More typically, parts of them emerge in response to deficiencies in other sources of information or the need for better organization of available information. Usually, they are developed in stages.

The development of an IIS in the Sheboygan Area School District happened in three stages. The first stage was our disillusionment with the lack of closeness and congruence between the district's standardized tests and the curriculum. The second stage, occurring a response to the first, was the creation of a simple Instructional Information System, using computer managed instruction (CMI) software. The third stage, currently under way, is converting the CMI software to a more feasible data base management system. The next sections will discuss each of these stages in more detail and describe five pilot tests of the system.

Stage I: Disillusionment with Test Results As a Source of Data

Many problems confront educators when we attempt to use test scores by themselves to improve instruction. We must abandon the notion that existing conventional modes of testing are adequate sources of information about student learning, even as we acknowledge that test scores should be part of any Instructional Information System.

By a conventional mode of testing, I mean one whereby teaching is stopped in order to have a special time for testing. The time of testing and the type of test is mandated by the board of education, district administrator, director of instruction, principal, or any individual other than the teacher. The directions and time limits for test-taking are standardized. Completed test forms are sent to a vendor (usually the testing company) for scoring. Reports are returned about four to eight weeks after the test. Principals and teachers are urged to review the test scores and make the appropriate modification in their instruction so that future scores will be higher. With a minimum amount of additional analysis, results are reported to the board of education, the public, and parents.

Such conventional achievement testing has several limitations in terms of being an effective tool for improving student achievement:

1. Tests purchased from a vendor may not match the district's curriculum. Or, tests may match the curriculum but not reflect actual instruction. Or, the test may match the curriculum and instruction but not be given at the right time of year to coordinate with either. Or, test results may be presented in different terms from the curriculum so that the relationship is unclear. Tests and the reports of their results must be absolutely congruent with both curriculum and instruction to be of use to teachers.

2. Tests scored by external vendors or even computer centers internal to the district generally take from two to eight weeks to be corrected, printed, and returned. In that time span, the instructional process continues, with the teacher moving to a different point in the curriculum. It is disruptive to return to reteach certain skills based upon the results of the test. To be of maximum use to the teacher, results need to be returned immediately, preferably within 24 hours.

3. In some districts, tests are given by district testing personnel or by a guidance counselor. As committed to testing as these people may be, they are rarely involved in the day-to-day instructional activities of teachers. Teachers do not have a sense of ownership of those tests, and do not perceive a use for the results. Tests that teachers give and score, and that produce results they can use in grading, grouping, or other instructional decisions, have greater meaning for teachers.

4. Teachers receive the results of traditional achievement tests on printouts. Further manipulation of the data is impossible unless the district orders a magnetic tape of the data and writes a computer program to perform those manipulations. Thus, many powerful techniques of electronic information processing are not available to answer teachers' questions. The teacher

cannot create and track individualized programs for gifted or remedial students, update student progress records after reteaching, combine testing information with other demographic or test information, regroup students for instruction, or print the test results for a small group. An electronic system could report the more recent information and archive the rest in an easily accessible manner.

Our district view is that testing should not be separate from normal classroom activities. Rather, to the extent possible, it should be an integral part of instruction. Advances in inexpensive computer technology have created the potential for even the smallest school district to be able to better integrate testing into instruction by scoring and recording their criterion-referenced test within a school. For less than $8,000, a complete test-scoring and recording system can be created in a district or school and stored on a microcomputer. Computer-managed instruction software, developed in the 1960s, can be used as a simple version of such a system.

Stage II: Computer-Managed Instruction as an Instructional Information System

We found that many, but not all, of the problems with conventional testing identified above could be addressed by use of appropriate computer-managed instruction (CMI) software. A CMI system keeps records on student achievement and prints reports. It supports instructional decision making by scoring tests, storing data, printing reports, grouping students for instruction, and prescribing courses of study. CMI systems do not provide direct instruction to students nor do students actually use a computer.

There are many versions of computer-managed instruction on the market today. Some are linked to specific textbook series and are structured only to store and record tests associated with that text series, while others are more generic and can be adapted to many curricula. A CMI system is more than a test-scoring system. To be effective in "managing" instruction, a school must have sufficient computer power to store and manipulate the test information in many formats. We found that our criteria for good CMI software included:

1. *Data capture.* Grades should be able to be entered through a keyboard or scanner by convenient sections of the curriculum. For scanner input, a wide variety of scan forms ought to be accommodated.

2. *Storing of information.* The grading structure should have sufficient flexibility to be defined by the user. Grades may be in the typical "A, B, C . . ." terminology, a percent correct test score, a mastery or nonmastery

symbol, or a raw score. Additionally, capability for weighting and aggregating grades for report card purposes is helpful. Information should follow the student, regardless of how the student is moved throughout the building or district. The user should have control over when and under what conditions the scores are either maintained, deleted, or updated.

3. *Reports.* The user ought to be able to control the types and formats of reports printed by the system. The system ought to produce reports for individual students over a specific time period, and reports of each class, grade, instructional group, and school or district. It ought to be able to produce grading or nonmastery reports of students who fail to meet a standard of achievement. In addition, the report-writing function should be able to print a report to verify whether or not information has been accurately entered and stored.

4. *Grouping operations.* The computer-managed instruction system should have the capacity to store and dynamically form and reform groups of students without affecting any of the other functions. In many instructional approaches, temporary groups are formed for the purposes of teaching specific skills. It ought to be able to grade students, access information, and print reports by group.

5. *Prerequisite functions.* Although they are not needed in many curricula, the system ought to have the capacity to store prerequisites to various skills. This is crucial for some mastery learning techniques where assignment to a group is dependent upon mastery of the prerequisite skills.

6. *Diagnosis and prescription.* The test file should be linked to the curriculum base and to a file containing the school resources. When a student test is scored, the results should be linked to specific school resources, such as a portion of text, specific review exercise, computer-assisted instructional software, or videotapes. For example, a student who received a high score on a test would be directed to a set of enrichment activities, while a student who did poorly would be directed to remedial materials.

7. *Curricular flexibility.* Different curricula have different methods of organization. Some are loosely ordered in a single sequence, others are tightly ordered in sequences with multiple paths, some are hierarchical, and still others are cyclical in organization. There are different organizational schemes for different curricula in the same district. In fact, some subjects may be organized differently during different times of the year. The software must have the capability of efficiently handling these organizational schemes.

Stage III: Planning for the Use of a Data Base Management System as an Instructional Information System

As computer-managed Instructional Information Systems become accepted and the demand for more and different uses of that information inevitably grows, Instructional Information Systems can then be organized under principles of data base management systems (DBMS). This would allow changes to be easily made in the way data is stored, reported, and linked to other data.

A data base management system is a collection of data that are shared and used for multiple purposes. The central concept of a DBMS is to create files that can be organized and accessed in many ways. Once appropriate data bases are in place, new types of applications can be created quickly without programs being written. Users can create their own reports, often without going through a programmer. It should be possible to enter students, teachers, grades, groups, and curriculum changes while the system is in operation without destroying the integrity of the data base.

The data base is a major resource for the system and provides a common pool of accurate, up-to-date data, with no duplication. If data need to be updated, one person makes the change for each application. Data must be available when required by the user, with due regard to security and integrity. As applications grow, and as data fields are added, one should not have to change existing programs. The need for users to retain the operation and control their own data must be present (Martin, 1980).

To be truly helpful and efficient, a data base management system must meet the following three criteria:

1. *The system must be easy to use.* The system envisioned here must possess all of the modern "user-friendly" capabilities of good software. It should be designed to be operated by a teacher or a teacher's aide with a minimum amount of training. The system should be menu-driven with choices clearly labeled. Each choice in any menu should have an on-line "help" function so that, with a single keystroke, an uncertain user can get an immediate explanation or example of each choice. It must be simple enough to encourage different people to fully use the system. A cost-efficient, flexible Instructional Information System can be built on top of a commercially available data base management system.

2. *The results should be returned to teachers fast.* The instructional process is time-sensitive. Teaching must go on, and the limited amount of time available for it must be utilized to its fullest, regardless of whether or not tests are back or new information about student progress is available. In order to have a significant impact on everyday teaching, information such as test scores and their implications must be available in a very short period of time.

3. *The system should link up with other data bases.* The system should have the capability of being linked to larger school data bases. Some school systems keep information on students in a system distinct from the Instructional Information System. The capacity to link to external data bases is important for ease of maintaining student files.

HISTORY OF AN IIS IN THE
SHEBOYGAN AREA SCHOOL DISTRICT

A series of pilot programs have been conducted in the Sheboygan Area School District to test the feasibility of different aspects of an information system, try out the software described above, and assess the potential of information systems to manage instruction.

Middle School Reading: The Skills Program

DESCRIPTION. In the fall of 1982, computer terminals and printers were installed in three middle schools and connected to a Digital Equipment Company LSI-1123 computer located in the central support facility. Computer-managed instruction software was purchased from MICE, Inc. of Madison, Wisconsin, and installed on the LSI. A district-developed middle school reading skills program was installed on the machine as the "curriculum." A set of mastery tests (one test per skill area) was developed and instruction was started.

During this implementation, the district was in the first year of a conversion from a grades 7 through 9 junior high school to a grades 6 through 8 middle school format. Teachers were in different buildings and were operating under a new concept that changed the mode of providing instruction from the single teacher, subject-specific classroom to a "pod" organization in which teams of three or four teachers were responsible for up to 125 students. Reading classes had not been taught in the junior high schools for several years, so roughly 60 percent of the teachers in the middle school had no experience teaching reading as a separate class. Scheduling and other organizational concerns were not completely resolved at the time of the conversion.

RESULTS. The program quickly met with failure. The faculty and administration at some of the schools did not completely accept the new curriculum. The software for the management system had a few serious problems that led to the scrambling of data. Student learning could not be measured with optical scanning equipment. Due to these problems, consistent implementation never occurred.

The Sixth-Grade Reading CMI Pilot at Horace Mann Middle School

DESCRIPTION. This pilot presented a revised reading program for 165 sixth-grade students taught by a team of ten teachers, including eight classroom teachers, a reading specialist, and a special education teacher. Four specific reading skill lessons took place over a four-week period in order to test:

- The potential for a computer-managed instruction system to provide rapid feedback of student mastery of skills
- The potential for entering test scores into a computerized record-keeping system using optical scanning from a remote site
- The practicality of combining pretests, posttests, and reassessment tests into an instructional cycle
- The potential of grouping students for instruction based upon test results
- The use of test data for team decision making

The pilot program consisted of four 5-day cycles, with each cycle focusing on a particular skill lesson. On day 1 of a cycle, all students took a skills pretest, which was then optically scanned, a score assigned, and a computerized record made. A score of 80 percent was considered mastery. Based on the scores of the pretest, students were assigned to an instructional group.

On day 2, a 30-minute skill development program focused on everyday reading tasks. On day 3, students who passed the pretest were assigned to a group and presented a literary lesson. Students who had failed the pretest were assigned to an instructional lesson on the skill for which they had failed to demonstrate mastery. Both lessons were 45 minutes long. At the end of the skill lesson, students were given a posttest on the skill, which was scored by the computer and then students were again regrouped. On day 4, reading was not taught. Students who failed the posttest were grouped for a reteaching lesson on day 5.

RESULTS. Connecting a remote scanner to the CMI system presented some problems. The scanner seemed to slow down computer response time, particularly if two users were using the system at the same time. At other times, the scanner would stop completely. This resulted in wasted time and uncertainty as to whether the computer was receiving information.

Another cluster of problems revolved around getting an accurate list of who took the test. A lot of time was wasted because of the inability of the system to determine whether a student had not taken the test or if the test sheet was not read properly.

The plan called for teachers to instruct homogeneous groups of students. But the software was not flexible enough to rank-order students on the basis of percent correct on the pretest or posttest.

Perhaps the most significant recommendation from the teachers was to have a longer instructional cycle so as to better organize instruction, better handle the logistics for the regrouping, and allow more time for reteaching before posttesting.

There was a problem with the relative difficulty level of pretests, posttests, and reassessment tests. This resulted in some students having difficulty on the pretest but passing the posttest with ease.

We concluded that the CMI concept seems to have potential for effectively teaching students if the logistics and instructional materials are improved and if the software could be enhanced to provide more power to scanning and more help to the aide in shortening time in data entry. Grouping and regrouping for instruction seems to have potential as an effective way to teach students. Students seemed to like the regrouping process and liked being with different teachers. The students also liked the rapid feedback on whether or not they had passed the test. However, we were unable to make a study of the effect of the teaching because of the inability to calibrate the levels of difficulty of the pre-, post-, reassessment, and retention tests.

The Revised Sixth-Grade Reading Pilot

DESCRIPTION. After a review of the Horace Mann Pilot program, the reading and language arts coordinator revised the sixth-grade reading program. First, the Houghton-Mifflin Reading Series was extended to the sixth grade with reordering of the curriculum due to the organization of the middle school.

This mode of organization extended the "cycle" concept used in the pilot program from five days to a nine-week quarter. This longer cycle gave teachers much more flexibility and permitted them to accommodate disruptions such as snow days, special programs, or teacher in-service days. Teachers had the flexibility to teach seven of the eight primary and secondary lessons in each quarter unit on any nine-week schedule they wished.

The testing required in the primary units consisted of a pretest, posttest, and end-of-quarter retention test. The pretest included all skills in the four primary lessons and was graded by computer and returned to the teacher immediately. After the teaching of each primary lesson, students took a posttest. The teacher had the option of scoring the posttest by hand or by machine. At the end of the quarter, a retention test was given on all primary lessons taught during that quarter. Again, the score for each skill was returned to the teacher during that quarter and remained on the system until it was tested again.

RESULTS. Using the Houghton-Mifflin series addressed several problems noted in the pilot test. It provided a well-developed set of skills and literary lessons to be taught. All three of the tests provided by the program were well developed and of equal difficulty. Many of the logistical problems of developing materials and matching them to the curriculum were solved. There were many curriculum materials for reteaching remedial skills or enrichment. Finally, word recognition, comprehension, reference, and literary skills were integrated.

The software was also rewritten to remove bugs that had previously disrupted the program. Further training in using the system and dealing with the hardware and software was given to the aides. Procedures were developed by which the aides were able to cross-check lists of students taking the tests with absenteeism.

Concerns still exist about the flexibility of the software and the fact that groups did not change as fast as achievement. Questions still remain as to what should be done when a student masters all of the skills on the pretest. A more detailed evaluation will be conducted, with program modifications in both software and curriculum to follow. Additionally, there are plans to expand the program into the seventh grade.

The James Madison Elementary School Mathematics Project

The curriculum, still in the planning stage, identifies 231 mathematics objectives from prekindergarten skills to quadratic equations. More importantly, it identifies prerequisite skills for each of the objectives needed for successful work. Students are not taught a skill unless they have mastered the prerequisites.

Instructional groups are formed when a minimum number of students are prepared to learn a skill, based upon the mastery of prerequisites. These groups may include students from several grades. Groups meet until the teachers have taught the skill and a mastery test is given. Students who pass the test for the objective are eligible for instruction at higher-level objectives. There are multiple routes through the curriculum and students who fail are not stigmatized by being placed in a "remedial class." They merely wait until enough students need to learn that skill and it is being taught again, although individual help is still given at the discretion of the teacher.

Before an instructional group is formed, students are given a pretest to determine if they have retained mastery of the *prerequisite* skills. Failure on a pretest results in immediate reteaching and/or additional practice of prerequisite skills.

This program seems to have several advantages over traditional "individualized" instructional systems. It does not fractionalize or isolate teaching and learning and does not present the management problems normally encountered when children in a single classroom work on multiple skills.

Each child moves at his or her individual pace, and is always actively involved in instruction as opposed to independent study.

A resource file on each of the 231 objectives will be developed for teaching and reteaching. As planning for this program continues, software is being developed to aid student placement, formation of groups, grading, and program evaluation.

Scott-Foresman Test-Scoring and Record-Keeping System

A second pilot program in mathematics, still being planned and not yet implemented, uses the Scott-Foresman Micro Management System. The software is still undergoing final correction of errors and has yet to be delivered to the school system. Other logistical supports are also slow in coming with this program. This pilot will test the usefulness of a simple testing and record-keeping system and will provide a contrast in terms of simplicity with some of the other programs.

CONCLUSIONS

Instructional Information Systems have tremendous potential to improve student achievement in our schools. As with any new technology, eventual success is dependent upon the ability of the technology to significantly change things for the better by making the day-to-day working of schools easier. Instructional Information Systems have not yet demonstrated that they can do this. As a whole host of past "innovations" give testimony, potential for improvement is not a guarantee for a lasting place in the educational process.

For those schools that want to improve instruction, Instructional Information Systems are not the first step. Changing classroom instruction is the first step. However, an IIS can make many of those changes easier by managing the logistics and giving teachers the ability to fine-tune those improvements, based upon rapid feedback.

The major problem currently confronting Instructional Information Systems is not primarily technological. Rather, it is changing people's thinking about what their informational needs are, or could be, given improved systems of instruction.

REFERENCES

Adams, A. S. (1962). Operation co-teaching. Dateline Oceano, CA. *Elementary School Journal, 62,* 203–12.

Allen, V. L. (Ed.). (1976). *Children as teachers: Theory and research on tutoring*. New York: Academic Press.

Block, James H., & Burns, R. B. (1976). Mastery learning. In L. Shulman (Ed.), *Review of research in education*. Itasca, IL: Peacock.

Bloom, B. S. (1976). *Human characteristics and school learning*. New York: McGraw-Hill.

Bloom, B. S. (1984, June/July). The 2 Sigma problem: The search for methods of group instruction as effective as one-to-one tutoring. *Educational Researcher, 13*(6), 4–16.

Bloom, B. S., Hasting, J., & Madaus, G. (1971). *Handbook of formative and summative evaluation of student learning*. New York: McGraw-Hill.

Calfee, R., & Juel, C. (1977, June). *How theory and research on reading assessment can serve decision makers*. Paper presented at Minnesota Perspectives on Literacy Conference.

Cohen, E. G. (1976). *Problems and prospects of teaming* (Memorandum No. 143). Stanford, CA: Stanford University, Center for Research and Development in Teaching.

Cohen, E. G., & Bredo, E. (1975). Elementary school organizations and innovative instructional practices. In J. V. Baldridge & T. E. Deal (Eds.), *Managing change in educational organizations: Sociological perspective, strategies and case studies*. Berkeley: McCutchan.

Cohen, E. G., Deal, D., Meyer, J., & Scott, W. R. (1976, October). *Organization and instruction in elementary schools: First results, 1973* (Technical Report 50). Stanford, CA: Stanford University, Center for Research and Development in Teaching.

Dawson, D. T., & Lunstrom, R. J. (1974). The expanded self-contained classroom. *The Elementary School Journal, 75*(4), 203–9.

Educational Research Service, Inc. (1983). *Effective schools: A summary of research*. Arlington, Va.: Author.

Frieder, B. (1970). Motivation: Least developed of teacher roles. *Educational Technology, 10*, 28–36.

Glaser, R. (1977). *Adaptive instruction: Individual diversity and learning*. New York: Holt, Rinehart and Winston.

Goodson, M., & Okey, J. R. (1978, November). The effect of diagnostic tests and help sessions on college science achievement. *Journal of College Science Teaching, 8*, 89–90.

Hickey, M. E., & Hoffman, D. H. (1973, October). Diagnosis and prescription in education. *Educational Technology, 13*, 35–37.

Jackson, P. W. (1968). *Life in classrooms*. New York: Holt, Rinehart and Winston.

Keller, F. (1968). . . . Goodbye teacher. *Journal of Applied Behavioral Analysis, 1*, 78–89.

Lippit, P. (1976). Learning through close-age peer tutoring: Why and how. In V. L. Allen (Ed.), *Children as teachers: Theory and research on tutoring*. New York: Academic Press.

Martin, J. (1980). *Managing the data base environment*. Lancaster, England: Savant Research Studies.

Rosenshine, B. V. (1979). Content, time and direct instruction. In P. L. Peterson & H. J. Walberg (Eds.), *Research on teaching: Concepts, findings, and implications*. Berkeley: McCutchan.

Rudman, H. C., Kelly, J. L., Wanous, D. S., Mehrens, W. A., Clark, C. M., & Porter, A. C. (1980). *Integrating assessment with instruction: A review (1922–1980)* (Research Series, No. 75). East Lansing: Michigan State University, Institute for Research on Testing.

Schmuck, P., Paddock, S., & Packard, J. (1977). *Management implications for team teaching*. Eugene: University of Oregon, Center for Educational Policy and Management.

Shavelson, R. J., & Borko, H. (1979, Summer). Research in teachers' decisions in planning instruction. *Educational Horizons*, 183–84.

Spartz, J. L., et al. (1977, September). *Delaware educational accountability system case studies: Elementary schools grades 1–4 (A report of results)*. Dover, Delaware: Delaware Department of Public Instruction.

Walberg, H. J. (1984). Improving the productivity of America's schools. *Educational Leadership, 41*(8), 19–27.

Wang, M. C. (1980). Adaptive instruction: Building on diversity. *Theory Into Practice, 19*(2), 122–27. Reprinted as *Reports to educators No. 2*, University of Pittsburgh, Learning Research and Development Center, 1980.

Wang, M. C., & Walberg, H. J. (1983). Evaluating educational programs: An integrative, causal-modeling approach. *Educational Evaluation and Policy Analysis, 5*(3), 347–66.

Wang, M. C., Gennari, P., & Waxman, H. C. (1984). *The adaptive learning environment model: Design implementation* (Publication 1984/4). Pittsburgh: University of Pittsburgh, Learning Research and Development Center.

Yeany, R. H., Dost, R. J., & Matthews, R. (1979, March). *The effects of diagnostic prescriptive instruction and locus of control on the achievement and attitudes of university students*. Paper presented at the annual meeting of the National Association for Research in Science Teaching, Atlanta.

18
Making Sense Out of Comprehensive School-Based Information Systems: An Exploratory Investigation

KENNETH A. SIROTNIK and LEIGH BURSTEIN

We have, in a number of other publications, described our exploration of the two concepts of systemic evaluation (Burstein, 1983, 1984a, 1984; Sirotnik, 1984a; Sirotnik, Burstein, & Thomas, 1983; Sirotnik, Dorr-Bremme, & Burstein, 1985) and contextual appraisal (Sirotnik, 1984a; Sirotnik & Oakes, 1981a, 1981b; Sirotnik, Burstein, & Thomas, 1983). Irrespective of terminology, however, our interest here is in what we call comprehensive information—data including but not limited to student achievement scores—as input into school improvement efforts at all levels of the educational enterprise. Perhaps even more central to our work is our contention that comprehensive information systems are not devices that can be packaged and forced upon school people; rather, all educators must be appropriately and nontrivially involved with them throughout the entire process of conceptualization, development, and implementation.

Our view, then, of ideal school-based information systems places such systems in the context of a general commitment to critical inquiry (Sirotnik, 1984b; Sirotnik & Oakes, 1986) at the school level—a commitment that should provide administrators and staff with significant time and resources for questioning what they do and collecting data that can help them decide how to go about doing it better.

Within this perspective, we clearly distinguish *information* from *knowledge*. Information is one—but only one—source of knowledge. Quantified facts and interpretations are simply inputs for interpretation, understanding, and critique. The process of encouraging dialogue, clarifying values, taking into account human interests and needs, and making, acting upon, and reevaluating decisions, therefore becomes as important as the empirical data bases required to undergird the process.

Beginning in 1984, we began to reality-test the information side of the critical inquiry idea in a typical secondary school setting. This school is a three-year senior high school of approximately 2,000 students located in a two-high-school suburban district (K–12 enrollment approximately 20,000 students) just outside the greater Los Angeles area. This school is in a district that had an information system already in place, but there was little teacher awareness of how it operated and why it might be helpful to them.

Our basic method was to work collaboratively with a selected group of teachers, administrators, and counselors to develop the means whereby the district's existing information system could be modified to meet needs at the school level. Towards this end, we were also in close working relationship with district staff, particularly in the data processing division, so that any changes or additions could be made in existing hardware and software configurations.

Our main concern was with questions about how school people made sense of the kind of data ordinarily found in comprehensive information systems. For example, when given the opportunity to become involved in developing such systems, on what basis do teachers, administrators, and counselors decide to include (or exclude) potentially relevant information? What are their operative paradigms of information use? What are the formats in which data should be transmitted to practitioners? How and why are (or are not) data used when reported in these formats back to practitioners? To what extent are consultative functions from outside collaborators necessary in order to develop, implement, and maintain minimally functional information systems at the classroom and school levels? These and other questions drove or emerged from the inquiry described in this chapter.

In what follows, we will describe both the process and outcome of developing and testing analysis and reporting formats that a select group of school staff found interpretable, meaningful, and useful in their day-to-day work settings. We will also discuss the perceptions of the entire school staff regarding the usefulness of the reports as developed by the smaller staff work group. It must be remembered that this was an exploratory case study in one suburban high school setting. Our inferences and conclusions, therefore, emerge as hypotheses deserving of further test rather than as generalizable confirmations.

THE PROCESS

Most of our development work took place collaboratively with school staff members. Specifically, a core group of five teachers who represented different subject matters, the principal and assistant principal, and sometimes a counselor, provided the main project input from the school. (In the last year, five more teachers joined this group.) We will refer to these representatives of the school and ourselves, collectively, as the "work group."

We also met regularly with district-level staff on two issues: (1) updating and negotiating with the assistant superintendent regarding the progress of the project and the material and resource needs as they occurred and (2) working closely with the director and senior programmer in data processing to study their information system's contents and capabilities as well as to facilitate their processing and use of the new information (e.g., student survey data) collected at the school level.

Initial Activities and Student Survey

Initial meetings during the first year were held with the work group to orient all participants to the general purposes and scope of the project and then to attend to the details of these activities:

- Identifying the kinds of information teachers, counselors, and building administrators view as useful for their own work—for example, for making student-level, class-level, school-level, and program-level decisions.
- Identifying what specific problems, at any level, the school staff would expect that information system to help them address.
- Ascertaining everyone's level of understanding about the computerized information currently available to school staff and the services provided.
- Reviewing the content of the existing computerized information system.
- Discussing the extent to which the system meets current and anticipated needs.
- Determining what additional information would be necessary to augment the system.
- Developing plans for collecting such additional information—for example, devising a student survey.
- Identifying information useful for characterizing the functioning and impact of ongoing programs—for example, of state-funded school improvement projects.

Among other things, it was clear from these activities that the teachers were aware of only a fraction of the information and reports that could be obtained from the existing system; they thought that the procedures for getting reports were slow, not responsive, and not flexible enough for specific needs, and that there were much more data of potential use that were not already in the information system.

The next few meetings of the work group centered directly on the task of constructing the student survey. This work was made easier because of an available compendium of student survey items, asking for student opinions on school and classroom issues that had been developed by the project in the previous year (Sirotnik, Burstein, & Thomas, 1983). Through an interactive process of dialog, sorting, sifting, priority-setting, revising, and subtracting irrelevant items and adding new ones, the group converged on a survey. It was completed by students in May 1984, scored and computerized by the district's data processing department, and subsequently analyzed at UCLA for the purposes of this project.

Analyses and Reporting Formats

Next, the work group tried to create analyses and reporting formats for this student survey data as well as other system data that might capture the interests and information needs of school staff. We held a two-day retreat during which the work group pursued an in-depth descriptive analysis of the survey results based upon marginal response percentages. A semistructured agenda moved the group toward consideration of the various ways in which the analyses could be graphically presented.

In the next couple of half-day meetings, the teachers, administrators, and CSE staff worked jointly on the details of analyses and reporting formats. These reports came to be known as the Students-at-a-glance, Class-at-a-glance, and School-at-a-glance reports. We will discuss how they were designed and produced in the next section. Suffice it to note here that this form-development process was an interactive one: ideas were generated by the work group, "brought back to the shop" and developed further by CSE staff, and presented again to the group until a working consensus was reached by all involved.

Once the at-a-glance reports were developed and we were certain that the district would produce them for all teachers, a total staff meeting was planned and held in November 1984. Its goals were to reiterate the purposes and scope of the project, share the progress to date, gain faculty-wide reactions, inform staff of upcoming next steps, and enlist more teacher volunteers to join the group. Particularly noteworthy was the fact that this meeting was planned and conducted primarily by the five teachers initially involved in our work group.

Based upon the results of this meeting, the report forms generated by the work group, and programming specifications outlined by CSE staff, the district developed the software and produced the reports approximately two week into the semester, after class enrollments stabilized. The reports were sorted and packaged for each teacher and disseminated in mid-February 1985 at meetings with teachers during their preparation periods. At this time, we talked with them about the purpose of the project, the report forms themselves, and issues regarding both use and abuse of information. We also suggested some general topics to keep in mind over the next couple of months that would help us evaluate the utility of the reports.

For approximately 10 weeks we left the teachers on their own in terms of using (or not using) the information in these reports. During this period, however, a senior staff member of the CSE project team interviewed 18 teachers (and five other staff members) who were selected to represent both the teachers in our work group and teachers generally in the school. These were one- to two-hour interviews. Summary results of these interviews will be given later in the chapter. (A more detailed analysis can be found in Dorr-Bremme, 1985.)

The interviews provided the basis for a teacher survey instrument about uses and nonuses of the students-at-a-glance and class-at-a-glance reports. In particular, we wanted teachers' views on how they used the forms or why they didn't use them; what information was most often used; which form was most often used; what deletions, modifications, additions, or format changes were desired; and what abuses might have occurred. These data were collected in early May of 1985.

This brief description is intended to set the stage for what follows—namely, a discussion of the analyses and at-a-glance report forms, followed by an analysis and interpretation of the interview and survey data regarding teachers' perceptions of the utility of these reporting devices. We will conclude with a discussion of the most critical issues, summarized across the entire project experience.

AT-A-GLANCE REPORTS

There is nothing inherent in information that automatically guarantees its usefulness. Even for information generated to fulfill a conceptual need—for example, to understand student attitudes and opinions—assessing the utility of the data actually obtained from the student survey is a whole new ballgame. What seems interesting in theory is not always of interest when the data are actually at hand. This was one of our primary reasons for having teachers and administrators face the tasks of data analysis and report design.

As already noted, three data displays were generated by the work group: students-at-a-glance, class-at-a-glance, and school-at-a-glance reports. We will discuss each in terms of its evolution, content, and anticipated use. We will then talk about the *actual* use of these reports.

Students-At-A-Glance

Of the various levels of aggregation at which reported information could be of use to school staff, teachers seemed to gravitate to the individual student level, particularly as information about individuals related to their own teaching. Early in the project, an interesting "tension" arose between teachers' predispositions to relate on the one hand to individually focused, diagnostic data and, on the other hand, to group or institutionally focused data (often aggregates of individual data). We have labelled these two perspectives regarding the use of information the clinical and the social, respectively. (See Sirotnik, Dorr-Bremme, & Burstein, 1985.) The clinical–social distinction is an important one in information use, and we will return to it in the next section. Suffice it to say that all teachers related to the clinical perspective on information use. Their main concern centered on which data to select and how to array them in a visually satisfying manner.

The work group already had a start on discussing these concerns because they had dealt with a district student information report and also a preliminary outline submitted by one of the teachers. Interestingly, not all the teachers were even aware of the availability of the district report. Nevertheless, all teachers reacted somewhat negatively towards the report in terms of its unclear variable definitions; its densely packed, difficult to read format; and the presence of both too much information and too much irrelevance.

Figure 18.1 shows part of the final version of the students-at-a-glance report, which provides teachers with a student roster for each of their classes. Information on each student is given by the column headings and defined by the keys at the bottom of the report. This report was based upon a merged file created from five separate district files, including the student survey data. This merged file was first used as input to the report generator subprogram of the SPSS system set up by CSE staff to produce a prototype report format. The district then wrote its own software and essentially duplicated this report format so that they could generate it for any class section.

Of the thirteen pieces of information selected by the work group to include in the report, seven came from the district information system and six were from responses to the student survey. It is interesting to note that one of the most influential criteria for the selection of information had little to do with content. To be sure, the group did struggle with the substance of the report. Yet the most restrictive criterion, on which all teachers were agreed, was that all the information for classes even as large as 40 should fit, uncluttered and easy to read, on a single 8½ × 11 page, so as to fit in their class notebooks.

At first blush, this may seem a rather trivial issue to get worked up about. Nevertheless, it was critical, and one that we will discuss further. Other critical issues emerging from the discussions about student-level data concerned the misuse and abuse of information, confidentiality, and creating self-fulfilling prophecies about students. These issues will also be addressed in a later section.

Finally, teachers anticipated several constructive uses for the students-at-

FIGURE 18.1. Students-At-A-Glance Report

```
                          STUDENTS AT A GLANCE

  SECTION:                                        PREPARED ON 10 OCT 84
  TEACHER:
                           C    E                                           
                           M    D       D    C    C    C              H    A    L
                                        A    T    T    T              O    C    I
                                S    E  Y    B    B    B         A    M    T    K
                           G    C    X  S    S    S    S         C    E    I    E
                           R    H    P                           A    D    W    V
                           A    O    E       R    L    M              O    J    I
  STUDENT   STUDENT        D    O    C    B  E    A    A    G    S    R    O    T    S
  NUMBER    NAME           E    L    T    S  A    N    T    P    C    K    B    Y    C
                                             D    G    H    A                        H

  0149043                  12   .    4Y   .  .    .    .    1.1  H    +    P    3    +
  0249052                  .    .    HS   .  .    .    .    .    M    +    P    0    +
  0341950                  12   6    HS  57  33   14   3    1.9  M    -    H    0    -
  0449274                  12   3    4Y  35  52   84   83   2.6  M    0    H    2    +
  0542468                  12   3    2Y  17  34   54   3    1.8  H    +    N    2    +
  0649341                  12   3    2Y  18  49   67   0    2.7  H    +    N    0    +
  0743686                  12   4    2Y  11  80   88   80   1.6  M    0    H    0    0
  0849048                  12   6    2Y  23  68   72   68   2 9  M    +    N    4    +
  0942771                  12   6    HS  30  .    .    3    1.5  H    .    N    0    -
  1049050                  11   6    ?   13  83   86   68   3.0  M    0    P    1    -
  ...                                       ...............
  3449323                  12   5    2Y  27  47   49   31   2.1  M    +    P    0    +
  3549109                  12   4    HS  10  61   74   26   1.9  M    -    H    0    +
  3641481                  12   5    4Y  15  42   17   23   1.3  H    +    N    3    -
  3744147                  12   6    2Y  56  54   73   40   2.9  H    +    P    2    +
  3849262                  12   1    2Y  31  92   52   95   3.1  H    +    P    0    +
  3949329                  12   8    2Y  27  63   50   60   3.0  M    +    H    1    -
  4043580                  12   4    2Y  25  12   12   23   2.2  M    -    P    1    -
```

. = MISSING

CM SCHOOL: CAREER MAGNET SCHOOL.
  1 = PHYSICAL SCIENCE AND TECHNOLOGY
  2 = INTERNATIONAL RELATIONS & POLITICAL SCIENCE
  3 = BUSINESS   4 = INDUSTRY   5 = PERFORMING VISUAL AND FINE ARTS
  6 = MENTAL, PHYSICAL & BIOLOGICAL SCIENCES   7 = LIBERAL ARTS
  8 = ENTRY AND ESSENTIALS   9 = DON'T KNOW

ED EXPECT: EDUCATIONAL EXPECTATION.
  CU = QUIT HIGH SCHOOL   HS = FINISH HIGH SCHOOL
  2Y = GO TO TRADE/TECHNIC SCHOOL OR JUNIOR COLLEGE
  4Y = GO TO 4-YEAR UNIVERSITY   ? = DON'T KNOW

DAYS ABS: NUMBER OF FULL DAYS ABSENT.

CTBS TEST RESULTS ARE REPORTED IN PERCENTILE RANK.

ACAD SC: ACADEMIC SELF CONCEPT. H = HIGH M = MEDIUM L = LOW

HOMEWORK: + = ALL/MOST OF THE TIME 0 = SOMETIME - = SELDOM/NEVER

JOB: F = FULLTIME(30+) H = HALFTIME(20-30) P = PARTTIME(10-20) N = NONE

ACTIVITY: NUMBER OF EXTRACURRICULAR ACTIVIES (1-5)

LIKE SCH: LIKE OF SCHOOL. + = LIKE 0 = NOT SURE - = DISLIKE a-glance report. Some of the teachers were experimenting with alternative forms of grouping to handle the wide range of ability differences in their classrooms. Using cooperative learning techniques, teachers needed to form heterogeneous ability groups. The information in the student report (particularly GPA and CTBS data) provided the teachers with an immediate basis for trial group assignments. As another example, the information derived from the survey's homework questions and the questions about after-school work and extracurricular activities were seen as providing teachers with some basis for dealing with those students having academic troubles or difficulty doing homework assignments. (The interview and survey data to be discussed shortly provide some interesting counterpoints to these expectations.)

Class-At-A-Glance

Teachers generally agreed that once the students-at-a-glance report was available, they could get a pretty good "feel" for their class by "eyeballing" the arrays of data in each column. However, there were additional data from the student survey that were not needed student-by-student but were useful aggregated at the class level. This information pertained to student perceptions of the relationship between classroom teaching and their own learning, and their preferences for particular subject matter or instructional techniques.

Again, unanimity among the work group members regarding the inclusion or exclusion of data for this report was not reached; nevertheless, there was a working consensus on three sets of items: student preferences for particular instructional grouping configurations, student preferences for various kinds of instructional activities, and the degree to which students liked the subject matter of a given class (e.g., mathematics).

Instead of the work group determining the format for this report, the CSE staff used this opportunity to get teacher reactions to several different report formats ranging from a straightforward tabular presentation to graphics using the SAS statistical system.

Although they had no trouble interpreting the results, teachers immediately rejected the tabular format. And although they were moderately impressed with the pretty graphics produced by SAS, they were again adamantly opposed to receiving three sheets of paper rather than one. Moreover, they actually liked the simplicity of a cruder graphics display (see Figure 18.2)—thus their decision was quick and easy to make.

During these discussions, the clinical-social distinctions regarding the importance and use of information emerged again. Aggregating data at the class level seemed to provoke another issue: a reaction to data as if they were

FIGURE 18.2. Class-At-A-Glance Report

```
                    CLASS AT A GLANCE
                        FALL 84

SELECTION NO:   XXX
NO. ENROLLED STUDENTS:    35
NO. STUDENTS TAKING SURVEY:  35
```

```
               INSTRUCTIONAL GROUPING PREFERENCES
   ALONE            XXXXXXXXXXXXXXXXXXXX--*************
   WHOLE CLASS      XXXXXXXXXXXXXXXXXX------************
   HOM SMALL CLASS  XXXXXXXXXXXXXXXXXXXXXXX----*******
   HET SMALL CLASS  XXXXXXXXXXXXXXXXXXXXXXX---**********

         XXX LIKE     --- UNDECIDED     *** DISLIKE
```

```
                    LIKING OF MATHEMATICS
   LIKE VERY MUCH
   LIKE SOME          *************************
   UNDECIDED          **********************
   DISLIKE SOME       *
   DISLIKE VERY MUCH  *
```

```
                    STUDENT ACTIVITY PREFERENCE
   LISTEN TEACHER     XXXXXXXXXXXXXXXXXXXXXX------********
   GO FIELD TRIPS     XXXXXXXXXXXXXXXXXXXXXXXXXXX---*****
   DO RESEARCH ETC    XXXXXXXXX---**********************
   LISTEN STUDENT     XXXXXXXXXXXXX------****************
   LISTEN SPEAKER     XXXXXXXXXXXXXXXXXXXXXXXXXX--*******
   CLASS DISCUSSION   XXXXXXXXXXXXXXXXXXXXXXXXX----******
   BUILD/DRAW THING   XXXXXXXXXXXXXXXX---------*********
   DO PROBLEM/ANSWER  XXXXXXXXXXXXXXX--------*************
   TAKE TEST/QUIZ     XXXXXXXXXXXX------*****************
   MAKE FILM/RECORD   XXXXXXXXXXXXXXXX--------************
   ACT THINGS OUT     XXXXXXXXXXX--------****************
   READ FOR FUN       XXXXXXXXXXXXXXXXXXXXX---------*******
   READ FOR INFO      XXXXXXXXXXXXXXXX------**********
   INTERVIEW PEOPLE   XXXXXXXXXXXXX---------************
   DO PROJECT PLNED   XXXXXXXXXXXXXXXXXXX-------**********
   DO PROJECT I PLN   XXXXXXXXXXXXXXXX----------**********
```

inherently directive. For example, teachers were concerned about whether the information in the sample class report "tells" the teacher *not* to assign research projects to a class because they are the least-liked class activity; or did the information merely provide a context for increasing teachers' understanding when dealing with student affect, dispositions, and so forth, when they assign research projects? We will return to this later.

School-At-A-Glance

Up to this point, information was organized by students in classes, either as individual data points or aggregated at the class level. In moving to the school level, a significant shift in orientation along the clinical-to-social data-use continuum is required; all teachers must now look at the same data set from the perspective of the organization's needs, decision making, planning, evaluation, and so forth.

Interestingly, it was when this level of information aggregation was considered that administrators became noticeably more involved and teachers became more inactive in the discussion of what to include. Perhaps this was due, in part, to the way CSE staff structured the work group meetings or to the obvious link between traditional roles and organizational structures: the teachers responsible for what goes on behind the classroom door and the principals responsible for school-wide issues that have impact at the building level.

In any case, the school-at-a-glance report that eventually emerged (see Figures 18.3 through 18.6) was influenced largely by the principal's interest in what he saw as the issues addressed by data from the student survey that were of immediate concern to the entire high school. These were:

1. What are the curricular goal emphases at the high school? What should they be?
2. What do students and parents want? How do these perceptions and expectations jibe with what students actually do upon graduation?
3. What are the implications of answers to these questions for the school's special career-focused program and for student comfort in selecting a career path in this program?

Basically, the analyses reported in Figures 18.3 through 18.6 explore data relevant to the first two issues by combining student survey results with other variables from the district's information system. It should be emphasized that although it was certainly the intent of our project to capture data relevant to the school in these reports, we were also concerned with more general analysis and reporting issues such as:

The optimal balance of descriptive text and graphics
The relative appeal of one graphical mode over another

Ease of interpreting graphical techniques for representing the relationships between two or more variables

The amount of information to be contained in any one report

To be sure, many graphic techniques are available. None that we have used thus far are particularly original. Nonetheless, knowing about bar charts, histograms, pie charts, frequency polygons, and so forth is one thing, while using them in certain contexts for certain purposes is quite another thing. It is quite clear that well-known graphic techniques can be misused or misinterpreted, or be irrelevant for the intended purpose (see, for example, discussions in Horwitz & Ferleger, 1980; Huff, 1954; and Tufte, 1983).

In an enlightening and creative book on graphic methods, Tufte (1983) notes that "Graphical excellence . . . is the well-designed presentation of interesting data—a matter of substance, of statistics, and of design" (p. 51). Following Tufte's principles underlying quality visual presentation of quantitative data (p. 15), the reports displayed in Figures 18.3 through 18.6 reflect deliberate attempts to:

- Include just enough narrative to explain the major trends embedded in the graphs and include only the most relevant numerical results upon which the graphs were based.
- Experiment with different graphical techniques that may represent the same data but highlight different emphases. The two graphs in Figure 18.3, for example, are based on the same survey questions but call attention to different comparisons. The first graph highlights relative emphases on the schooling functions (social, intellectual, personal, vocational), while the second highlights the difference between perspectives (school's emphasis versus students' preference).
- Organize visual displays thematically, with one theme per page, each successive page building upon previous ones, and all pages adding up to a reasonable (not overly data-laden) foray into the issues of concern to the group.
- Go beyond a simple univariate treatment of information but not overly complicate the analytical and graphical treatments of data. The comparisons by grade level and sex (Figures 18.4 and 18.5) and bivariate relationships in Figure 18.6 are illustrative.
- Bring to bear a variety of information from a variety of sources (e.g., student survey, extant information systems, and district records).

We must emphasize again that our reports were designed primarily as experiments to test the feasibility of various data displays; as such, they only

(Text continues on p. 200)

196 Instructional Information Systems and Educational Realities

FIGURE 18.3. School-At-A-Glance Report, Page 1

Student Survey Results
May, 1984   School-At-A-Glance

FUNCTIONS OF SCHOOLING

Social Development
 Instruction that helps students learn to get along with others, prepares students for social and civic responsibility, develops students' awareness and appreciation of our own and other cultures.

Intellectual (Academic) Development
 Instruction in basic skills in mathematics, reading, and written and verbal communication and in critical thinking and problem solving abilities.

Personal Development
 Instruction that builds self-confidence, self-discipline, creativity, and the ability to think independently.

Vocational Development
 Instruction that prepares students for employment, developing the skills necessary for getting a job, developing an awareness about career choices and alternatives.

Some Student Perceptions:
(see survey questions 90 & 91; note wording --
students could only choose one)

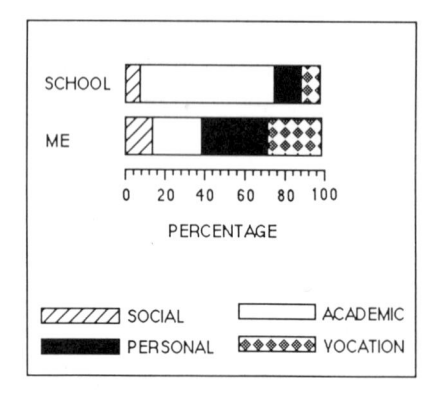

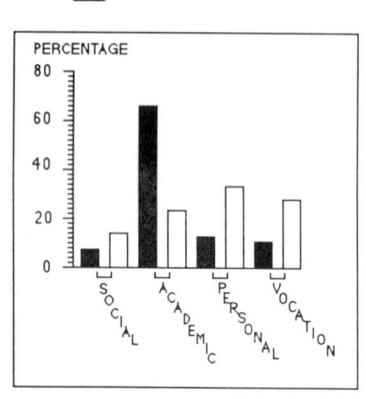

Students perceive the school as emphasizing mainly the academic function; from the students' point of view, however, they tend to spread the emphasis around to the other goal areas, particularly the personal and vocational functions.

> Congruency:
> 35% of the students place the most importance on the same goal area they see the school as emphaasizing. To put it the opposite way, nearly 2/3 of the students would prefer a different goal emphasis than the one they perceive.

FIGURE 18.4. School-At-A-Glance Report, Page 2

Page 2

DO THESE PERCEPTIONS CHANGE DEPENDING UPON GRADE LEVEL?

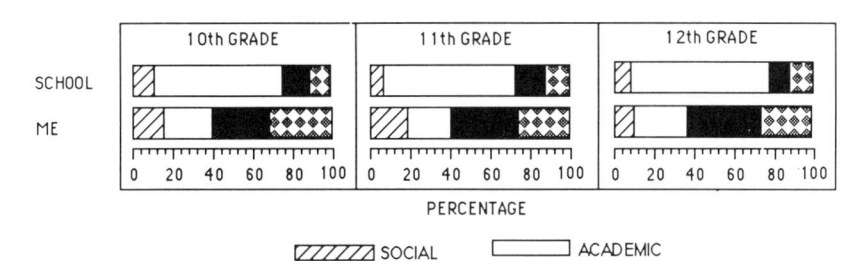

[Bar charts for 10th GRADE, 11th GRADE, 12th GRADE showing SCHOOL and ME percentages, 0-100]

PERCENTAGE

////// SOCIAL   ▭ ACADEMIC
███ PERSONAL   ◆◆◆◆ VOCATION

The trends, if any, are slight. Emphasis on Personal Development increases across grades (29% of 10th graders, 33% of 11th Graders and 38% of 12th graders) while emphasis on Social Development (16% in 10th grade, 17% in 11th grade, 11% in 12th grade) and Vocational Development (31% in 10th grade, 26% in 11th grade, 25% in 12th grade) decreases.

DO THESE PERCEPTION CHANGES DEPEND UPON SEX?

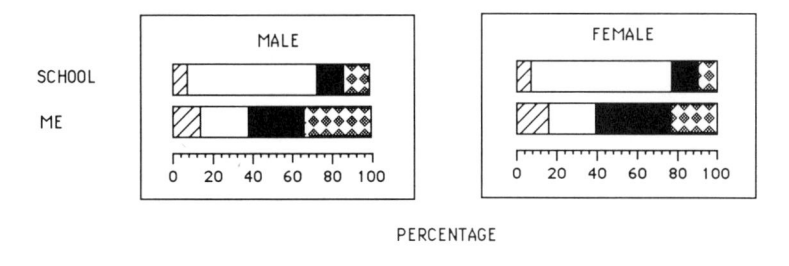

[Bar charts for MALE and FEMALE showing SCHOOL and ME percentages, 0-100]

PERCENTAGE

////// SOCIAL   ▭ ACADEMIC
███ PERSONAL   ◆◆◆◆ VOCATION

Boys place greater emphasis on vocational development than girls (33% of boys versus 22% of the girls) while girls place greater emphasis on Personal Development than boys (37% of girls versus 29% of boys).

198   *Instructional Information Systems and Educational Realities*

FIGURE 18.5. School-At-A-Glance Report, Page 3

Page 3

STUDENT ASPIRATIONS AND EXPECTATIONS
(Survey questions 6, 7, and 8)

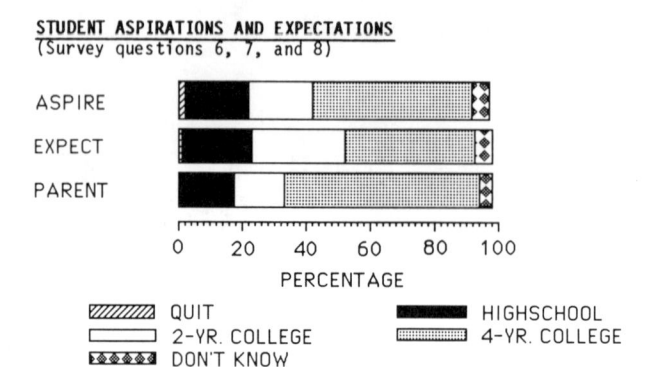

ASPIRE
EXPECT
PARENT

0   20   40   60   80   100
PERCENTAGE

▨▨ QUIT	■■ HIGHSCHOOL
☐ 2-YR. COLLEGE	▦▦ 4-YR. COLLEGE
✸✸✸ DON'T KNOW	

MAIN TREND: Half of the students would like to go to a 4 year college or university in contrast with only 22% aspiring to attend a 2-year college. Their expectations, however, drop by about ten percent; 40% expect to go to university and 30% expect to go to vocational school/junior college. Students perceive their parents' attitudes to be more in line with students' aspirations than with students expectations.

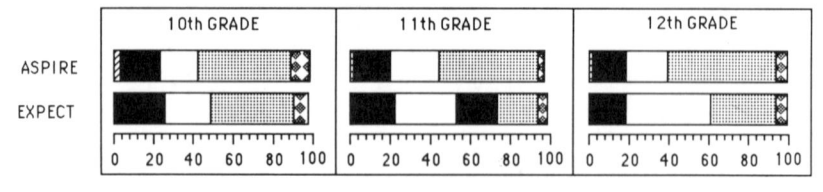

	10th GRADE	11th GRADE	12th GRADE
ASPIRE			
EXPECT			
	0 20 40 60 80 100	0 20 40 60 80 100	0 20 40 60 80 100

PERCENTAGE

▨▨ QUIT	■■ HIGHSCHOOL
☐ 2-YR. COLLEGE	▦▦ 4-YR. COLLEGE
✸✸✸ DON'T KNOW	

The general trend in <u>aspirations</u> is toward more education (both 2 year and 4 year college) across grades while the trend in <u>expectations</u> is toward less four-year college and more two-year college. While the percentage of students <u>aspiring</u> to attend a four-year college increases slightly across grades (from 48% at 10th grade to 53% at 12th grade), the percentage of students that <u>expect</u> to attend a four-year college decrease slightly (44% at 10th grade to 38% at 12th grade). The percentage of students expecting to attend a trade school or junior college increases substantially across grades (22% in 10th grade, 30% in 11th grade, and 39% in 12th grade).

> NOTE: According to district records, only 5-7% of all graduating seniors go on to a 4-year college.

FIGURE 18.6. School-At-A-Glance Report, Page 4

Page 4

GPA: Averages for Males and Females at Each Grade Level

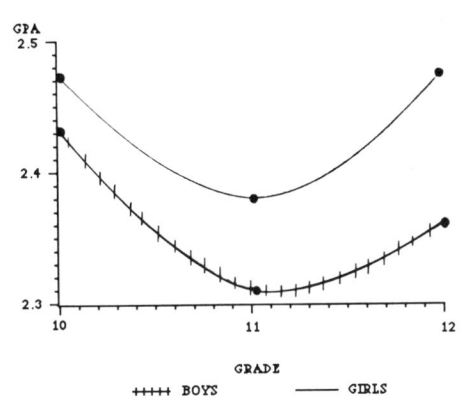

++++ BOYS   —— GIRLS

Two slight tendencies are apparent: (1) Boys show lower GPA averages than girls, and (2) GPA goes down in the 11th grade.

DAYS ABSENT: Averages for Males and Females at Each Grade Level

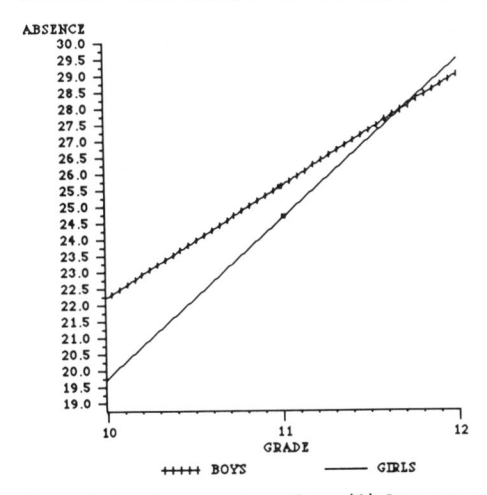

++++ BOYS   —— GIRLS

Several trends are noteworthy: (1) Boys are generally absent more days than girls; (2) Absences increase almost linearly from the 10th through the 12th grades (roughly 3 to 4 more days absent in each grade level); (3) The increase in days absent over grade levels is more exaggerated for girls than boys (in fact, girls slightly surpass boys in the 12th grade).

scratch the surface of what can be done analytically with the data in a comprehensive information system.

School-at-a-glance data, obviously, are useful primarily at the school level. Since promoting and studying school-level planning and development activities were beyond the scope of our project, we did not inquire about the use of these reports. However, at-a-glance reports for students and classes were produced for each teacher, and it is the use of these reports that we turn to next.

TEACHERS' REACTIONS TO AT-A-GLANCE REPORTS

It will be recalled that only a select group of five to 10 teachers, out of a staff of 83, participated heavily in the development of the student and class report forms. Even so, these teachers were eager to see how, if at all, they could use these reports in their classrooms. We were particularly interested, therefore, in the reactions of the remaining school staff. Their reactions were obtained through interviews and a written survey.

Our interview data is remarkably compatible with and supportive of the survey's findings. We will simply summarize these combined findings here. They are reported in more detail elsewhere (Dorr-Bremme, 1985; Sirotnik & Burstein, 1985).

The results suggested that nearly two-thirds of the teachers used the students-at-a-glance report one or more times during the study period. Little use was reported for the class-at-a-glance form. Only two instances of organizational (versus individual) uses of data were recorded; these occurred within departments and were focused on student placement. None of the teachers indicated that they were aware of any misuse of the information provided in the reports. A few nevertheless expressed their concern about the possibilities of bias and prejudgment made possible by easy access to the information. Only a few teachers had any recommendations for changing either form; those that did had different ideas for what to delete and what to add.

The information on the students-at-a-glance report that received the most attention from teachers included grade point average, educational expectations, self-concept, CTBS scores, and absenteeism. The predominate pattern of use was the juxtaposition of each student's GPA and CTBS scores first, followed by a comparison of that contrast with the student's educational expectations. By inference, and given the interpretive context of teacher remarks in many discussions of these data, we concluded that most teachers accepted the CTBS and GPA data as unconditional indicators of student ability and performance.

We turn now to a discussion of the many concerns and issues that have emerged over the course of our investigation.

CLINICAL VERSUS SOCIAL USES OF INFORMATION

Often in the deliberations over which items from the student survey data might be useful, particularly for class- and school-level reports, considerable differences of opinion occurred among work group members. Usually the debate seemed to take the form, "I don't see how I could use this piece of information in teaching a student" versus "I think these data could help us (me) make planning decisions about the school (my class)." In effect, the disagreements were more a matter of differing orientation to information use than about content.

CSE staff members intervened a number of times in these discussions attempting to distinguish the individual, diagnostic, clinical perspective on the one hand, from the organizational, planning, social perspective on the other. These interventions helped clarify and facilitate the discussion and also permitted us to observe that some teachers placed less value than others on the social use of information. Nevertheless, teachers could sort out what substance to include in the reports. They did, for example, agree that student answers to the question "How much do you like mathematics?" had little diagnostic use at the individual level, yet when aggregated at the classroom level could help the teacher better understand class climate and learning environment issues.

Judging from our interviews and surveys of teachers, the social perspective for information was generally a foreign concept for most of the high school teaching staff. This is not to say that when given the appropriate opportunities (purpose, setting, time, training, and so forth), teachers were unable to work with information at levels other than the individual student. It was clearly the case, however, that without such opportunities, teachers were not inclined towards selecting items for, or using analyses based upon, aggregated data for groups. Our working assumption was and continues to be that multilevel analyses and interpretations of school-based information have potential for facilitating individual–diagnostic, class–instructional, and school–planning decisions and evaluation. The results from this study suggest to us the importance of an educative or training function for collaborators, teachers, and administrators.

The clinical–social distinction is a familiar one when assessing organizational settings, but its manifestation within a school as people try to design and make sense out of comprehensive data sets deserves further study.

Clearly, this distinction has a direct bearing upon statistical and psychometric concerns arising out of multilevel analysis. Also worthy of study are the interacting effects of the sociocultural context and the circumstances of schooling and teaching that may predispose teachers to "think clinically." We refer here to institutional features such as the hierarchical organization of schooling, traditional roles of administrators vis-à-vis teachers, and the ways teachers have for developing and organizing their "working knowledge" (Kennedy, 1984).

The clinical-social distinction cuts across all the issues discussed below. The interested reader should refer to our paper on this topic (Sirotnik, Dorr-Bremme, & Burstein, 1985).

TEACHERS AS RESEARCHERS/DATA ANALYSTS

During our meetings with the work group, teachers and administrators came to behave more and more like trained researchers. They asked probing questions of the data and wanted more sophisticated treatments of the data (e.g., bivariate and multivariate analyses). This corresponds with the observation we made earlier that school staff members can interact with information in a sophisticated manner when given the opportunity to do so. Certainly part of their behavior may have been due to our presence and our deliberate suggestions regarding the ways in which data can be explored. However, this question-asking approach to data exploration was apparent in the work group from the beginning and was evidenced by several teachers who had never been involved in the work group.

Our point here is to cast some doubt on the often-heard researcher's lament that teachers don't really care about having more and better information and, even if they did, wouldn't know what to do with it. The fact of the matter may be less one of caring and more one of professional opportunity. The usual circumstances of teaching and administrating do not permit the kind of time necessary for *informed* dialog, decision making, action-taking, and evaluation that characterize a dynamic and renewing organization (Goodlad, 1975).

As the age of information explodes upon us, along with the technology to handle it, the pressures for organizational response become impossible to ignore. Many organizations in the private sector have welcomed, for example, a new role for workers as informed decision makers (Peters & Waterman, 1982). Our belief is that schools and school districts will need to respond in similar ways, encouraging administrators and teachers to participate more fully as professionals and engage in inquiry processes that can be significantly advanced by the kind of information systems we have been discussing.

THE POWER OF NUMBERS

Teachers presented with quantitative data usually treat it *prescriptively*—standardized test scores are the prime example. It is not surprising to see school staff, therefore, reacting to survey data as if they contain the prescription of educational change instead of providing just one more heuristic for helping to understand the possible directions for change.

The typical way in which we observed this phenomenon is illustrated in the following exchange (paraphrased here) that occurred among the members of our work group:

> *Person A*: If we allow these data to make decisions for us, then we must be concerned with the validity of the student responses.
> *Person B*: I give tests—I have a vested interest, as a teacher, in student assessment. Would I reconsider this method of evaluation just because kids say they don't like tests? Maybe so.
> *Person A*: I think learning to read is more important than any subject matter per se. So I assign reading both for content and skill development. If the survey indicated students don't like textbooks, should I not bother to teach them to read?
> *Person C*: It seems that the dilemma here is more a question of perceptions regarding what the data mean.

Person C, of course, hit the nail on the head. We added our own two cents worth to this discussion by noting that data do not make decisions—people do. Thus, information is best used not as a blueprint for action but as a catalyst for, and adjunct to, staff discussion and decision making. These kinds of discussions occurred a number of times throughout the course of the project, and it seemed to be of some considerable relief to the work group to know that it's OK to be proactive rather than reactive in regard to information and the use of information.

INFORMATION AND SELF-FULFILLING PROPHECIES: ISSUES OF MISUSE AND ABUSE

The potential for misusing information—violating confidentiality, creating self-fulfilling prophecies regarding individuals, misinterpretations, overinterpretations, inappropriate applications of data, and so forth—has always been a possibility in districts and schools. The presence of comprehensive and accessible information systems exacerbates the problem.

It is a serious problem and we have been sensitive to it in the more general context of developing and using computerized information systems (Sirotnik, 1984a). The teachers in the work group, as well as several others on the faculty, also worried about the abuse of people through the misuse of data, and they voiced their concern several times over the course of this project. Interestingly, this concern was provoked by the presence of information related to self-concept, homework compliance, and educational expectations. Yet the ever-present standardized test scores have always had the potential for misuse by disenfranchising many students in low-tracked classes from full participation in the call for academic excellence (Oakes, 1985).

Clearly related to the "power of numbers" is the concern of teachers about the potential for biasing and prejudging created by giving teachers student profiles—particularly CTBS-type test scores and GPA—early in the semester. We would not be troubled about this if it were only a theoretical possibility. Unfortunately, it is not. As teachers went about exploring the information on the students-at-a-glance form—comparing GPA, test scores, and academic expectations—no explicit instructional concern was evidenced for the many students who were low on all three variables. We do not mean to imply that teachers were not, in fact, concerned about and responsive to these students' needs in classes; we did not observe these teachers at work in their classrooms. Our observations are based strictly upon teachers interacting with information. From these observations, we infer that low-achieving students are seen by teachers as living up to, or perhaps "down" to, their abilities and expectations. (Pedagogically, of course, this assumption conflicts with everything we know about the power of individualization, small group instruction, mastery learning, and so forth.)

Our inference is supported by the way teachers did make use of the student information. They flagged those students not living up to their abilities and expectations—that is, the college-bound, high-CTBS-scoring students with low GPAs. In our view, then, those teachers who expressed great concern over the prejudicial effects of student information had an important point to make. Moreover, we find no comfort in the old notion that it is people, not the information, that carry the potential for abuse. It may well be that the costs associated with the misuse of information outweigh the advantages of individual reports like students-at-a-glance.

Our recommendation at this point, however, is not to throw out the baby with the bath. If information has the *potential* to be useful—and we believe it has—then those who use it must reflect seriously on the purposes for use and the training required for using information appropriately. For example, do CTBS scores represent useful, valid, and reliable diagnostic information, measures of scholastic ability, and so forth? If not, what information might be more useful to classroom teachers and how would it be more appropriately utilized? Needless to say, this whole issue is bound to become messier before it becomes clearer. Our view is that we should remain sensitive to the misuse of data within the context of the constructive use of information systems.

INFORMATION VERSUS KNOWLEDGE

Implicit in all of these emerging themes is the distinction between information and knowledge. It is widely acknowledged that we have passed from an industrial society into one of information and technology. Much of the relevant information on any given school can now be stored on a few diskettes and manipulated at will with relatively inexpensive microcomputer hardware and software. With the invention of laser disk storage and retrieval technology, information for an entire large school district will be able to be stored on one or two devices small enough to carry around in a shirt pocket.

Our concern is the "tail wagging the dog" phenomenon, the technological seduction of practitioners and evaluation researchers, into collecting information simply because it's there. Information is now cheap; knowledge, however, is still at a premium.

The importance of this observation is highlighted by our experience in this project. We have noted throughout our discussions how teachers become trapped by the apparent veracity of computerized information and fail to critically evaluate the meaning of information in the context of their own practice. When we speak of knowledge, therefore, we have in mind the pursuit of understanding, the search for interpretive meaning of phenomena in context. We have in mind, obviously, the idea of *informed* understanding. Information serves as a catalyst for this process; as does, more importantly, the process serve as a catalyst for seeking out appropriate information.

THE PERSONAL KNOWLEDGE OF TEACHERS

Yet another issue related to what we have been discussing is the competing epistemological paradigms inherent in the contrast between rigorous, operationally defined, comprehensive information systems on the one hand, and the primary way in which teachers go about establishing meaning in what they do (personal knowledge), on the other. A number of researchers who have done in-depth case studies of how teachers make day-to-day decisions in their classrooms have arrived at similar conclusions: teachers make decisions based on unique, even artistic, ways of combining intuition, experience, conventional wisdom, and so forth, accumulated over their years of teaching and their socialization into the school setting. Moreover, the minute-to-minute decisions teachers make during an instructional period are laced with interacting contingencies not easily touched by information systems, no matter how responsive (MacKay, 1978).

The idea of personal knowledge, of course, is not new; we have borrowed the term from its inventor, Michael Polanyi (1958). In particular, we are interested in his notion of the *"personal participation* of the knower in all acts of understanding" (p. vii). Others have made use of similar ideas in their studies of how teachers and administrators develop and make use of knowledge in practice; see, for example, Kennedy's concept of "working knowledge" (1984) and the inquiry paradigm suggested by Tharp and Gallimore (1982).

It is not surprising, therefore, that the teachers in our study said they used the at-a-glance reports primarily at the beginning of the semester. Moreover, in those instances where teachers were in year-long classes, they said they had little need for the reports since they were already familiar with each of their students. In truth, it takes only a short amount of time before teachers learn about students based upon their own personal "information systems." At a minimum, therefore, it seems clear that an essential feature of a viable information system must be its flexibility; that is, it must be able to produce student and class reports tailored to the immediate requests of individual teachers anytime during the school year.

Although we noted the epistemological conflict between the personal knowledge base of teachers and the data base of an information system, this may be more a conflict in philosophy than in practice. The trick in bringing together information and working knowledge is to acknowledge the "scientific" credibility of both approaches and establish a genuine process of critical inquiry that involves the users in the construction and use of their own information system.

THE QUEST FOR SIMPLICITY IN COMPLEXITY

Connected to teachers' reliance upon their own personal representations of "data" was their recurrent demand that the report forms be as simple as possible. Although content was of importance to work group members, of equal or greater importance was their wish for simple, short, uncluttered, nonnumeric displays of data. Whatever they contained, the students-at-a-glance and class-at-a-glance reports must each fit on a single 8½ × 11 page.

Notwithstanding the group's concern for simplicity, schooling and its assessment are extraordinarily complex; there are multiple data sources, multiple domains of potential data, multiple levels at which information is used, multiple methods for obtaining data, and multiple analytic and reporting techniques. Yet given this complexity, teachers still seek simple representations of it.

We do not mean to imply that this is an unworthy goal or that a complex problem necessitates a complex solution. In fact, as a society, we face a growing need to provide a more human side to the products of an increasingly technological world (see Naisbitt's 1982 "high tech/high touch" megatrend). Our point here is merely to note the tension between the legitimate requirement for simplicity and the complexity of schooling and the school setting.

THE EDUCATIVE FUNCTION IN COLLABORATION

Finally, we have been quite self-conscious regarding our role in this project. Our presence in the work group was not unobtrusive, but neither was it unduly interventionist. We tried to walk the fine line separating the observer-researcher from the participant-director.

Throughout the discussion here, we have tried to make clear how we ourselves may have shaped events in what we hope was an educative rather than a directive role. We did not intend to be university-based educators bringing their words of wisdom to the less informed levels of school practitioners. We think that the educative function in collaborative research is reciprocal; during this project we have learned from teachers and administrators about the realities of schools and about the meaning of information in the context of practice.

What this suggests to us is the need for someone or some group to fill such an educative and collaborative role about issues in the development and use of information systems. Given the trends toward increased use of technology, decentralization, and the reconfiguration of resources, it is easy to imagine a staff position at the building level explicitly set aside for inquiry activities using comprehensive information systems.

CONCLUDING REMARKS

As we reflect upon our immediate experience in this project, our more general experience as educational researchers and evaluators, and what we have heard from others working in similar areas of investigation, we are led to the conclusion that the comprehensive information system for local school improvement, developed and used by staff at the building level, is a viable concept. Moreover, computerized Management Information Systems are probably the wave of the future whether teachers and administrators like it or not. Regardless of how sanguine or cynical one might be regarding the potential usefulness of school-based information systems, it would seem wise to investigate carefully the conditions and circumstances under which such systems can serve the needs and interests of those who use them.

Our own investigation, like most of the other studies we have seen to date, was far from definitive. Clearly, it will be from an accumulation of such investigations that significant and generalizable directions for schools will emerge. Immediately accessible information systems are a relatively new phenomenon for schools and school people. It is our hope that the idea will not be packaged and sold to districts and schools like so many other unsuccessful school interventions over the years. It is our hope, rather, that the concept will be explored collaboratively by researchers and practitioners in the context of educational practice.

ACKNOWLEDGMENTS: We would like to thank Don Dorr-Bremme, who made significant contributions throughout all phases of the project, and Phil Ender and Chi-Ping Chou, who were responsible for the development of software for the prototype computerized reports that were later implemented by the school district's data processing division. Needless to say, the project itself could not have been done without the cooperation and collaboration of the teachers and administration of the participating school, the staff of the district's data processing division, and the district administrators who supported the project effort.

REFERENCES

Burstein, L. (1983). *Using multilevel methods for local school improvement: A beginning conceptual synthesis*. Los Angeles: University of California, Center for the Study of Evaluation.

———. (1984a, April). *Information use in local school improvement: A multilevel perspective*. Paper presented at the Annual Meeting of the American Educational Research Association, New Orleans.

———. (1984b). Use of existing data bases in program evaluation and school improvement. *Educational Evaluation and Policy Analysis*, 6(3), 307–18.

Dorr-Bremme, D. (1985, November). Contextual influences in developing a school-based comprehensive information system. In *Comprehensive information systems for local school improvement: A reality test in secondary schools* (Report to National Institute of Education, NIE-G-84-0112, P1). Los Angeles: University of California, Center for the Study of Evaluation.

Goodlad, J. I. (1975). *Dynamics of educational change*. New York: McGraw-Hill.

Horwitz, L., & Ferleger, L. (1980). *Statistics for social change*. Boston: South End Press.

Huff, D. (1954). *How to lie with statistics*. New York: Norton.

Kennedy, M. M. (1984). How evidence alters understanding and decisions. *Educational Evaluation and Policy Analysis, 6*(3), 207–26.

MacKay, R. (1978). How teachers know: A case of epistemological conflict. *Sociology of Education, 51*, 177–87.

Naisbitt, J. (1982). *Megatrends*. New York: Warner Books.

Oakes, J. (1985). *Keeping track: How schools structure inequality*. New Haven: Yale University Press.

Peters, T. J., & Waterman, R. H. (1982). *In search of excellence*. New York: Harper & Row.

Polanyi, M. (1985). *Personal knowledge*. Chicago: University of Chicago Press.

Sirotnik, K. A. (1984a, April). *Using vs. being used by school information systems*. Paper presented at the Annual Meeting of the American Educational Research Association, New Orleans.

―――. (1984b). An outcome-free conception of schooling: Implications for school-based inquiry and information systems. *Educational Evaluation and Policy Analysis, 6*(3), 226–39.

―――. (1984c). *Principals and practice of contextual appraisal for schools* (Occasional Paper No. 5). Los Angeles: University of California, Laboratory in School and Community Education.

Sirotnik, K. A., & Burstein, L. (1985). *Making sense out of comprehensive school-based information systems: An exploratory investigation* (NIE-G-83-0001). Los Angeles: University of California, Center for the Study of Evaluation.

Sirotnik, K. A., Burstein, L., & Thomas, C. (1983). *Systemic evaluation* (Report to National Institute of Education, NIE-G-83-0001). Los Angeles: University of California, Center for the Study of Evaluation.

Sirotnik, K. A., Dorr-Bremme, D., & Burstein, L. (1985). *Social vs. clinical perspectives on the use of information: Implications for school-based information systems* (Report to National Institute of Education, NIE-G-83-0001). Los Angeles: University of California, Center for the Study of Evaluation.

Sirotnik, K. A., & Oakes, J. (1981a). *Toward a comprehensive educational appraisal system: A contextual perspective* (Occasional Paper No. 2). Los Angeles: University of California, Laboratory in School and Community Education.

―――. (1981b). A contextual appraisal system for schools: Medicine or madness? *Educational Leadership, 39*, 164–73.

―――. (1986). Critical inquiry for school renewal: Liberating theory and practice. In K. A. Sirotnik and J. Oakes (Eds.), *Critical perspectives on the organization and improvement of schooling*. Boston: Kluwer-Nijhoff.

Tharp, R. G., & Gallimore, R. (1982). Inquiry process in program development. *Journal of Community Psychology, 10*, 103–18.

Tufte, E. R. (1983). *The visual display of quantitative information*. Cheshire, CT: Graphics Press.

19
Making Instructional Information Systems Teacher-Friendly

JEAN A. KING

This year a friend of mine who teaches two sections of English in a nearby middle school decided to take to heart the message of a supervisor who recommended that she collect and review her students' standardized test scores at the beginning of the year. The logic was flawless. With objective test data about each of her 63 students, she could start the year knowing where students stood relative to each other, knowledge important to her early in the year for such activities as developing units, selecting materials, and creating groups. So my friend innocently asked in the main office where the computer printouts for last year's CTBS (Comprehensive Test of Basic Skills) results were kept.

The clerk said she thought they were in the green filing cabinet. They weren't.

The school secretary said they must be in the principal's office. They weren't.

The principal said perhaps the counselor had them. She didn't. After a day the counselor succeeded in locating a dusty cardboard box that contained *last* year's scores; unfortunately, those students had been promoted to ninth grade in a different school.

Because my friend's school is part of an educational improvement project sponsored by an outside advocacy group, my friend—somewhat bewildered but by no means defeated—asked the project leader for assistance. Having time for activities such as these, the project leader called the district's testing office and asked for another copy of the test results. The testing director wondered what had happened to the first copy—it apparently *had* been sent—but was persuaded to send a second. It came a week later.

Meanwhile, the project leader volunteered to help my friend make a chart showing the results of a supplemental reading test (the DRP or Degree of Reading Power) that he had just administered to her students. He also agreed to add to this chart the results of a diagnostic spelling test my friend had given. Out of the 63 students, 45 had scores on both of these. Within a week, the project leader tested the students with missing scores on the DRP and the spelling test. Now all students had at least two scores listed on the chart. When the copy of the computer printout arrived, the project director's secretary added to the chart CTBS scores for the 37 students whose scores had been recorded. (It's not known why the remaining 26 students had no CTBS scores; numbers were never found for them.)

The final result of all this effort, then, was a chart containing CTBS scores, a DRP score, and a diagnostic spelling test score for 37 out of 63 students, or roughly 60% of the students in two classes. It took two and a half weeks and seven people's energy to gather an incomplete set of data that, my friend later told me, was of little value because too many scores were missing and the available scores were so uniformly low that little discrimination was possible. Subscores had not been included on the chart.

And we wonder why teachers don't take advantage of existing data bases in local schools?

Few can deny that the recent emergence of computerized Instructional Information Systems in school districts marks another addition to the long list of technological advances with the potential to improve American education. School systems are now able to have an IIS store information on student demographics, placement, achievement, instructional materials, teachers, finances, or whatever, so that the compilation of relevant data that would once have taken days or weeks can literally be done in seconds. It is vital to discuss how such systems can improve reporting, projecting, and decision making in local central offices—and even in state departments of education, because aggregated data should inform the activities of top-level administrators.

However, the effect of an IIS on teachers is arguably more important than its effect on central office policymaking because the effect of such systems will be most potent if they can help classroom teachers do a better job of teaching children. Student learning is, after all, what schools are all about, and to the extent that an IIS can help teachers teach better and ultimately help students learn better, information systems will become a meaningful and permanent part of current reform efforts.

With computer technology, placing this kind of information directly into teachers' hands becomes much easier. But this very ease brings with it the capacity to frighten good teachers like my friend, causing them to ask about the worth of such information and making them question the value of the technology itself.

This chapter therefore asks two questions: (1) What are the likely reactions of classroom teachers to the installation of an IIS? and (2) How can administrators increase the likelihood that teachers will take advantage of an IIS?

TEACHERS' REACTIONS TO INSTRUCTIONAL INFORMATION SYSTEMS

Although an optimistic outlook is an essential prerequisite for people working in schools, misplaced optimism about the likely reaction of teachers to an IIS may delay its successful implementation and use in the classroom. Three factors mitigate against teachers' use of an IIS and make it improbable that teachers will greet these systems with open minds and arms. These factors are: (1) the acknowledged difficulty of successfully implementing *any* instructional change; (2) the potentially negative attitude of teachers in particular towards a computer-based innovation; and (3) the low probability that such an innovation, in the form of an Instructional Information System, will provide meaningful information of value for classroom decision making.

The history of American education documents how difficult it is to effect change in the classroom. A study by Larry Cuban demonstrates how little change has occurred in instructional techniques in secondary school classrooms from 1900 to 1980 (Cuban, 1982). As Cuban puts it, his research shows how "impervious high school classrooms have been to reform efforts over the last half century" (p. 113). The few innovations that have occurred were "overshadowed by the persistent continuity of teaching practices" (p. 117). With the exception of instructional methodology from the progressive movement, the same continuity can be found at the elementary and middle-school levels as well (Goodlad & associates, 1970). To paraphrase a line from an old poem, innovations may come, and innovations may go, but large group instruction and the lecture method go on forever.

Two examples suffice to make the point. The advent of educational television in the 1950s and 1960s led some to suggest that the role of teachers in the classrooms of the future could be radically altered (Asheim, 1962; Chataway, 1965). Today, television programs do play a small role in many classrooms, but they have certainly not altered classroom practices as dramatically as early advocates hoped they would. A second example of the difficulty of changing classrooms comes from the "alphabet soup" curriculum reform efforts of the early 1960s (for example, BSCS—Biological Sciences Curriculum Study; SAPA—Science, A Process Approach; and MACOS—Man, A Course of Study). Despite carefully developed "teacher-proof" curricula including top-quality audiovisual materials and expensive in-service efforts, these new curricula were often unable to get through the classroom door. And when they did, they were often adapted to fit existing practice. Millions of dollars spent in development led, finally, to a dime's worth of change (Atkin & House, 1981).

To expect that today's Instructional Information Systems will necessarily or even possibly break a long tradition of educational inertia is foolhardy. Common sense and the research literature suggest that IIS developers cannot take implementation for granted. Care and attention must be paid to teachers' reactions if change is to happen in the classroom.

The second factor that may adversely affect the implementation of an IIS in a school system is the negative attitude of many classroom teachers toward technological innovations and particularly toward a computer-based innovation. Cyberphobia (fear of computers) is an affliction affecting millions of Americans, and there is no reason to expect that teachers are excluded from this group. Despite some evidence that teachers hold positive attitudes toward microcomputers in the classroom (e.g., Ingersoll, Smith, & Elliott, 1983-84), Norris and Lumsden (1984) report that most studies indicate that teachers and principals range "somewhere between apathetic and hostile in their attitudes towards computers" (p. 129). In their own study of 450 teachers and administrators, Norris and Lumsden found that educators were "positive toward computers as long as the function of the computers is removed from their experiential world of practice" (p. 132). In other words, as long as someone else has to do the using, teachers are in favor of the computer revolution, but when they themselves are asked to work with a computer, they no longer react positively. Anxiety towards computers in general can make teachers reluctant to work with an IIS, and, as Lane (1982) notes, such resistance "will not be easily brushed aside by helter-skelter enthusiasm" (p. 184).

Another aspect of teachers' negative attitudes is equally important. Many are cynical about instructional innovations—past, present, or future—and choose not to participate until such time as they see that the current change, whatever its form, is either useful to them or here to stay. There are numerous examples of this phenomenon. For example, teachers participating in a million-dollar mastery learning curriculum improvement program in a large urban system reported continual frustration with the logistics of computer-generated and computer-scored tests. One teacher noted, "I've been in this system for 17 years and innovations like this come and go. I just waited for this one to pass me by" (King, 1982).[1]

Computer-assisted instruction (CAI) is a good example of a computer-based innovation with tremendous potential for improving instruction, but one that has yet to be adopted enthusiastically by most teachers. Fisher (1982) gives several reasons why the promise of CAI still remains a promise—for instance, that much software reflects poor pedagogy and that much software does not fit into existing curricula. Smith and Pohland (1974) describe a tearful little girl sitting in front of a terminal after a computer with a particularly malicious glitch had told her to "cry again."

It may not only be computer anxiety and negative experiences with computer innovations that make teachers slow to accept an IIS. Part of classroom teachers' reluctance to adopt a computer-based innovation may be the frequent connection between computers and an approach to curriculum that emphasizes accountability and, in many cases, low-level but easily observable skills. That computers help school systems keep regular tabs on such kinds of student achievement may make computers seem to be on the side of the enemy. Walker (1983) points to the difficulty of using computers to teach subject matter that involves "judgment, intuition, improvisation, and creativity" (p. 104), suggesting that a teacher interested in developing reasoning and critical thinking may well dislike basic-skills objectives that will be measured repeatedly on a system-wide test.

Teacher attitudes, then, are the second factor that may affect the implementation of an IIS. For many teachers, an IIS may be just another technological assault on their classroom that they hope will disappear.

A third factor affecting teachers' responses to an IIS is the likelihood that the system will provide little information of value in classroom decision making. Teachers may not value the kind of objective data typically stored in an IIS. Two studies (David, 1981; King & Thompson, 1983) suggest that many teachers and principals feel that the "objective" information collected in evaluations may well fail to measure the success of their programs. One administrator told David an accepted school system truth when he noted that test scores can always be discredited. As David (1981) puts it: "When people invest their time and energy in a cause they view as worthy, they will seek out and readily accept evidence that their work has not been in vain. Likewise, they will ignore or explain away information that suggests they have failed" (p. 38).

Although it is true that qualitative data can be coded for use in an IIS, even in those rare instances when this is done, teachers can justifiably argue that something is lost in the translation. For people who work on a daily basis with students, computer printouts generated by an IIS may never provide convincing or useful evidence on which to base instructional changes. Evidence supporting teacher judgments seems unnecessary; that contradicting their judgments is not credible.

In their discussion of the use of evaluation and testing data, Kennedy, Apling, and Neumann (1980) note that the decisions teachers make on a regular basis are clinical in nature, dealing with students' instructional, social, and emotional needs or with referrals to special programs. Achievement test scores are of value only if they provide clues that tell a teacher how to adapt instruction to accomplish specific ends. Criterion-referenced tests (CRTs) are far more useful to teachers than tests that rank-order students on a national norm. Data on students' social and emotional needs are subjective, anecdotal, and hard to collect and code, and there are ethical as well as technical problems in using them in information systems. Nonetheless, it is these kinds of data that teachers often rely on to get an intuitive sense of their students' problems. To assume that an IIS can be programmed with data that a teacher can readily apply to classroom decisions is inappropriate. This is unlikely to happen unless someone makes it happen.

An article by Burstein (1984) supports, through omission, my point about the lack of teacher-oriented IIS thinking. Burstein lists what he sees as five current functions for computerized data bases in local districts: long-range planning, pulse monitoring, student decision making, program decision making, and educational policy formulation. Long-range planning, pulse monitoring, and policymaking clearly fall outside the teacher's domain; and as defined in Burstein's article, student and program decision making do not relate directly to classroom activities. Student decision making refers to the "computerized maintenance of student educational histories" for use in individual counseling. Program decision making refers to the use of information by decision makers at the program level (e.g., course offerings, year-to-year class assignments, and monitoring of curriculum suitability).

In other words, of the five possible functions of existing data in local districts listed by Burstein, not one refers to the use of data in the classroom to make instructional decisions. That such *can* be done is documented in Williams and Bank's article (1984) discussing how teachers in Baker District used CRT data to monitor student progress on the system's scope and sequence and alter instructional practices accordingly. But unless an IIS is designed and implemented with the classroom in mind, the strong probability exists that teachers will not see how data can be used instructionally.

The three factors discussed previously—the difficulty of making far-reaching changes of any kind in classroom practices, the negative attitudes of teachers toward computer innovations in particular, and the likelihood that Instructional Information Systems as they are currently conceived will not provide useful information to teachers—must not be ignored by those who want to implement such systems in their schools. However, the impressive potential for an IIS to make valuable new information available to teachers makes it worthwhile to address the question of what can be done to increase the chances that teachers will be both able and willing to use IIS information.

CREATING TEACHER-FRIENDLY SYSTEMS

As other chapters in this book have shown, not every IIS need be designed for use by teachers. Those designing such systems must decide whether or not classroom-level decision making is a priority for their situation. If it is, I would argue that the responsibility for whether or not teachers take advantage of an IIS lies squarely on the shoulders of school system administrators and those technical staff members charged with developing and implementing the system. This is not to say that even if these individuals do everything right the system will work perfectly and please everyone. But if the teachers' perspective is not taken into account when an IIS is established, the likelihood that teachers will run or even walk to the terminals is greatly diminished.

If this is the bad news, the good news is that there *are* things that can be done to encourage teacher participation in an IIS. I will discuss five such activities: (1) including instructional improvement data in the system; (2) insuring quick, easy, and reliable information retrieval; (3) involving *all* teachers in the development and implementation process; (4) creating a professional support system for teacher-users; and (5) leaving teachers' clinical responsibilities alone.

Including Instructional Improvement Data

In the example given at the beginning of this chapter, my friend was unable to do much with the information she finally obtained because it did not speak to her instructional concerns. For her, it was simply not enough to know that many members of her fourth-period class were at the 19th percentile on the CTBS reading test or that they were capable of reading independently only at the second-grade level.

Information for instructional improvement can take two forms in an IIS, curricular achievement and pedagogical.[2] IIS curricular achievement information—for example, tests measuring student achievement of specific learning objectives—can show teachers weak areas in need of additional instruction. The Baker District case study in Williams and Bank (1984) documents the fact that data from an IIS *can* be used by classroom teachers when the information relates directly to a detailed, meaningful curriculum. In the Baker District writing curriculum, for example, teachers use both a district-developed scope and sequence manual and the accompanying computer-scored CRTs for instruction, planning, and monitoring. The system works because the information available to teachers pinpoints specific content with which students are having difficulty. Teachers can then alter their teaching accordingly. Any curriculum person will be quick to point to a necessary caveat in the use of such a system: the level of specificity needed to make objectives explicit may trivialize what students are to learn. The IIS developer as well as the teacher must recognize that the whole of the learning is greater than the parts, and not allow themselves to become like the spider whose entangled students struggle through a web of objectives.

Pedagogical information from an IIS would be distinct from the foregoing type of curricular achievement data. While achievement information would be student-centered, pedagogical information would be teacher-centered. Entries might include lists of instructional resources such as specific chapters in supplementary texts, filmstrips, and other media; alternate teaching strategies; and perhaps summaries of pertinent research. Teachers could use such information to inform and broaden their own instructional practice. To summarize, then, my view is that the best way in which IIS administrators can encourage teachers to use their systems is to include in them practical information for teaching. If IIS information is not immediately applicable to their own classroom concerns, teachers are unlikely to use an IIS.

Insuring Quick, Easy, and Reliable Information Retrieval

The example given at the beginning of this chapter illustrates an obvious point. If it is time-consuming or complicated to use an IIS, teachers—all of whom will attest to being pressed for time—will simply give up. And they can't be blamed. Having functioned in classrooms for years without an IIS, they will continue to do so unless IIS-generated information somehow appears in their hands reliably and with ease. An interactive system through which teachers can access their district's data base and immediately locate information on their students' past performance (grades, standardized tests, attendance, and so forth) is an exciting prospect, particularly if the system will also handle time-consuming bureaucratic chores like averaging grades and generating report cards.

Involving All Teachers in the Process

The danger of the bulldozer approach in installing an IIS is that the few teachers who have been involved early-on may well be the ones who insure its failure. Teachers who are offended or angered during the initial implementation of the system may refuse to participate. They may go through the motions without actually using the available information, or, worse yet, they may sabotage the entire operation by giving bad publicity to their peers. Fullan (1982) notes that simply including a token teacher or two on a development team is insufficient motivation for other teachers to accept a proposed innovation.

I suggest that *all* teachers who will be expected or encouraged to use an IIS should be somehow involved throughout the development and implementation of an IIS. I am not advocating that committees of 150 be established, but rather that administrators charged with installing an IIS provide mechanisms for the meaningful participation of all teachers if teachers are identified as important users of the planned system.

Such participation could range from minimal to maximum. Minimal participation might include receiving regular written updates on what is happening, attending after-school informational meetings with IIS developers, periodic in-service training sessions, and being asked for input in an ongoing formative evaluation. Maximum participation would be reserved for those volunteers who are truly interested in working with an IIS in their classrooms. Early in the development process these teachers could be given access to IIS data and, with the help of the IIS developers, allowed to experiment with inputting data, querying the data, and generating report formats.

Creating a Professional Support System

My fourth suggestion is closely related to the third. Two critical points from the educational change literature must not be overlooked if an IIS is to succeed. The first of these is the failure of one-shot or short-term in-service sessions with teachers (Joyce & Showers, 1980). If teachers are politely introduced to an IIS in an afternoon meeting and then abandoned by those who know how the system works, it is likely that the negative factors discussed above will encourage teachers to stick to their previous tried-and-true methods.

The second point IIS developers must not overlook concerns different types and stages of use. In studying the acceptance of innovations, Hall and his colleagues (1975) have identified at least six levels of use of innovations, starting with nonuse and proceeding through orientation and preparation, to integration and eventual renewal. Classroom teachers newly faced with an IIS may need assistance in moving from lower levels of use toward the higher, more sophisticated levels.

These points suggest the value of a support system to provide teachers with a network of colleagues all of whom are struggling with the same questions. Such support can take many forms. For example, one readily accessible person in the central office can be responsible for helping teachers use the IIS; an IIS manager might come on-site to respond to problems; or periodic in-service discussions of IIS implementation could be scheduled. With such support, teachers will be far more likely to become intelligent and enthusiastic users than without it.

Leaving Teachers' Clinical Responsibilities Alone

I noted earlier that if teachers are to take advantage of an IIS, the system must provide information for use in the classroom. But I would also add as an essential restriction that IIS administrators not *require* that teachers make use of their information in any prespecified way. The autonomy of the classroom teacher once his or her door is closed is well known (Jackson, 1968; Lortie, 1975). Because an IIS designed for instructional use has the potential to open the classroom to administrative scrutiny, teachers may hesitate before becoming involved. Teachers are used to assuming responsibility for their own instructional decisions. They will be appropriately reluctant to yield this task to a computer, regardless of how well it is programmed.

In my opinion, those installing an IIS will be most successful if the system provides information for use in classrooms without specifying exactly what must be done with it. Making instructional decisions is, after all, what teachers have been trained to do, and by giving teachers additional information to help them do it better, an IIS becomes a vital asset to the clinical decision-making process. To go beyond this is to risk offending the very individuals who must make the system work.

My original title for this chapter was "What Teachers Would Like to Do to Computers," because I wanted to emphasize that many teachers view the classroom computer revolution with apprehension and distaste. Given the choice, many would be happy to be left behind. Administrators who consider adding an IIS to their system, therefore, must not assume that classroom teachers will easily integrate computer-generated data into their instructional activities. I changed the title, however, because I do believe that thoughtful administrators *can* work to involve teachers in creating systems that will help make them better teachers and that by so doing, Instructional Information Systems *can* gain a welcomed place in the classroom. We will know we have succeeded when union contracts require that every classroom comes equipped with an IIS terminal.

ACKNOWLEDGMENT: My thanks to Fanny Sosenke for her help in preparing this manuscript.

NOTES

1. The teacher in this instance was right. Within two years, a highly negative evaluation of the project led to its disgraceful demise. The teachers, many of whom had predicted this end, smiled smugly and began waiting for the next innovation to arrive.

2. My thanks to Brian Stecher for pointing out this distinction to me.

REFERENCES

Asheim, L. (1962). A survey of informed opinion on television's future place in education. In *Educational television: The next ten years*. Stanford, CA: Institute for Communication Research.

Atkin, M. J., & House, E. R. (1981). The federal role in curriculum development, 1950–1980. *Educational Evaluation and Policy Analysis, 3*(5), 5–36.

Burstein, L. (1984). The use of existing data bases in program evaluation and school improvement. *Educational Evaluation and Policy Analysis, 6*(3), 307–18.

Chataway, C. (1965). *Education and television*. London: Conservative Political Centre.

Cuban, L. (1982). Persistent instruction: The high school classroom, 1900–1980. *Phi Delta Kappan, 64*(2), 113–18.

David J. (1981). Local uses of Title I evaluations. *Educational Evaluation and Policy Analysis, 3*(1), 27–39.

Fisher, F. D. (1982). Computer-assisted education: What's not happening? *Journal of Computer-Based Instruction, 9*(1), 19–27.

Fullan, M. (1982). *The meaning of educational change*. New York: Teachers College Press.

Goodlad, J. I., Klein, M. F., and associates. (1970). *Behind the classroom door*. Belmont, CA: Wadsworth.

Hall, G. E., Loucks, S. F., Rutherford, W. L., & Newlove, B. W. (1975). Levels of use of the innovation: A framework for analyzing innovation adoption. *Journal of Teacher Education, 26*(1), 52–56.

Ingersoll, G. M., Smith, C. B., & Elliot, P. (1983-84). Attitudes of teachers and reported availability of microcomputers in American schools. *International Journal of Instructional Media, 11*(1), 27–37.

Jackson, P. (1968). *Life in classrooms*. New York: Holt, Rinehart and Winston.

Joyce, B., & Showers, B. (1980). Improving in-service training: The messages of research. *Educational Leadership, 37*(5), 379–85.

Kennedy, M., Apling, R., & Neumann, W. F. (1980). *The role of evaluation and test information in public schools*. Cambridge, MA: Huron Institute.

King, J. A. (1982). *Evaluation use in a curriculum improvement project*. Unpublished manuscript.

King, J. A., & Thompson, B. (1983). How principals, superintendents view program evaluation. *NASSP Bulletin, 67*(459), 46–52.

Lane, J. (1982). Teachers and the new technology—Servant or master? In R. Garland (Ed.), *Microcomputers and children in the primary school*. Lewes, Sussex, England: Falmer Press.

Lortie, D. C. (1975). *School–teacher*. Chicago: University of Chicago Press.

Norris, C. M., & Lumsden, B. (1984). Functional distance and the attitudes of educators toward computers. *T.H.E. Journal, 11*(4), 129–32.

Smith, L. M., & Pohland, P. A. (1974). Education, technology, and the rural highlands. In R. H. P. Kraft, L. M. Smith, P. A. Pohland, C. J. Brauner, & C. Cjerde, *Four evaluation examples: Anthropological, economic, narrative, and portrayal* (American Educational Research Association Monograph Series on Curriculum Evaluation). Chicago: Rand McNally.

Walker, D. F. (1983). Reflections on the educational potential and limitations of microcomputers. *Phi Delta Kappan, 65*(2), 103–7.

Williams, R. C., & Bank, A. (1984). Assessing instructional information systems in two districts: The search for impact. *Educational Evaluation and Policy Analysis, 6*(3), 267–82.

PART V

Inventing the Future: The Development of Instructional Information Systems

The two essays in Part V synthesize, for different audiences, major points made throughout the book. In the first, "An agenda for Developing Instructional Information Systems," Bank and Williams assume the role of consultant-at-a-distance to educators who might want to think about creating an IIS. Some of the questions that those interested in introducing an IIS into their organization must wrestle with are presented, along with activities that may produce answers. The authors caution against do-it-yourself or go-it-alone development strategies, but urge that administrators become wise consumers of expert advice by knowing in advance some of the issues that the experts will need to address.

In the second essay, "An Agenda for Research and Inquiry on Instructional Information Systems," Williams and Bank speak to researchers and policymakers. They suggest that rather than waiting until the field ripens solely through trial and error efforts, we anticipate some of the research and inquiry issues that will arise for practitioners and for policymakers as Instructional Information Systems become more commonplace. Longitudinal and comparative studies of IIS development strategies, costs, impact on organizational functioning, and effects on instructional decision making, would move us to a better conceptualization of IIS models and their appropriateness in different settings. Legal research might reveal to us the implications of matters such as access to information, unwarranted use of information, and protection of privacy, while reviews of related literature such as information management and Management Information Systems might help us anticipate and avoid dilemmas others have experienced.

The authors note that inquiry and conceptualization are needed to develop common understandings among educators about what is worth knowing; the considerations governing the growing relationship between education and industry, between schools and vendors; and the opportunities Instructional Information Systems can provide for us in significantly restructuring the basic organization of schools and school districts.

20

An Agenda for Developing Instructional Information Systems

ADRIANNE BANK and RICHARD C. WILLIAMS

Anyone seriously interested in introducing an Instructional Information System into a school or district must eventually come face-to-face with the uncertainties of how to proceed. What are the first steps? Is there some logical sequence of activities or decisions to follow? Where is it possible to learn what others have done and thereby avoid unnecessary errors and expense?

These few pages may provide direction to those who are actively considering some form of Instructional Information System. We will begin with some basic observations.

- Districts and schools differ greatly with regard to the presence of some important components for Instructional Information Systems, such as computer hardware and software, data bases consisting of standardized test scores or criterion-referenced test scores, and an orientation towards instruction that includes an articulated curriculum and measurable objectives.
- Districts and schools differ greatly with regard to the number and kinds of people who are enthusiastic, trained, or knowledgeable about computers and computer-managed instruction.
- Districts and schools differ greatly with regard to their liking for technology, commitment to systematic management of instruction, and the urgency they feel about moving ahead with system development.
- At the present time, developing an information system to manage instruction requires a combination of careful planning, creativity, and fortuitous circumstances. Given the current state of the art, such a system cannot be purchased ready-made. And creating a customized system will not likely occur in an orderly or sequential manner. There are too many activities, conditions, and components to which a system planner must attend concurrently and iteratively. There are too many unknowns that can be dealt with only as they arise. Although you may want to conceptualize and create your Instructional Information System in as efficient a

way as possible, your own priority list and the sequence in which you should do things will probably be different from that of your neighboring district.

Given these observations, it is neither possible nor wise for us to prescribe a step-by-step procedure that will guarantee an effective Instructional Information System. Instead, each district or school must assess its unique situation in terms of present conditions, district goals and plans, resources available, and sense of urgency, and begin from those realities.

One's usual first response to an ambiguous complex problem such as this is to call in the experts—get a consultant. This is a good idea here. Only the most daring would attempt a do-it-yourself or go-it-alone approach. In these pages, we cannot act as experts, but we can help you become a more knowledgeable consumer of consultant advice. We can list some of the questions a consultant would ask, and some things you might do to get the answers. In this section, we will assume the role of "consultant-at-a-distance." Our questions and a menu of possible activities are grouped into three chronological phases, namely: exploring the need for an IIS, planning and designing an IIS, and operating and monitoring an IIS.

Clearly, the questions and activities in the first phase should receive major attention at the start; but if you are considering an IIS, review all phases early-on so as to anticipate problems that might lie ahead.

EXPLORING THE NEED FOR AN IIS

It is not necessarily the case that every district or school should install an Instructional Information System. It is likely, however, that within the near future, many larger districts and schools may find it necessary to make a reasoned decision about purchasing computers for other purposes, either for the business office or for the classroom. At this point, it will become important to think about whether those same computers should, either immediately or eventually, become part of an IIS. Since computers are becoming omnipresent in our society, computer vendors are using persuasive sales techniques even to the point of substantial hardware discounts, and parents may see computers as an important element in their child's schooling, districts and schools may be pushed to formulate a policy: to have no computers at all, to have separate unconnected systems for different purposes, or to have coordinated multipurpose systems organized in centralized or decentralized fashion.

Before making such decisions, a rather lengthy period of fact-finding is needed. Since there is at present no single source of good information, and no single vendor or technical group that clearly dominates the field, fact-finding must be done through accessing experts—through talking with those who have already ventured ahead (or who have decided not to) and through discussions with all the "stakeholders" in the district or school who would be affected by decisions about such a system. At this stage you should be addressing the following questions:

1. What would be the goals and purposes for establishing a computerized information system? Would you want to use it for business, administrative, or instructional functions, or all three?
2. What might your organization want to do with a computerized Instructional Information System (e.g., store records, generate reports, search the data for answers to questions)?
3. Who would be the primary users of an information system (e.g., central office administrators, principals, teachers, board members, clerks)?
4. What might be the difficulties in installing such a system (e.g., costs, time involved, getting adequate technical assistance, resistance of staff)?
5. What might be the benefits of installing such a system (e.g., greater efficiency in planning, managing, monitoring, keeping track of student progress, problem-spotting)?
6. With what other ongoing systems would such a system need to be coordinated (e.g., state, district, classroom)?
7. With what other instructional activities would such a system need to be coordinated (e.g., curriculum, instructional resources, classroom organization)?
8. Who would take leadership responsibility and who would provide the needed support?
9. Who else would be involved in decision making (e.g., individuals, groups)? When and how?
10. Who would need to be kept informed about the decision-making process (e.g., supporters, opponents, parents, community members)?
11. What are the fears, concerns, anxieties that an Instructional Information System might generate (e.g., in the short term, over the long term, personal, organizational, instructional)?

There are many possible approaches to answering these questions. Listed below are some of the activities you might undertake to gather the necessary information.

- Talk with opinion leaders, idea champions within the district or school, about what they see as the needs and uses for an Instructional Information System.

- Organize a series of meetings to discuss the desirability of an information system.
- Develop an IIS attitude survey for use with staff, parents, and community groups.
- Ask what new information about student performance, attitudes, and characteristics various groups (e.g., principals, teachers, parents, school board) would value and use.
- Do a "Report of Reports not Reported"—or an "Analysis of Analyses Never Analyzed"—to discover what information now collected, stored, or distributed is not valued or used.
- Brainstorm with various groups about their concerns, fears, anxieties regarding an IIS.
- Do an "Assets Analysis" of the resources presently available to devote to an IIS (e.g., persons, skills, equipment, funds, time).
- Assess environmental factors such as impediments and incentives to an IIS.
- Make a list of decision makers and interested persons who would most strongly advocate or oppose such a system.
- Think about past change efforts in the organization, why they worked or didn't work.
- Make a list of specific past and present catalysts which might serve as motivations or arguments for introducing change.
- Create a metaphor depicting your own vision (with both positives and negatives) of the organization after an IIS has been installed.
- Visit functioning IIS in other institutions. Ask about the satisfactions, problems, evidence that various groups have about how their IIS works.
- Read early memos, documents, notes, plans which describe how others got started.
- Ask leaders elsewhere how they got started, what would they do differently if they were starting over.
- Ask other schools or districts about the financial, personal, and organizational costs, both anticipated and unanticipated, related to development of an IIS.
- Observe the systems in other organizations; consider pros and cons of replicating their systems. Ask them to be peer consultants and advisors.
- Find out about grants, loans, and other available financial resources.
- Convene a working group of principals, parents, teachers, advisory council, and citizens' representatives to define purposes/procedures for getting started.
- Talk to people from nearby universities, technical assistance or research centers who have provided assistance to schools and districts about the human, financial, and technical resources needed for an IIS.

PLANNING AND DESIGNING AN IIS

One's impulse, when considering computerized systems, may be to look at the available hardware in order to decide about the type of computer (mainframe, mini, or personal computer), brand of computer, and number of terminals one could purchase for a given price. It is the opinion of many experts, however, that software purchase decisions should precede the hardware purchase decisions, not the other way around. It is the software that will make your system work as you intend. It is your decision about which software will meet your needs, and whether to purchase an existing package or to commission a unique program, that are the crucial first steps.

It is early-on at this planning and design phase that expert advice is critical. And since experts are only helpful if they can solve your particular problems, shop carefully for your expert advisors. You will find great variation in the type of advice you will receive and what you will pay for it. It is at this time, also, that the considerations of cost must be faced. Some experts suggest that you estimate your costs as completely as possible, double the amount, and regard this as a conservative figure. Focusing on the questions below will help to assure that planning and design are carried out thoroughly and effectively.

1. What decision-making sequence should you follow? (Whose approval do you need? How quickly or slowly should you proceed?)
2. What experts are essential? (Needed skills? An individual or a team? On a continuing or one-time basis?)
3. Who will work with the experts? (A representative user group? Inside experts? With what time constraints?)
4. What software will meet your needs?
5. What hardware should you purchase or lease?
6. What costs should you anticipate?

INITIAL DECISIONS. It is a serious mistake to begin by asking, "What computer should we purchase?" The first step should always be an analysis of your organization's needs for an IIS. Only after the needs assessment has been completed should you begin to look into expertise requirements, software, and finally hardware. As you consider these three, you will also want to examine the later expansion possibilities for the system.

ANALYZING YOUR NEED FOR EXPERTS. You may want a consultant team, or a single consultant who can access others. You may need different consultants for different parts of the process. Ideally, you want people familiar with data management processes who also know about educational environments. The experts you may need include:

Systems analyst—the person who looks at the complete operation and breaks it down into segments. From the work of a systems analyst comes a set of specifications and a program design.

Programmer—the person who works from the set of specifications and program design to write the program. (This could be the same person as the systems analyst, or someone else.)

Manual developer—the person who writes the procedures for using the program in your situation. (Generally, programmers can't write readable manuals. Manuals may need to be revised several times before they are workable.)

Trainer—the person who can train others to input and access data and be knowledgeable users. (This person may come from the software vendor or from within the school or district.)

Troubleshooting consultant—the person who handles routine "bugs," software and hardware problems. (This person should be available and accommodating.)

Overseers—the people representing various user groups, as well as financial, administrative, and technical interests, making sure the system is meeting the organization's needs; they can modify the first-generation system and create a second-generation system when needed.

Operations manager—the person who makes day-to-day decisions about system use.

Once you have decided what kind of help you will need, locate the best experts for your purpose. The best way is "word of mouth" from organizations similar to yours that have been well satisfied by their consultants. Other sources are software manufacturers, who often keep lists of consultants; big-8 accounting firms; technical assistance centers; and universities, schools of education, computer science departments, or business schools.

Be sure to negotiate the best arrangements possible. Get competitive bids and written estimates from several consultants. It is to your advantage to work with a consultant who sets a fixed price for a defined job—with interval payments for milestone accomplishments (dollars per hour with an estimate of hours)—rather than an open ended per-hour or per-day arrangement. Consider building in penalties for late delivery or improper installation. Check references carefully.

Consultants who purchase software or hardware may add a fee or percentage, but they may also be able to get you discounts. Both of these possibilities should be double checked, as should final ownership of system.

Usually, the end product should be the property of the organization, not the developer.

REVIEWING THE SOFTWARE SITUATION. There are two types of software: off-the-shelf software, which doesn't require programming, and scratch or custom programs, which are written in a language like PASCAL and can be designed by programmers to meet your exact needs. Off-the-shelf software in turn divides into two kinds: data base management programs, which cannot be customized but can do simple jobs well and inexpensively (e.g., DB Master), and data base language programs, which can be programmed and customized to your specification. There are advantages and disadvantages to each type. Off-the-shelf programs are less expensive and can be acquired more quickly, but you may have to adjust your specifications (e.g., for the kind of report you will get) to meet their constraints. Customized programs are more expensive, but they are essential for complex or unique operations.

EXAMINING HARDWARE. Major considerations for hardware purchasing decisions are: hardware compatibility with software; disk size; disk storage capacity; and number and kind of work stations needed (e.g., input only, output only, input/output, single, multiple). In addition, there are the "intangibles." Cost is often not a major factor; your best initial deal may not be the best long-term deal. Look for a company that is established in the business and likely to continue in it. Choose a company that has a track record working with educational institutions and has service centers everywhere.

Anticipate your repair and maintenance needs. You will have to make decisions about a service contract vs ad hoc repairs. You may want to consider a service contract that promises on-site repairs if the system is critical to your operation; or you may want a cheaper off-site repair arrangement. Software also requires fixing sometimes. You'll probably need on-site troubleshooting. Sometimes software companies provide free advice for a specific time and charge a fee for advice thereafter.

ESTIMATING INSTALLATION AND MAINTENANCE COSTS. In addition to the obvious expenses involved in setting up and maintaining an Instructional Information System—that is, the purchase of hardware and software—there are numerous other costs that must be considered. Among these costs are those for:

> Training—including wages for temporary replacements for those being trained and salary increments for upgraded personnel scales

Running the old and the new system simultaneously for a period of time
Supplies such as paper, ribbons, and disks
Dedicated telephone lines and other communications equipment
Security for equipment—anchor pads, window bars, etc.—as well as insurance
Furniture, such as printer stands, computer desks, and the like
Upgrades for the electrical system
Additional personnel, such as an operations manager and an oversight group

IMPLEMENTING AND MONITORING AN IIS

While the system is being developed, it is important to anticipate all the elements that contribute to successful implementation. Installing the system and then finding and dealing with all the "bugs" in it can be a trying period for many. There may be disruptions in usual work flow. Some people will have to change their routines and learn new skills. Once the shakedown period is over, and the major training and maintenance problems are being handled, it is time to develop monitoring, fine-tuning, and improvement strategies to insure effective and efficient operations. Careful attention to the questions listed below will greatly increase the chances for a successful system.

1. What training needs will there be? (Who will be trained? By whom? When? To what level of skill? At what cost?)
2. What personnel adjustments will be needed? (New hires? Staff reductions? Reclassifications? Promotion?)
3. How will the system be maintained? (Physical security? Repairs? Replacement? Insurance?)
4. Who will have access to the system? (When? On what priority basis?)
5. How will quality control of data be handled?
6. How will confidentiality of information be maintained?
7. What safeguards will be built to prevent abuse of the system?
8. How will the system be monitored and fine-tuned to reduce irritations and minor frustrations?
9. How will the system be evaluated and upgraded to meet changing needs?

Anticipating these considerations can help to avoid the disruption that might otherwise occur. Here are some steps you can take to keep things running smoothly:

- Encourage staff to work together, collegially, on purposeful projects related to IIS development and installation.
- Provide opportunities for professional development and advancement for people associated with the IIS.
- Provide training so that key staff can help others to do their own troubleshooting.
- Encourage ongoing expressions of fears, concerns, anxieties and provide mechanisms to handle grievances.
- Maintain good records on IIS performance for various user groups.
- Monitor IIS operations at sample sites or for sample user groups.
- Contract for an implementation evaluation.

ACKNOWLEDGMENT: The authors gratefully acknowledge the valuable input of Philip Ender, Graduate School of Education, UCLA, a seasoned and expert information systems consultant who contributed many of the insights and suggestions contained in this essay.

21

An Agenda for Research and Inquiry on Instructional Information Systems

RICHARD C. WILLIAMS and ADRIANNE BANK

Frequently in an emerging field, such as that of Instructional Information Systems, considerable attention is given to detailing the how-to-do-it activities listed in the preceding chapter. And rightly so. These short-term, pressing decisions must be made before an IIS can be built, installed, and evaluated. Somewhat less attention is paid to defining the research that might be done to clarify our understanding of the factors leading to success or failure, or to inquiries that should be conducted in anticipation of longer-range policy issues.

For example, it was only after the successful development and marketing of home videocassette recorders (VCRs) that the courts began to hear cases about the legal issues surrounding the widespread home copying of programs off the air. The industry might have anticipated this problem somewhat earlier than it did. More recently, the impact of this invention on the commercial movie industry's traditional theatrical movie release system is being considered in producers' offices and on Wall Street. These and other such unanticipated issues will likely play a prominent role in influencing the development of the videocassette recorder industry.

In this chapter, we will suggest some of the nontechnical research studies and areas for inquiry that could speed up our understanding of the new field of Instructional Information Systems. Whereas the previous chapter was addressed to school and district staff members who are interested in actually developing and implementing an Instructional Information System, these pages are meant for researchers and policymakers whose activities—although not directly related to the details of day-to-day operation of Instructional Information Systems—are nonetheless critical to furthering this field.

A RESEARCH AND INQUIRY AGENDA

Research and inquiry are normally thought of as subsets of one another. For indeed, the purpose of research is to inquire into some phenomenon of interest. However, research does not constitute the whole of inquiry. For our purposes here, we make the following distinction between research and inquiry. Research implies learning about a phenomenon through empirical means—that is, interviews, record examination, questionnaires, and fieldwork. Inquiry refers to conceptualizing and negotiating policies relative to Instructional Information Systems in areas that do not readily yield to empirical research or that are sufficiently urgent that they cannot await empirical answers. For this agenda, we are putting aside all of the technical and statistical areas relating to the collection, storage, analysis, and retrieval of data that must be resolved before Instructional Information Systems are fully practical.

Research Possibilities

The following sections highlight some research studies that might yield insights into critical policy questions and issues. No one kind of study can answer the variety of questions raised. Thus, we have included several approaches. The selection is not intended to be exhaustive, only suggestive.

LONGITUDINAL STUDIES. Sample districts and schools that are now in the early stages of developing an IIS might be chosen because of their similarities or their differences, depending on the questions to be answered. Longitudinal studies, especially if they are comprehensive, will shed light on a whole series of questions about the process of developing these systems: the problems that develop; the nature of the solutions devised and their effectiveness; how districts and IIS systems mutually adapt to one another; the stages, if any, that naturally occur in developing and implementing an IIS; and the role of various stakeholders in the process. Much of the fieldwork on this subject to date has been *ex post facto* case studies (Bank & Williams, 1984) or recollections by those, such as Cooley, Dussault, and Idstein, who have developed an IIS in their districts (see Chapters 8, 17, and 6, respectively, in this volume). These studies are useful but the research base would be greatly strengthened by independent, comprehensive, longitudinal case studies, because critical details are lost when events are explored after the fact.

Of particular interest would be studies that examine the effects Instructional Information Systems have on various aspects of school and school district functioning. It is comparatively easy to trace how a district develops and implements an IIS and to learn about the technical configurations and training used. It is difficult but essential to measure IIS impact. For example, what influence does the system itself or the information it generates have on district instructional decision-making processes and on the attitudes and activities of those who use the system? On the quality of the instructional program? On the careers and job opportunities of those who operate the system? On the distribution of power among and between levels and individuals? We don't know much about the causal links between Instructional Information Systems and these phenomena, and it is important to explore whether they can be established.

Another topic for longitudinal studies might be the role of user groups in IIS development and the ways in which those roles shift over time or in different phases of the development sequence. What, if any, is the relationship between the quality and quantity of user participation in creating the IIS and users' ultimate acceptance of such systems?

Still another topic should be studies of start-up and maintenance costs. What ingredients should be considered in determining the costs? Ultimately such studies must attend to not only the more obvious costs of technology, staff training, materials, and security measures, but also the hidden costs incurred by the earlier system (such as testing costs already paid for under an existing program) and the often unanticipated costs of personnel who, after learning a new technology, leave the district for better employment opportunities elsewhere.

Finally, and importantly, we should attend to the consequences the system has for student achievement. Does student achievement increase, and if so, why? Is there a relationship between teachers' use of information, their decisions, their classroom practices, and student performance? Again, it is important to acknowledge the difficulty of developing causal links between an IIS and these occurrences, but attempts should be made.

COMPARATIVE STUDIES IN SEVERAL DISTRICTS SIMULTANEOUSLY. Topics may be similar to those suggested for the longitudinal studies above. Here, we are suggesting that parallel data collection be carried out in several districts—be they comprehensive case studies or more restricted examinations of specific components or phases of an IIS, such as user attitudes, costs, or staff training activities.

LEGAL RESEARCH. IIS use in school districts raises a number of legal questions: for example, the whole set of freedom-of-information issues related to who should have access to IIS information, how procedures can be created to protect individuals from unwarranted use of personal data, and the rights of a student or teacher to refuse being included in the data base. These and other questions might be examined through law reviews and other types of legal research.

REVIEWS OF STUDIES FROM RELATED FIELDS. Instructional Information Systems are, after all, an educational version of Management

Information Systems. There is a large and growing MIS literature that has dealt with many of the problems that are and will be cropping up in IIS (see Bank & Craig, Chapter 4 in this volume). What can we learn from the MIS literature that will help us avoid predictable dilemmas and problems and also shed light on the unique characteristics of these systems when applied to education, thereby adding to the MIS literature?

Some Policy Inquiries

Although more policy questions might eventually be answered through empirical research, many decisions and policies must be made before such studies can be completed. And some issues simply do not lend themselves to empirical methods. Sometimes thoughtful and careful analysis is required before decisions are made. The following are some issues that would likely gain from such consideration.

What is worth knowing? An IIS cannot store data on everything. What is more, data collection and storage costs a lot, and districts are typically constrained financially, so tough choices have to be made among those data that might be included in a large, comprehensive system. What data should we collect? Why? How? For what purpose? A good deal of thought needs to be put into answering these questions.

What are the ethical and financial considerations arising from the working relationships between school districts and the commercial vendors of information systems? Schools districts and schools, given their limited financial resources, are receptive to special offers from computer software and hardware enterprises. But these offers can later come to haunt districts if they make commitments that limit their degrees of freedom in future IIS developments. How can we define the danger? And how do such agreements affect the competitive bidding practices normally followed in governmental agencies?

What policies should govern the appropriate use of IIS data? For example, should test results that have been collected for several years, and that could be easily aggregated to obtain a record about the classes taught by an individual teacher, be used to evaluate that teacher's performance? To do so will limit the likelihood that the IIS will be acceptable to teachers and their organizations. Yet, if discernible and dramatic trends emerge, should not such data be used at least to signal that a problem might exist?

And what about the employment security of those whose jobs directly relate to this system? For example, school secretaries might find that the need for their services is diminished by an IIS and their unions might demand job protection clauses in their contracts. Or, teachers might find that an IIS requires that they conduct their teaching in ways that some find objectionable. Are these condition-of-employment issues? And what considerations should be given to employee groups whose very jobs are threatened by this development? What kinds of retraining should be provided? Should new salary schedules or job classifications be worked out for those who have been trained in IIS use? How should such changes be negotiated?

In what ways might the development of an IIS offer opportunities for significantly restructuring the school district's basic organization and functioning? For example, one reason for abandoning the team teaching and nongraded approach to schooling so popular in the 1960s was the difficulty of keeping track of progress data for all students. The self-contained classroom at least gives the teacher the illusion that he or she has a pretty good notion of the individual differences of the students in the class and the progress they are making in their studies. But a large, nongraded, team-taught arrangement makes it much more difficult to keep track of everyone. An IIS can change that. An IIS can allow teachers to record and retrieve the individual characteristics and the progress of large numbers of students quite easily. Also, it provides teachers with the means to aggregate data in many different ways, thereby allowing them to group and regroup for instructional purposes. Thus, the development of this technology can provide the opportunity to change important structures that have persisted over many, many years in education because of technical limitations. We haven't yet begun to discover the other ways in which the traditional delivery and organization of schooling might be changed by the use of an IIS.

Much of the progress to date in IIS development has come from the efforts of "idea champions" in pioneering districts. Mostly they have designed their district system independent of other agencies. But this idiosyncratic R&D "model" is costly and slow, and will likely not result in substantial national development and diffusion of Instructional Information Systems. If the idea is to spread, there must be a closer working relationship between the various organizations and agencies that have potential roles in their development. What should state legislatures, state departments of education, technical assistance centers, schools of education, and educational research and development organizations do in relation to this field? For example, should there be legislation to provide school districts with the financial support and incentives to invest the time and energy involved into developing an IIS? And once such systems are developed, should the government and universities evaluate the relative merits of different approaches and further the dissemination of the most promising ones?

The research and inquiry topics that have been touched on here hardly constitute an agenda. We don't yet know enough to outline a full-fledged agenda of researchable issues, of policies that will need formulation. But just as great effort will be needed to create solutions for the technical problems relating to Instructional Information Systems, similar levels of energy are called for in order to invent strategies to handle the political, economic, and social ripples that these systems may cause.

REFERENCE

Bank, A., & Williams, R. C. (1984). Assessing instructional information systems in two districts: The search for impact. *Educational Evaluation and Policy Analysis*, 6(3), 267–82.

About the Contributors

ADRIANNE BANK is Senior Research Associate at the UCLA Center for the Study of Evaluation, and Associate Director of UCLA's Seeds University Elementary School. She is an independent consultant who works with non-profit institutions and parochial school systems on organizational change, planning, decision making, and evaluation. Dr. Bank has been Codirector of CSE's Instructional Information Systems project for a number of years. She has written extensively on this and other educational subjects.

ROBERT E. BLUM is Director of the Goal Based Education Program at the Northwest Regional Educational Laboratory in Portland, Oregon. In this capacity, he directs a major portion of the Laboratory's work on effective schooling and high school improvement, including the development and widespread use of the "Onward to Excellence" research-based school improvement program. Dr. Blum has taught at junior high, high school, and university levels, was an assistant principal in a junior high school, and served as career education coordinator in the Jefferson County (Colorado) Public Schools.

LEIGH BURSTEIN is a Professor in UCLA's Graduate School of Education and Faculty Associate of the Center for the Study of Evaluation. His long-term interest in methods for analyzing multilevel educational data has been directed in recent years toward the implications of this research for the development and implementation of information systems for educational decision making at multiple levels (student, class, school, district, state, and nation) of the educational system. The Systemic Evaluation Project, codirected by Sirotnik and Burstein, explored the methodological issues in developing a comprehensive information system in a secondary school. Dr. Burstein has also been working on information systems at the state and national levels.

JOCELYN A. BUTLER is Development/Dissemination Specialist for the Goal Based Education Program at the Northwest Regional Educational Laboratory in Portland, Oregon. She is responsible for monitoring reports of effective schooling research and for the development and preparation of training materials and research reports, and has authored many Laboratory publications. Ms. Butler has an extensive background in communications, including work in the arts, politics, film, and television.

TERENCE R. CANNINGS is a Professor of Education at the Graduate School of Education and Psychology, Pepperdine University, Los Angeles. Dr. Cannings is also Program Director for the M.S. in Educational Computing, a program that emphasizes the application of computers in the educational setting. He is interested in how teachers and administrators utilize computers to assist in instructional decision making as well as in future developments in technology and how they will impact learning and teaching.

WILLIAM M. CAREY is Coordinator of Computer Services and Staff Development for the Santa Monica-Malibu Unified School District. He is a partner in RW & Associates, Santa Monica, a software application and consulting company. Carey designed and implemented the Elementary Office Management System, a student Management Information System for elementary schools that links student profiles with test data and manages attendance.

WILLIAM COOLEY is currently Director of the Evaluation Research Unit at the Learning Research and Development Center, University of Pittsburgh. His current interests include how to conduct decision-oriented research in the context of an operating educational system and the use of microcomputers in support of school-based student information systems. He is a past president of the American Educational Research Association.

ELAINE CRAIG specializes in the uses of computers in education. She teaches computer education courses in UCLA's Teacher Education Lab and is a researcher on the Management of Instructional Information Systems project at UCLA's Center for the Study of Evaluation. Her current research involves expert/novice problem-solving in an instructional computer game.

NICHOLAS F. DUSSAULT is currently Coordinator of Research and Evaluation for the Sheboygan (Wisconsin) Area School District. Dr. Dussault received his Ph.D. degree from the University of Wisconsin-Milwaukee. He is currently interested in more closely linking teaching with testing and improving the management and provision of instruction by the use of current technology. This interest has led him to work with computer-managed instruction systems and to develop sophisticated Instructional Information Systems.

STEVEN M. FRANKEL is Director of Educational Accountability, Montgomery County (Maryland) Public Schools. He is also president of The Assessment Group, Ltd., and a contributing editor and columnist for *The Washingtonian* and *Baltimore Magazine*. He has a doctorate in Instructional Systems Technology with a minor in Marketing from Indiana University, and never has less than six computers and an equal number of audio/video systems in his home.

J. RICHARD HARSH is currently an independent consultant in educational research and evaluation. His previous experience has been as Director of the Educational Testing Service (ETS), Los Angeles; Assistant Director, Research and Guidance, for the Los Angeles County Superintendent of Schools; and Lecturer in psychology at Occidental College, Claremont Graduate School, and University of Southern California. He is a certified psychologist. Dr. Harsh's activities include evaluation of school districts and of innovation programs in education at colleges and universities.

WALTER E. HATHAWAY is currently Director of Research and Evaluation for the Portland (Oregon) Public School System. His duties include leadership of the district's educational research, evaluation, and testing systems related to the performance and satisfaction of students and staff. He received an undergraduate degree in the classics, and graduate degrees in philosophy and mathematics from Fordham University, and in computer science and educational psychology from the University of Pennsylvania. He serves on a number of national, regional, and state advisory boards. He has published on a wide variety of subjects: most recently he has been responsible for the development of a national report on secondary school reform in large urban school systems and a book on testing in the nation's schools. Dr. Hathaway has been President of the Oregon Educational Research Association and Vice President of the American Educational Research Association for Division H—School Evaluation and Program Development.

PETER IDSTEIN is currently Supervisor of Instruction for the Christina School District in Newark, Delaware. For the past five years he has headed a team that developed and implemented a school-based information management system consisting of an objective-based testing program, an attendance package, and a data base management system. Dr. Idstein's instructional areas of specialization are mastery learning and cooperative learning strategies.

JEAN A. KING moved to New Orleans seven years ago to become the Coordinator of Secondary Education at Tulane University. In this capacity she teaches methods courses to students becoming junior and senior high school teachers and works extensively in New Orleans schools, both public and private. Dr. King's research interests include curriculum and evaluation use and specifically looking for ways to increase the effective use of available information at the school and classroom level.

JOHN LESLIE KING is Associate Professor and Chair of the Department of Information and Computer Science at the University of California, Irvine. For the past 10 years his research has focused on the management and economics of computer applications to government at various levels. Recently, he has been conducting a large-scale longitudinal study of computing change in selected organizations to determine the drivers of change in the evolution of computer system use. Dr. King is the coauthor of *Computers in Local Government* (Praeger), *The Dynamics of Computing* (Columbia University Press), and *Computerized Models in Federal Policymaking* (Columbia University Press), as well as many articles in academic and professional journals.

MICHAEL QUINN PATTON is a social scientist on the faculty of the University of Minnesota. His interests in information systems derive from his program evaluation work. He is the author of five evaluation books, including *Utilization-Focused Evaluation* (Sage, 1986), which sets the context for using information in the information age. He is Futures Editor for the *Journal of Extension*. Dr. Patton was the 1984 recipient of the Myrdal Award from the Evaluation Research Society "for outstanding contributions to evaluation practice and use."

LINDA POLIN recently joined the Pepperdine University Graduate School of Education and Psychology as Assistant Professor. She teaches primarily in the Educational Computing masters program. Her research has focused upon instructional and administrative uses of computer labs, computers in the English classroom, and measurement and teaching of writing (composition) skill. Prior to her arrival at Pepperdine, Dr. Polin codirected a four-year study of college writing instruction.

SAUL ROCKMAN is Director of Technology Programs for the Far West Laboratory in San Francisco. His work has focused on the effective use of technology in schools and the evaluation of television and computer materials. For many years, he was the Director of Research for the Agency for Instructional Technology, in Bloomington, Indiana. While at AIT Dr. Rockman was involved in the design and creation of many instructional television series and computer programs.

KENNETH A. SIROTNIK is a Research Professor at the College of Education, University of Washington. For a number of years, he was at UCLA as a

Senior Research Associate in the Laboratory in School and Community Education and at the Center for the Study of Evaluation. He has participated in many educational research studies including the recent nationwide study of elementary and secondary schools, *A Study of Schooling*. Dr. Sirotnik's interests and publications range broadly from topics in measurement, statistics, evaluation, and educational technology to issues in local school improvement and educational policy and change.

BRIAN STECHER is a Professional Associate in the Los Angeles office of the Educational Testing Service, and is interested in both the role of technology and the role of assessment in education. His current research activities involve an examination of effective in-service strategies for training teachers to use technology in education. Dr. Stecher has trained teachers to use microcomputers in the classroom and is coauthor of a recent book, *The Electronic Schoolhouse*, that examines the impact of a large-scale computer education program.

RICHARD C. WILLIAMS is Faculty Associate at the UCLA Center for the Study of Evaluation, and Professor in the UCLA Graduate School of Education, where he teaches courses in educational administration. He is Director of UCLA's Seeds University Elementary School and a member of the school board of the Santa Monica-Malibu Unified School District. Dr. Williams has been Codirector of CSE's Instructional Information Systems project for a number of years. He is the author of many articles and monographs on this and other subjects.

Index

Accountability strategies, 7
Adams, A. S., 172
Adaptive instruction, 169–71
Administrators, 6, 8, 9, 41–43
   computers and, 4–5, 39–56, 126–27
   IIS applications for, 6
   IIS training programs for, 159–66
Advisory Council of National Organizations, 139
Albright, A. D., 160
Aldridge, W. D., 160
Alkin, M. C., 161
Allen, V. L., 172
American Association of School Administrators, 160
Anderson, B. F., 13, 15
Anderson, C., 162
Anshen, M., 23
Apling, R., 214
Argyris, C., 30
Armsey, J. W., 139
Asheim, L., 212
Atkin, M. J., 212
Automated Information Systems (AIS), 86–96
   effective, characteristics of, 90–93
   functions of, 89–90
   goals of, 88–89
   need for, 86–88
   prototype development for, 93–95
   steps in, 95–96
   see also Computerized information systems

Bank, Adrianne, 3–10, 22–34, 105–6, 145–51, 215, 216, 225–33, 234–39
Barabba, V. P., 4, 30
Becker, G. L., 160
Becker, S. W., 8, 10
Berman, P., 161
Bitter, G., 162
Block, James H., 169–70
Bloom, B. S., 169–70

Blum, Robert E., 76–85
Borko, H., 169
Brady, Matthew, 115
Bredo, E., 172
Burdeau, H. B., 23
Burns, R. B., 169–70
Burstein, L., 5, 10, 185–209, 215
Butler, Jocelyn A., 76–85

Calfee, R., 169
California, 17, 137
Camuse, R. A., 162
Cannings, Terence R., 39–56
Carey, William M., 97–102
Carroll, L., 67
Carroll, T., 162
Carson, Johnny, 13
Carter, L. F., 20, 21
Chataway, C., 212
Christina Instructional Management System (CIMS), 58–65, 68–75
   acceleration and, 70
   curriculum review and test development in, 59
   curriculum standardized by, 71–72
   data base problems of, 63–64
   equal protection and due process concerns and, 70
   equipment problems of, 62–63
   integration of data bases in, 60–61
   logistical problems of, 61–62
   mastery learning and, 68–69
   minimum requirements vs. excellence and, 72
   multi-user system problems of, 64–65
   operations in, 59–60
   privacy issues and, 69
   purpose of, 58
   for special education, gifted and talented students, 70–71
   strategic vision of, 73–75
   training problems of, 63
   see also Information management

247

248   Index

Chu, G. C., 139
Clark, C. M., 169
Classrooms
  computers in, 19–20
  IIS in, 146–47
Coburn, P., 107
Cohen, E. G., 139, 172
Commission on Instructional Technology, 139
Computer-Assisted Instruction (CAI), 45
Computerized information systems, 24, 29–32
  advantages of, 47
  centralized, 49–52
  data in, 50–51
  decentralized, 45–49
  defining purpose of, 29–30
  evaluation of, 32
  installation of, 47–48
  problems of, 48–49
  requirements for, 45–46
  role of leadership for, 30
  role of users in design of, 31–32
  selection of, 46–47
  technical consultants for, 30–31
  training and, 109
  uses of, 51–52
  wish lists for, 52
  see also Automated Information Systems
Computerized office management systems, 97–102
  cautions for, 101
  development of, 97–98
  evaluation of, 101–2
  reactions to, 98–99
  uses of, 99–100
Computers, computing, 7, 112–13
  as administrative tools, 4–5, 39–56, 126–27
  application domain of, 133–35
  for business tasks, 4–5
  as classroom innovation, 19–20
  demand side of, 122–23, 128–30
  developing inside expertise in, 131–32
  as entertaining hassle, 121–24, 127–28, 132–33
  essential resources for, 132
  fact vs. faith in, 131
  future uses of, 43
  general impressions about, 52–54
  instructional, 124–25
  learning and, 114–16
  location of, 40
  maintenance and repair of, 110
  management and, 113–14
  with multi-user systems, 64–65
  realities of living with, 130–31
  research, 125–26
  salient issues in increasing use of, 54–56
  student users of, 4, 19–20
  supply side of, 122, 128
  teachers as dedicated users of, 147, 148–49
Cooley, William W., 86–96, 235
Craig, Elaine, 22–34, 105–11
Cuban, Larry, 212
Curriculum
  for accelerated students, 70
  review of, 59
  standardization of, 71–72

Daft, R. L., 8, 10
Dahl, N. C., 139
Daillak, R. H., 161
Daniel, D. R., 23
Data, data bases
  backup copies of, 110
  for business, 18–19, 29, 51
  in computerized information systems, 50–51
  instructional, 18–19, 29
  integration of, 60–61
  personnel, 51
  problems of, 63–64
  rights of privacy and, 69
  student, 5, 9, 50–51
  teachers as analysts of, 202–3
David, J., 214
Dawson, D. T., 172
Deal, D., 172
Decisions Support System (DSS), 4, 5
Deschooling, 72–73
Deschooling Society (Illich), 72–73
Devaney, K., 136–37
Diebold, J., 23
Dirr, P. J., 138
Dorr-Bremme, D., 185, 189, 190, 200, 202
Dost, R. J., 169–70
Dussault, Nicholas F., 167–84, 235

Education
  accountability movement in, 17

dreams and hopes for, 11
IIS and realities of, 152–58
improvement of, 16–21
Educational Research Service, 170
Educational Testing Service, 17
Education for the Handicapped Act (1975), 70
Elementary schools
  automated information systems for, 86–96
  computerized office management systems in, 97–102
  see also Schools
Elliot, P., 213
Ender, P. B., 108
Estes, Nolan, 39
Eurich, N. P., 137

Farquhar, R. H., 160
Ferleger, L., 195
Fisher, F. D., 213
Frankel, Steven M., 112–18
Frederick, W. A., 23
Frieder, B., 169–70
Fullan, M., 161, 217

Gallimore, R., 206
Gates, Bill, 112
Gennari, P., 170
Ginzberg, M. J., 31
Glaser, R., 87, 169
Goal setting, using profiles for, 79–83
Goldhammer, K., 160
Goodlad, J. I., 202, 212
Goodson, M., 169–70
Government, research and evaluation supported by, 7–8, 11
Greenwood, P. W., 161
Gruber, W. H., 31
Grupe, F., 137

Hall, G. E., 161, 218
Hall, T. P., 30
Hardware, 108–9
Harsh, J. Richard, 16–21
Harvard Business Review, 22
Hastings, J., 169–70
Hathaway, Walter E., 152–58
Hickey, M. E., 169–70
Hiscox, M. D., 30, 106
Hoffman, D. H., 169–70

Holland, W. E., 23
Hord, S. M., 160–62
Horwitz, L., 195
House, E. R., 212
Hoyle, J. R., 160
Huff, D., 195
Hunt, J. G., 24

Idea champions, 8
Idstein, Peter, 57–75, 235
Illich, Ivan, 72–73
Individual Education Plan (I.E.P.), 70
Information
  clinical vs. social uses of, 201–2
  collection and summarization of, 77–79
  computerization of, 24, 29–32
  criteria for determining value of, 13
  knowledge vs., 205
  teachers in need of, 168–69
  upclassing and rise of, 119–21
Information management, 3–4
  in Christina School District. *See* Christina Instructional Management System
  deschooling in, 72–73
  policy issues and, 67–73
  promotion requirements and, 68
  sociology of change and, 65–67
Information utilization, 11–15
  current understanding of, 14–15
  focus important for, 12–13
  as inherently constrained, 14
Ingersoll, G. M., 213
In Search of Excellence (Peters and Waterman), 154
Instructional computing, 124–25
Instructional Information Systems (IIS)
  alternative types of, 35–102
  development of, 152, 223–39
  educational realities and, 143–221
  exploring need for, 185–209, 226–28
  impact of, 149–51
  implementation and monitoring of, 232–33
  integrating instructional processes with, 167–84
  plan and design of, 229–32
  research and inquiry agenda on, 234–39
  teacher-friendly, 210–21
  technical aspects of, 103–42
  views on, 1–34

Instructional techniques
  adaptive, 169–71
  information systems integrated with, 168–73
  personal nature of, 19
  technological additions for, 19–21
International Council for Educational Development, 139

Jackson, P., 219
Jackson, P. W., 169
Johnson, N., 162
Joint Committee on Standards for Educational Evaluation, 15
Jones, R., 30, 106, 109, 110
Joyce, B., 218
Juel, C., 169

Keen, P. G., 32
Keller, F., 169–70
Kelly, J. L., 169
Kelman, P., 107
Kennedy, M., 214
Kennedy, M. M., 202, 206
Killman, R. H., 4, 30
King, Jean A., 210–21
King, John Leslie, 119–35
Klein, M. F., 212
Kling, R., 30, 31
Knowledge, 13, 205
Kretlow, W. J., 23
Kroeber, D. W., 24, 26

Lane, J., 213
Learning
  computers and, 114–16
  diagnosis and monitoring of, 171
Leavitt, H. J., 26
Leonard, G. B., 89
Leonard, George, 154
Levitan, K. B., 4, 10
Ligon, J. C., 23
Lippit, P., 172
Lortie, D. C., 219
Loucks, S. F., 161, 218
Lucas, H. C., Jr., 24, 26, 30, 31–32, 106
Lumsden, B., 213
Lunstrom, R. J., 172

MacKay, R., 206

McLaughlin, M. W., 161
McLean, E. R., 31
McLuhan, M., 89
Madaus, G., 169–70
Management, computers and, 113–14
Management by Objectives (MBO), 16
Management Information Systems (MIS), 4, 5, 22–34
  lessons for educators from, 29–32
  life cycle of, 25–29
  literature of, 22–25
"Management in the 1980s Revisited" (Hunt and Newell), 24
Management Science, 22
Markus, M. C., 30, 31
Martin, J., 177
Mastery learning, 68–69
Matthews, R., 169–70
Meals, D. W., 32
Megatrends (Naisbitt), 73
Mehrens, W. A., 169
Meyer, J., 172
Microcomputers, 112–13. See also Computers, computing
Middleton, J., 139
Mies van der Rohe, Ludwig, 131–32
Millsap, M. A., 7–8, 10
MIS Quarterly, 22
Mitroff, I. I., 4, 30
Multi-age grouping, 172
Multinovich, J. S., 30, 32
Multi-user systems, problems of, 64–65

Naisbitt, John, 73, 207
Neumann, W. F., 214
Newell, P. F., 24
Newlove, B. W., 161, 218
Norris, C. M., 213

Oakes, J., 185, 204
Okey, J. R., 169–70

Packard, J., 172
Paddock, S., 172
Patton, Michael Quinn, 11–15, 161
Pedone, R. J., 138
Peters, T. J., 154, 202
Piele, P. K., 160
Pincus, J., 161
Pohland, P. A., 213

Poirot, J. L., 162
Polanyi, Michael, 206
Polin, Linda, 39–56
Porter, A. C., 169
Powell, J. D., 162
Principals
 computers used by, 41–43
 IIS applications for, 6, 8, 9
 see also Administrators
Privacy, rights of, data bases and, 69
Profiles, 76–85
 checklist for, 83–85
 collecting and summarizing information for, 77–79
 preparation of, 79
 for schools, 77–79
 use of, for goal setting, 79–83
Profiling process, 76
Promotions, requirements for, 68

Ragosta, M., 20, 21
Research computing, 125–26
Riccobono, J. A., 138
Roberts, N., 107
Robey, D., 30, 31
Rockman, Saul, 136–42
Rosenshine, B. V., 169
Rubinstein, Seymore, 112
Rudman, H. C., 169
Rumberger, R. W., 4, 10
Rutherford, W. L., 160–62, 218

Schmuck, P., 172
School board members, IIS applications for, 6
School districts, 8–9
Schools
 computerization in, assessment of, 119–35
 heterogeneity of, 6–7
 management guidelines for administration of, 16–17
 profiling for improvement of, 76–85
 readiness factors of, 9–10
 reform of, 7, 11
 see also Elementary schools
Schramm, W., 139
Scott, W. R., 172
Shavelson, R. J., 169
Showers, B., 218
Sirotnik, Kenneth A., 185–209

Sloan Business Review, 22
Smith, C. B., 213
Smith, L. M., 213
Smith, R. L., 162
Snyder, T., 107
Society, historical perspective of, 11–12
Software, 107–8
 backup copies of, 110
Spartz, J. L., 170
Special education, 70–71
Standards for Evaluation (Joint Committee on Standards for Educational Evaluation), 15
Stecher, Brian, 159–66
Stoddard, A. J., 139
Students
 data on, 5, 9, 50–51
 gifted and talented, 70–71
 as users of computers, 4, 19–20
Stull Bill, 17
Suttle, J. E., 160
Sykes, G., 136–37
Synnott, W. R., 31

Taffe, W. J., 162
Taylor, R. P., 162
Teachers, teaching
 as dedicated group of users, 147, 148–49
 IIS applications for, 6, 8, 9
 information needed by, 168–69
 objectives of, 17
 personal knowledge of, 205–6
 reactions to IIS by, 212–15
 as researchers-data analysts, 202–3
 specific strategies of, 169–73
 team, 172–73
Technological issues, 105–11
 hardware as, 108–9
 information system implementation as, 20–21, 109–11
 software as, 107–8
Technology
 assumptions and, 136–42
 availability of, 7
 future implications of, 117–18
 instructional techniques and, 19–21
 new, 112–18
 predictions for future of, 116–17
Teilhard de Chardin, P., 152
Tharp, R. G., 206

Tharrington, J. M., 30
Thomas, C., 105–6, 187–88
Thompson, B., 214
Through the Looking Glass (Carroll), 67
Thurber, J. C., 160–62
Toch, T., 137
Toffler, A., 11, 15, 154
"Tonight Show," 13
Training, 109–10
  for administrators, 159–66
  computerized information systems and, 109
  problems of, 63
Tricker, R. I., 29
Trivia, 12, 17
Tufte, E. R., 195

Upclassing, 119–21

User Needs Analysis (UNA), 30

Vlahovich, V., 30, 32

Walberg, H., Jr., 169, 170
Walker, D. F., 214
Wang, M. C., 169, 170, 171, 172
Wanous, D. S., 169
Waterman, R. H., Jr., 154, 202
Watt, D., 107
Waxman, H. C., 170
Weiner, C., 107
Weissmann, S., 162
Whisler, T. L., 26
White, P., 161
Williams, Richard C., 3–10, 23, 105–6, 145–51, 215, 216, 225–33, 234–39

Yeany, R. H., 169–70